Science Fiction across media
adaptation/novelization

A *Gylphi Limited* Book

First published in Great Britain in 2013
by Gylphi Limited

Copyright © Gylphi Limited, 2013

A CIP catalogue record for this book is available from the British Library.

ISBN 978-1-78024-012-1(pbk)
ISBN 978-1-78024-013-8 (Kindle)
ISBN 978-1-78024-014-5 (EPUB)

Cover image from *Fahrenheit 451* with permission from Photofest, Inc. Design and typesetting by Gylphi Limited. Printed in the UK by imprintdigital.com, Exeter.

Gylphi Limited
PO Box 993
Canterbury CT1 9EP, UK

Every effort has been made to obtain permissions to reproduce copyright material and if any proper acknowledgement has not been made we apologize and invite copyright holders to inform us of the oversight.

A previous version of the interview with Christopher Priest was published in *Image [&] Narrative*. Special thanks to Jan Baetens and Christopher Priest for their permission to include it in this book.

The excerpts from Ray Bradbury's unpublished teleplay of 'A Sound of Thunder', held in the collection of the Center for Ray Bradbury Studies, University of Indiana, are reprinted by permission of Don Congdon Associates, Inc. © 1989 by Ray Bradbury.

Science Fiction across media
adaptation/novelization

edited by Thomas Van Parys and I.Q. Hunter

Gylphi SF STORY WORLDS
Critical Studies in Science Fiction

SF Storyworlds

Edited by Paul March-Russell, this new and exciting book series aims to explore the evolution of Science Fiction (SF) and its impact upon contemporary culture. The series will argue that SF has generated a series of storyworlds: first, in terms of SF's own internal landscape – the extent to which SF has grown self-referentially – and second, in terms of SF's external effect – the extent to which SF storyworlds have influenced the vocabulary of political, social and cultural discourse. The series is interested in rethinking the possibilities of the genre, in particular, by engaging with different media (literature, film, television, radio, the Internet and the visual arts), critical and aesthetic theory, and reading in translation, including SF from Africa, Asia and Latin America. Although the series focus is on SF, it is open to writers who have alternated between genres (M. John Harrison, Ursula Le Guin) or who have cross-fertilized SF with Gothic and fantasy (China Miéville, Christopher Priest). We are interested in the current and future directions of SF.

Series Editor

Paul March-Russell (University of Kent)

CONTENTS

PART III: NATION, POLITICS AND GENDER

PART IV: NOVELIZATION

Acknowledgements

This book is 'based on' a conference, *Science Fiction across Media: Adaptation/Novelization*, at the Faculty of Arts, KU Leuven in 2009, which was made possible by the support of FWO Vlaanderen (Research Foundation Flanders) and the Institute for Cultural Studies as well as the Faculty of Arts at KU Leuven. The keynote speakers were Andrew M. Butler, I.Q. Hunter, Peter Verstraten and Peter Wright.

The editors would like to express their gratitude to all the contributors, series editor Paul March-Russell, Anthony Levings and everyone at Gylphi, and Jan Baetens, who inspired this whole project. They are also indebted to FWO Vlaanderen, whose generous grant helped realize this publication. Thomas Van Parys would like to dedicate this book to his parents, Christine (†) and Eric, and to his sister Liese. I.Q. Hunter would like to thank the Faculty of Art, Design and Humanities at De Montfort University for granting him study leave during which he wrote his chapter and completed editing this book; the staff of the BFI Library, where he carried out research; and Elaine Street, whose support made all the difference. He dedicates his work on this book to his two sons, Tom and Will.

Notes on Contributors

Mark Bould is Reader in Film and Literature at the University of the West of England and co-editor of *Science Fiction Film and Television*. He is the author of *Film Noir: From Berlin to Sin City* (2005), *The Cinema of John Sayles: Lone Star* (2009) and *Science Fiction: The Routledge Film Guidebook* (2012), co-author of *The Routledge Concise History of Science Fiction* (2011) and co-editor of *Parietal Games: Critical Writings by and on M. John Harrison* (2005), *The Routledge Companion to Science Fiction* (2009), *Fifty Key Figures in Science Fiction* (2009), *Red Planets: Marxism and Science Fiction* (2009) and *Neo-Noir* (2009). He is an advisory editor of *Extrapolation, Historical Materialism, Paradoxa* and *Science Fiction Studies*.

Andrew M. Butler is the author of Pocket Essentials on *Cyberpunk* (2000), *Terry Pratchett* (2001), *Postmodernism* (2003), *Film Studies* (2005) and *Philip K. Dick* (2007), and co-editor of *The Routledge Companion to Science Fiction* (2009) and *Fifty Key Figures in Science Fiction* (2009). He has also edited or co-edited collections of essays on Terry Pratchett, Ken MacLeod and Christopher Priest and is a co-editor of *Extrapolation*. He is currently working on science fiction in the 1970s and exploring the notion of the cognitive uncanny.

Aristea Chryssohou holds a BA in French Language and Literature and a BA with Honours in English Language and Literature, both from the Aristotle University of Thessaloniki, Greece. She also holds an MA in European Literature and Culture from AUTH and is currently working as a state school teacher of French in the Greek primary and secondary education. She has presented papers at international conferences and her main research interests are in the areas of comparative literature, cultural studies and intermediality.

Teresa Forde is Senior Lecturer in Film and Media and Programme Leader for the MA Humanities and the MA pathway in Horror and Transgression at the University of Derby. Teresa's publications include an article on science-fiction film and soundtrack, "The Sunshine Soundtrack as Aural Attraction", in the *New Review of Film and Television Studies* (2011) and has both guest-edited and contributed to an issue of *Image [&] Narrative* entitled "Memory Screens" (2011). Her research interests are in science fiction, soundtrack, memory and consciousness in film and television.

I.Q. Hunter is Reader in Film Studies at De Montfort University, Leicester, UK. He has published widely on science fiction, horror, exploitation cinema and literary adaptation, including, as editor, *British Science Fiction Cinema* (1999) and, as co-editor, *British Comedy Cinema* (2012), *Controversial Images* (2012) and six books in Pluto's Film/Fiction series, including *Pulping Fictions* (1996), *Alien Identities* (1999) and *Retrovisions* (2001). He is currently completing *British Trash Cinema* for BFI/Palgrave.

Cynthia J. Miller is a cultural anthropologist, specializing in popular culture and visual media, and her writing has appeared in a wide range of journals and anthologies across the disciplines, including the recent *Télévision: le moment expérimental* (2011) and *Science Fiction Film, Television, and Adaptation: Across the Screens* (2011). Cynthia serves as series editor for Scarecrow Press's Film and History series. She is also the editor of the forthcoming volume *Too Bold for the Box Office: A Study in Mockumentary* and is on the editorial board of the *Encyclopedia of Women and American Popular Culture*. Cynthia is currently at work on several edited volumes: *Steaming into a Victorian Future: A Steampunk Anthology* with Julie Taddeo and Ken Dvorak, *Cadets, Rangers, and Junior Space Men: Televised "Rocketman" Series of the 1950s and Their Fans* with A. Bowdoin Van Riper and *Undead in the West: Vampires, Zombies, Mummies and Ghosts on the Cinematic Frontier* also with A. Bowdoin Van Riper.

Phil Nichols holds an MA in Screenwriting, has a background in video production and teaches all aspects of Video & Film Production. He is a Fellow of the Higher Education Academy and is currently working on a PhD at Liverpool University, supervised by David Seed. His research interest is in the screenplay as an interface between film production and literature, and adaptations to/from literature, film and other media. His primary focus is the American writer Ray Bradbury, who is best known for his short stories and novels in the popular genres of horror, fantasy and science fiction, but is also a writer whose authorship is most heavily engaged with self-adaptation. Phil serves on the advisory board of the Center for Ray Bradbury Studies and the editorial board of *The New Ray Bradbury Review*. His website at www.bradburymedia.co.uk catalogues and reviews Bradbury's work across all media, and is the most extensive bibliography and filmography of Bradbury on the web.

Nicholas Ruddick is professor and head of English at the University of Regina. He is the author of *Christopher Priest* (1989), *British Science Fiction: A Chronology, 1478-1990* (1993) and *Ultimate Island: On the Nature of British Science Fiction* (1993), and the editor of the critical anthology *State of the Fantastic* (1992). He has published scholarly editions of *The Time Machine* by H. G. Wells (2001), *Caesar's Column* by Ignatius Donnelly (2003), *The Woman Who Did* by Grant Allen (2004) and *The Call of the Wild* by Jack London (2009). He has written book chapters and articles on a wide variety of North American and European authors from Atwood to Zola. His most recent book was *The Fire in the Stone: Prehistoric Fiction from Charles Darwin to Jean M. Auel* (2009). He has chapters forthcoming on 'faithful' cinematic adaptations of Mary Shelley's *Frankenstein* and on film adaptations of the cold war thriller *Fail-Safe*. He is currently writing a book provisionally entitled *Science Fiction Adapted to Film: Attack of the Mutant Parasites* to be published by Gylphi.

Jamie Sherry is a Lecturer in Screenwriting at Bangor University, where he teaches writing for film and television, and critical and cultural theory. His research focuses on the transformative relationship of literature to film through the process of screenwriting, providing new concepts on literary adaptation. He is a Trustee for the Association of Adaptation Studies and serves on the steering committee for the Screenwriting Research Network.

Michael A. Stackpole is a novelist with over 41 published novels to his credit. Roughly two-thirds of his work has been in licensed universes including *Star Wars*, *BattleTech* and *Shadowrun*. His latest novel is *At the Queen's Command* (2010), which is the first in a series of his own creation. He resides in Arizona.

Gwilym Thear is currently completing a PhD on apocalyptic narratives in contemporary British culture at the School of Journalism, Media and Cultural Studies, Cardiff University.

Thomas Van Parys has recently finished his PhD thesis on science-fiction novelizations at the University of Leuven, Belgium. His research interests include adaptation and novelization, literary description and serialized TV narratives. His articles on novelization have been published in *Literature/Film Quarterly*, *Science Fiction Studies* and *Belphégor*.

Peter Verstraten is Assistant Professor of Film and Literary Studies as well as chair of the MA Film and Photographic Studies in Leiden. He has published *Film Narratology* (2009) at the University of Toronto Press as well as some studies in Dutch, among others on cinema and postmodernism. Currently, he is co-editing a book on directors of photography. His dissertation on westerns has been published as *Screening Cowboys: Reading Masculinities in Westerns* (1999), and he has written articles on the relation between attraction and narrativity, on early film fairy tales and on *Imitation of Life*. Articles on cult movies *Pierrot le fou* and *Hadewijch* are forthcoming.

Jennifer Woodward is a lecturer in English Literature and Film Studies at Edge Hill University. She has a Masters degree in Science Fiction Studies from the University of Liverpool and she is currently writing her PhD on British disaster science-fiction literature (1898-1945). Her published output covers work on psychoanalytic theory and adaptation studies, as well as science-fiction film, television and literature. Jennifer has contributed a chapter on J. Michael Straczynski, creator of the television science-fiction show *Babylon 5* for Routledge's *Fifty Key Figures in Science Fiction* (2009). She has also written chapters on *Deluge*, *No Blade of Grass* and *The World, the Flesh and the Devil* for the forthcoming *The Critical Companion to Science Fiction Film Adaptations*.

Andrea Wright is a senior lecturer in Film Studies at Edge Hill University. The focus of her doctoral thesis was gender, representation and the appeal of 1980s screen fairytales. Fantasy/fairytale cinema, aesthetics, costume, set design and location, and New Zealand cinema are central to her current research. She has written for the *Journal of British Cinema and Television*, *Anglo Files: Journal of English Teaching*, *British Review of New Zealand Studies*, and contributed chapters to the edited collections *New Zealand: A Pastoral Paradise?* (2000) and *Postmodern Reinterpretations of Fairy Tales: How Applying New Methods Generates New Meanings* (2011).

Peter Wright is Reader in Speculative Fictions at Edge Hill University in the North West of England. He is author of *Attending Daedalus: Gene Wolfe, Artifice and the Reader* (2003). He has written numerous articles and has contributed to Blackwell's *A Companion to Science Fiction* (2005), *The Routledge Companion to Science Fiction* (2009) and *Fifty Key Figures in Science Fiction* (2009). In 2005, he co-edited *British Science Fiction Television* with John Cook. His *Shadows of the New Sun: Wolfe on Writing/Writers on Wolfe* (2007) was a finalist for the Locus Award for non-fiction in 2008. Peter's *Teaching Science Fiction*, co-edited with Andy Sawyer, was published by Palgrave Macmillan in 2011. He is currently working on *When Worlds Collide: The Critical Companion to Science Fiction Film Adaptations* and an article on the BBC children's sf television serial *The Changes*.

Martin Zeller-Jacques has recently finished his PhD thesis on television narrative and endings at the University of York. He has published articles on adaptations, television narrative and televised sexuality in several edited collections and has also contributed to recent volumes of the Directory of World Cinema and the World Film Locations series.

LIST OF ILLUSTRATIONS

List of Illustrations

PART I

SCIENCE FICTION AND ADAPTATION

INTRODUCTION
SCIENCE-FICTION ADAPTATION ACROSS MEDIA

Thomas Van Parys and I.Q. Hunter

This book belongs to a new wave of adaptation studies, interested not only in detailed comparisons between novels and their screen versions, but in intertextuality and the proliferation of textual material across multiple media platforms. Case studies comparing originals and their screen copies remain the life-blood of adaptation studies, but they are significantly augmented by analyses of the 'adaptation industry' and the commercial exploitation of copyrighted properties in franchises, remakes and spin-offs of all kinds.[1] The familiar dyad of novel and film is joined by studies of comics, novelizations, toys, video games, theme-parks rides, remakes, reboots, extended and director's cuts, TV versions and the numerous other ways in which adaptations borrow from and relentlessly reproduce and commodify narratives and story worlds. In this way, adaptation can be seen as a key function in a 'vast narrative', which is a concept from new media studies that helps to understand how narratives are constructed across different forms of media (see Harrigan and Wardrip-Fruin, 2009). This book tries to illustrate how adaptations are elements of that 'vast fictional quilt' (Harrigan and Wardrip-Fruin, 2009: 2). The intention is that 'adaptation will become part of a general theory of repetition, and adaptation study will move from the margins to the center of contemporary media studies' (Naremore, 2000: 15). A ca-

3

sualty – sidelined rather than disproved – has been the automatic assumption that the novel is superior to the film. It is not entirely true that adaptation studies have always fetishized fidelity. That the most successful adaptations are often the freest and least faithful (*Throne of Blood* [Akira Kurosawa, 1957], *Apocalypse Now* [Francis Ford Coppola, 1979] and *The Shining* [Stanley Kubrick, 1980], for example) is as much a cliché as 'the book is always better than the film'. But qualitative comparisons based on reductive generalizations about what novels can do and films (usually) cannot have generally yielded to nuanced understandings of adaptation in production and reception contexts that make studies of betrayal simply unhelpful.

It is this view of adaptation that energizes this collection of essays on a significant field, that of science-fiction adaptations.[2] Science fiction (sf) is an important niche literary genre, but it is an absolutely central genre in contemporary film production, even if the films are often promoted as action films or epics rather than as sf movies. Sf novels have often provided source material for films and TV programmes, and major sf writers from H. G. Wells to Philip K. Dick have been adapted many times over. But it is fair to say that the relationship between sf literature and sf cinema has not been an easy one. To some extent there are the usual, qualitative issues around adaptation – the critical preference for the Word over the Image, the literary over the popular, and *anything* over Hollywood. From the point of view of enthusiasts for sf literature, this is compounded by some often repeated essentialist assumptions about the genre in the two media. Although cinema, with its ability to concretize immersive imaginary worlds, might seem sf's ideal platform, it is often seen as inimical to the 'true' purpose of the genre. Sf is regarded as 'idea-driven', while, adding a new spin to the old generalization that film cannot deal with ideas, cinema tends to literalism and empty-headed spectacle. The sf novelist Robert Silverberg, for example, commended *THX 1138* (George Lucas, 1971) and *Blade Runner* (Ridley Scott, 1982) for embodying 'the highest virtue the science fiction film can offer', as 'they show the way the future looks' (Silverberg, 2004: 172). But, he argued, if they were novels, 'they would be undistinguished ones' – 'Science fiction is, among other things, a literature of ideas; and the problem that each of these movies has *as science fiction literature* is its mediocrity on the level of idea' (Silverberg 2004: 173). Sf cinema also suffers from temporal intellectual drag. Whereas sf literature might be seen as a progressive genre, formally as well as intellectually, cinema is wedded to ideas and images sf literature got out of its system with the pulps, especially alien Bug-Eyed Monsters and a fear of science that allies sf films more closely to Gothic horror than to scientifically literate extrapolation. The case is summed up forcefully in *The Encyclopedia of Science Fiction*:

> Sf as literature is analytic and deals with ideas; film is the opposite of analytic, and has trouble with ideas. The way film deals with ideas is to give them visual shape, as images which may carry a metaphoric charge, but metaphors are tricky things, and, while the ideas of sf cinema may be potent, they are seldom precise. [...] Few influential sf filmmakers are literate in contemporary sf; at best, they draw groundwater from their adolescent reading a generation behind the calendar date. So, on its surface, sf cinema has often been simplistic, even though complex currents may trouble the depths where its subtexts glide. (Nicholls and Lowe, 2011)

Moreover, as John Baxter noted, sf literature and sf cinema have little common ground in terms of reception, too; the audience for an sf film 'is not a science fiction audience, but merely part of the great mass audience of the cinema generally' (Baxter, 1970: 8).

Sf on film, as a branch of escapist SFX-laden fantasy, is also often identified as symptomatic of contemporary Hollywood itself, dating from what Robin Wood called the 'Lucas-Spielberg Syndrome' in the wake of the release of *Star Wars* (George Lucas, 1977) and other 'children's films conceived and marketed largely for adults – films that construct the adult spectator as a child, or, more precisely, as a childish adult, an adult who would like to be a child' (Wood, 1986: 163). The influence of the success of *Star Wars* on cinema and on science fiction has been well-documented and indeed well-lamented, especially in regard to sf literature. Lou Anders's collection of essays by sf writers and critics is full of arguments why '*Star Wars* was the worst thing that ever happened to science fiction' (Sawyer, 2004: 160). For such critics *Star Wars* was Year Zero of cinema's infantilization, which found its apotheosis in Michael Bay's *Transformers* franchise, in which are combined all the negative qualities of today's post-classical sf cinema of spectacular eye-candy for kids. Like fantasy, sf is important to contemporary film and TV production because it allows the creation of secondary worlds – 'world-building', as Henry Jenkins has called it (see Jenkins, 2006) – and synergy across video games, comic books, novelizations, toys, websites and other spin-offs. After the downfall of the studio system, New Hollywood gradually developed their conglomeration politics, which led to the transformation of a film into an entire multimedia experience – which Sean Cubitt calls the 'neobaroque' cinema. The neobaroque film 'moves away from the promotion of fantasy anchored in the star persona to situate it in the diegetic universe from which it springs [...] and which it further promotes and develops' (Cubitt, 2005: 218). This encourages the consumption of sf as cult: novelizations, making-of books, DVD packages and extras and other paratexts, as well as the 'original' text, clamour to orientate us, involve us in the text, and relate to it commercially. Ernest Mathijs and Jamie Sexton make this point about blockbuster films, which have the possibility of further adaptation and franchising built into them:

> When the consumption of a blockbuster film is not merely accompanied but in fact *constructed* through satellite texts and dispersed discourses it develops characteristics strikingly similar to those of cult viewing, such as multiple exposure, immersion, and the invitation to create interpretations far beyond the single film-text. (Mathijs and Sexton, 2011: 216)

Adaptation is not supplementary but absolutely central to how a blockbuster works. The film itself is 'a starting place as much as an end product of adaptation: just one reference point in a matrix of intertextual relations created by synergic cross-promotion' (Hunter 2007: 154). Ideally, as with sf franchises like *Star Trek*, *Planet of the Apes*, *Star Wars*, *Alien* and *Predator*, stand-alone films may develop into immersive intertextual myths, designed for cult appropriation as well as mass-market appeal. But the blockbuster tradition of escapist spectacle is far from the only manifestation of sf on contemporary screens. As well as *Transformers* (Michael Bay, 2007) and *Avatar* (James Cameron, 2009) – the most successful film ever made – sf on screen also embraces exploitation cinema (*Evil Aliens* [Jake West, 2005]), art-house and small-scale independent films such as *Crash* (David Cronenberg, 1996) and *Moon* (Duncan Jones, 2009), literary adaptations such as *Children of Men* (Alfonso Cuarón, 2006) and *Never Let Me Go* (Mark Romanek, 2010), and of course cult TV series such as *Doctor Who* (1963–89; 2005–), *Battlestar Galactica* (1978–9; 2003–9) and *Firefly* (2002–3), all of which testify to the vitality of sf at every level of screen culture.

As part of the approach to adaptation as a process within a larger textual network, one of the central aims of this book is to highlight the under-discussed phenomenon of novelization, which may function as a kind of link between the new theoretical paradigms and the traditional literature/film approach in adaptation studies. Basically, 'novelization' means adaptation into a novel; those novels can be based on films, TV series, videogames or other media. Most of the time, however, a ('commercial') novelization is not actually adapted from the film itself, but from the screenplay of that film. It is also – in contrast with a novel-to-film adaptation – released concurrently with the film, functioning as a marketing tool to heighten visibility and awareness of the title in places like bookshops, supermarkets, newspaper kiosks or airport stands, where there is no space for regular film advertisements to reach the casual yet potential filmgoer. On that same book market, however, novelizations are very easily confused with novels republished as film tie-ins after they have been adapted into films, which has created a general unfamiliarity with the phenomenon.

As Randall D. Larson signals, 'there has been a tremendous increase in the popularity and output of these movie novelizations' over the last couple of decades, 'especially of films in the science fiction, fantasy, and horror genres, and it is these novelizations which traditionally have been the most successful' (Larson, 1995: 5). With regard to novelizations of sf films or TV series, it must be emphasized that the science-fiction novelization is usually not regarded as an entity in itself, but it is first and foremost associated with the category of 'novelization', since novelization (at least the 'commercial' Hollywood variant) constitutes a genre itself. Additionally, sf novelizations have been repulsed by sf literature and lumped into the general category of novelizations and spin-off novels. Science fiction has a history of striving for emancipation and legitimation, which it tried to attain, at least until recently (with the phenomenon of 'genre-morphing'), by distinguishing itself from other genres like fantasy and all 'impure' forms of literary sf. An indication of this categorization of sf novelizations in tandem with other novelizations (especially fantasy and horror) is the habits of collectors, especially concerning (but not restricted to) novelizations from the studio system era; usually these collections even encompass both novelizations and adapted books, for the attracting feature for the collector is the book cover of the tie-in (or 'photoplay edition') with the movie poster and/or the movie star (e.g. Davis, 2002; Miller, 2002; Wadle, 1994).

The new blockbuster film, already blamed for turning science fiction into escapism and spectacle, also had considerable influence on the market for novelizations because of its tendency to give rise to an endless number of tie-ins. In the US, 'the sales of science fiction books that aren't related to *Star Trek*, *Star Wars*, or other media properties, are the worst they've ever been' (Larson, 1995: 165). The novelization of *Star Wars* (1976), ghost-written by Alan Dean Foster, together with David Seltzer's *The Omen* (1976) made Hollywood realize that, besides raising awareness, novelizations could also be bestsellers in their own right (even though book-length novelizations go back to the first long movie serials and narrative films). Among all other ancillary products, this generated innumerable spin-off or 'continuation' novels, which developed the universe of many franchises. And it was the success of these books that sf literature had to rival with: 'although publication and sales of SF, fantasy, and horror (often overlapping and lumped together) soared in succeeding decades, the increase was in media-related *Star Wars* and *Star Trek* novels, and novelizations of almost every other SF TV series and film' (Gunn, 2004: 54).

In many ways, therefore, the sf novelization stands as a symbol for the clash between sf literature and sf cinema, which largely emanates from the projection of sf writers' ideas of what science fiction should be and aspire to be onto sf cinema. Silverberg, referring to the novelization of *THX 1138* (1971) by 'the experienced science fiction writer Ben Bova', claims concretely that 'not even Bova's professionalism could lift the story beyond the level of the perfunctory' (Silverber, 2004: 173). As with adaptation, the crux of the problem here lies with, and always arises with, direct comparison. Instead of weighing up its shortcomings vis-à-vis science-fiction literature, which in the end it does not share much with contextually speaking, this book will acknowledge the science-fiction novelization as a text that negotiates between sf literature and sf cinema – inheriting from both these media in the sf genre. For instance, on the one hand a novelization can add a scientific explanation or historical foundation to the story; on the other hand it can foreground the 'sense of wonder' which the visuality of the film should elicit from the reader/viewer, or overlay a filmic point of view over the text, for example: 'The whole background of nothingness seemed to change as a camera changes focus, bringing objects that were blurred into invisibility suddenly into clear, sharp view' (Bova, 1978: 113). This specific negotiation is what makes novelization interesting, since it can put both sf literature and sf cinema in a different light; at the same time a novelization may enhance and enrich our view on a given film, or on a given multimedia network of texts.

In this book, a wide range of adaptations will be discussed, moving from art films and the classic subjects of film adaptation theory, over more obscure films, over novelization of the film, to texts that have been adapted across various media. There is a distinct focus on concrete case studies, in which the authors analyse adaptation from the viewpoint they consider as appropriate to the given case – whether it is a traditional comparative approach or there is more attention to intertextuality and intermediality. After all, as Christine Geraghty says, 'there is no one model for creating or analyzing an adaptation' (Geraghty, 2008: 5). The first section of the book includes two longer essays that deal with the core issues of science-fiction adaptation in general, providing a framework and foundation for the entire book. Parts II and III consist of case studies of film adaptations, the former concentrating on a few classic art films and the latter engaging with the key thematic transformations involved in the process of adaptation. Parts IV and V, moving away from the traditional book-to-film adaptation, offer a much-expanded intertextual understanding of sf adaptation.

Going back to the formal roots of science-fiction criticism, Peter Wright proposes a taxonomy that lays out the different types of cinematic estrangement and their enunciation in science-fiction cinema. His model charts the structural principles behind the cinematic adaptation of literary sf, showing how sf adaptations are exemplary texts in order to understand the conceptual and aesthetic differences between sf literature and sf cinema. I.Q. Hunter, focusing on reception rather than formal analysis, argues that adaptation studies could make useful links with audience and cult/fan studies. He investigates how an emotional investment into a given film leads cinephiles to continually reframe it by layering all kinds of source texts, adaptations and intertexts over that film. With *2001: A Space Odyssey* (1968), Stanley Kubrick also thematizes and allegorizes the evolution of cinema beyond literature, running counter to the alleged superiority of the novel over film – despite the widespread influence of Arthur C. Clarke's novelization (1968), which represents all the traditions of science-fiction literature that Kubrick rejects and transcends.

Opening the book's series of case studies are two analyses of Nicolas Roeg's *The Man Who Fell to Earth* (1976). Peter Verstraten addresses the countercultural elements in the film, which represent a deviation from Walter Tevis's novel (1963). In the film, he shows, the continually defamiliarizing style mirrors the estranged experience of the alien protagonist, who is placed between the Alien Chic of popular sf cinema (aliens resemble yet differ from humans) and the similitude in marginal sf cinema (aliens are humans). Andrew M. Butler focuses on how the discontinuity editing in the film represents the abnormal consciousness of the alien, reversing the traditional male gaze in Hollywood cinema. Despite the fidelity of the film to the novel with regard to the theme of 'falling', the auteur Roeg makes the film his own through his distinct editing style. Lastly, he shows how this feeds into Philip K. Dick's *VALIS* (1981), which is strongly linked to Roeg's film structurally and intertextually.

Teresa Forde compares two film versions of Stanislaw Lem's *Solaris* (1961), one, by Andrei Tarkovsky (1972), a classic of art-house cinema and the other, by Steven Soderbergh (2002), a high-minded multiplex movie. Forde deconstructs the chronological order of the novel and its adaptations. Drawing a parallel with the story of *Solaris,* she argues that the reader/viewer (as well as the author) processes the various texts by building memories of Lem's novel and the adaptations, and in this way goes on a (Derridean) archival search for the meaning of the *Solaris* texts. Jamie Sherry, on the other hand, draws a parallel between genre theory and adaptation studies. He investigates how Andrei Tarkovsky's *Stalker* (1979) shakes loose the sf genre characteristics of Arkady and Boris Strugatsky's source novel *Roadside Picnic* (1971), but is then reintegrated into the sf genre as the film itself reshapes the definition of what science fiction is and should be. Precisely by breaking down sf, Sherry argues, *Stalker* inspires new understandings of both genre and adaptation. In this way, the source material becomes dynamic, as it is continually repositioned by adaptations, which are themselves always in a state of flux.

Nicholas Ruddick compares J. G. Ballard's *Crash* (1973) and David Cronenberg's film (1996), which are both highly respectable – and allegedly compatible – texts in their own medium. Via an analysis of the spatial specificity of each text, he demonstrates how the adaptation is far from faithful to the source, and then weighs up the novel and film on the basis not of fidelity but of their generic, semantic and aesthetic traits, arriving at the conclusion that Cronenberg's film is a supplement rather than a complement to Ballard's novel. Aristea Chryssohou, going back to the basics of adaptation studies, provides a narratological comparison between Ray Bradbury's novel *Fahrenheit 451* (1953) and François Truffaut's 1966 film adaptation. Illustrating Truffaut's transformation of the source text with Roland Barthes's breakdown of narrative functions, she gives special attention to how both texts deal with the theme of orality in such a dystopian society.

Two further case studies then focus on thematic links between novels and their adaptations. Andrea Wright takes a look at the New Zealand film *The Quiet Earth* (Geoff Murphy, 1985), by discussing its similarities and contrasts with the rare source novel by Craig Harrison (1981). Her essay proving the importance of contextualization, she situates each text by tracing their representation of gender, race and nation. Notably, the influence of the differing contexts of production is exemplified by the variety of interpretations of the apocalypse in novel and film. In the next case study, an analysis of Felix E. Feist's obscure film adaptation (1933) of Sydney Fowler Wright's disaster novel *Deluge* (1927), Jennifer Woodward, too, addresses the cultural and political context of the texts. She shows in detail how, as they comment on their modern societal circumstances, novel and film both re-establish patriarchal values through their differing representation of women.

The traditional corpus for case studies, novel-to-film adaptation, is turned on its head for the next section on novelization, which also gives the floor to two writers who have personal experience in the field. In an interview, Christopher Priest gives an illuminating account of how he concretely set about the task to novelize David Cronenberg's *eXistenZ* (1999). He reveals some of the additional problems and demands that may crop up, showing how a novelization is not just a transcription, but necessarily requires adaptational changes, which the novelizer can seize to make improvements. Also based on personal experience as a distinguished novelizer, Michael A. Stackpole draws up a taxonomy for novelizations and continuation novels that differentiates between the various kinds of non-creator-owned novels and highlights the wide range of franchise work. Based in practice, his model provides a highly pertinent counterpoint to a recently published 'typology' of novelization (Van Parys, 2011), which maps the phenomenon through the prism of novelization studies. By means of apt examples, Stackpole carefully unravels the artificial opposition between creativity and fidelity to the canon established by the primary source material.

Thomas Van Parys focuses on Orson Scott Card's novelization (1989) of *The Abyss* (James Cameron, 1989), asking if film and novel are truly as complementary as they claim to be. The thread running throughout his analysis is that the criterion for a respected novelization, fidelity to the film, is opposite to the Romantic view on adaptation, which dictates that a good adaptation is one that is unfaithful and creative. Gwilym Thear, too, discusses a novelization with an unusual authorship, namely Terry Nation's novelization *Survivors* (1976) of the cult television series from the 1970s (1975–7). As it has been republished as source novel for the recent remake of the series (2008–10), the novel negotiates an interesting and ambivalent position between novelization and adaptation, further complicated by the fact that Nation has also created the series. Even though the same label, 'Terry Nation's *Survivors*', is virtually applied to all three texts, Thear shows they are in fact quite divergent.

Moving away from one-on-one adaptation and novelization, the last section illustrates the vast span of certain sf texts, characters and themes, across time and across media. Cynthia J. Miller focuses on adaptations not of a given text but of a specific theme, as she discusses the various incarnations of the third eye in science fiction across all media. She devotes special attention to two television episodes, 'Will the Real Martian Please Stand Up?' (1961) from *The Twilight Zone* (1959–64) and 'The Martian Eyes' (1950) from the anthology series *Lights Out* (1946–52), which represent the American Cold War fear and paranoia of the day. In the next chapter, Phil Nichols breaks down the assumed link between the controlling influence of the original author and fidelity to the source text on the basis of the various incarnations of Ray Bradbury's short story 'A Sound of Thunder' (1952). Even when the author's name turns into a brand, he shows that Bradbury's control or self-adaptation can lead to a more creative and better adaptation, regardless of how far it remains faithful.

The final two chapters both explore the vast story universe of one particular fictional character, discussing the ensuing complications of all the adaptations, remakes, reboots – in fact of intertextuality itself. Martin Zeller-Jacques demonstrates how each new iteration of the *Superman* mythos struggles to free itself from its predecessors; it inscribes itself into the vast *Superman* meta-text in order to affirm that it is part of the authentic canon, while at the same time establishing Superman in its new context, thereby necessarily rejecting previous *Superman* texts. Rather than an attempt at accurate copying, adaptation is a series of crises. Mark Bould's study of *Flash Gordon*'s numerous 'extraordinary renditions' similarly shows that fidelity is no longer a useful model for understanding adaptation. As he suggests, perhaps it is possible to conceptualize an adaptation as a Derridean supplement – at the same time an addition to and a substitution of the source text. However, each adaptation as well as each source text has multiple sources; both are equally complex intertextually. In this way, according to Bould, adaptation is better seen as a complex transformation of all the different discrete elements of the source intertext.

As these last two chapters explicitly indicate, this book moves the understanding of adaptation away from fidelity to one source text towards 'misprision' – a deliberate creative misreading of a text. Adaptations not only refer back to their sources but present themselves as new texts that supersede previous versions, as upgrades as much as copies. The ambivalent connection between related texts often entails a complex web of, and play between, a canon and ancillary texts, complementary and supplementary status, auteur and adapter. At the same time, misprision refers to the interpretive acts that both the adapter and the reader/viewer undertake. Everyone assigns their own set of salient characteristics to a given text: the adapter transforms the source text on the basis of his or her understanding of that text; the reader/viewer holds the selected features of the adaptation against those of the source. What this book thus shows is that adaptation is not only a process of transmedialization from one text to the other, but also a way of approaching a certain text. As a way of reading, adaptation sheds new light on familiar science-fiction texts; studying sf in light of adaptation also brings under-discussed incarnations of certain sf texts to the fore. Conversely, genre also brings something to the table of adaptation studies: on the one hand, genre is an essential component of the study of adaptation (for it is not only the text, but also the genre that is being adapted); on the other hand, it also shows how a comparison with the original text is not necessarily the only, or even the most significant, way of approaching an adaptation (for 'the most important thing about an adaptation might precisely not be its adaptation status' [Geraghty, 2008: 193]). Genre opens up many other avenues of exploring a given adaptation, as the diversity of the essays in this book testifies. In the end, this very book of course tries to be a supplement itself, in that for all its references to previous adaptation theories it wants to substitute those at the same time. And it is our hope that this collection of essays may prove to be a fertile starting point for further supplements and misprisions.

Notes

1 The key recent books in adaptation studies, which supersede earlier 'profoundly moralistic' studies (Stam, 2005: 3) that 'reinscribe the axiomatic superiority of literature to film' (Stam, 2005: 4), are Stam and Raengo (2005), Hutcheon (2006), Cartmell and Whelehan (2007), Leitch (2007), Geraghty (2008), Gray (2010), and Saint Jacques (2011).

2 Currently there is a great surge of interest in science-fiction adaptation. Recently published and forthcoming books in this field are Jay Telotte and Gerald Duchovnay's collection *Science Fiction Film, Television, and Adaptation: Across the Screens* (2011), which chronicles the adaptive journey of a selection of popular sf films and TV series; Peter Wright and Sue Short's volume *When Worlds Collide: The Critical Companion to Science Fiction Film Adaptations*, which provides a comprehensive overview of sf film adaptations; and Nicholas Ruddick's book, provisionally entitled *Science Fiction Adapted to Film: Attack of the Mutant Parasites*.

References

Baxter, J. (1970) *Science Fiction in the Cinema*. New York: A. S. Barnes & Co.

Bova, B. (1971/1978) *THX 1138*. London, Toronto, Sydney and New York: Granada Publishing.

Cartmell, D. and Whelehan, I. (eds) (2007) *The Cambridge Companion to Literature on Screen*. Cambridge: Cambridge University Press.

Cubitt, S. (2005) *The Cinema Effect*. Cambridge, MA and London: MIT Press.

Davis, A. (2002) *Photoplay Editions and Other Movie Tie-In Books: The Golden Years 1912–1969*. East Waterboro, ME: Mainely Books.

Geraghty, C. (2008) *Now a Major Motion Picture: Film Adaptations of Literature and Drama*. Lanham, MD: Rowman & Littlefield.

Gray, J. (2010) *Show Sold Separately: Promos, Spoilers, and Other Media Paratexts*. New York and London: New York University Press.

Gunn, J. E. (2004) 'The Tinsel Screen', in L. Anders (ed.) *Projections: Science Fiction in Literature & Film*, pp. 43–59. Austin, TX: MonkeyBrain Books.

Harrigan, P. and Wardrip-Fruin, N. (eds) (2009) *Third Person: Authoring and Exploring Vast Narratives*. Cambridge, MA and London: MIT Press.

Hunter, I.Q. (2007) 'Post-classical Action Cinema: *The Lord of the Rings*', in D. Cartmell and I. Whelehan (eds) *The Cambridge Companion to Literature on Screen*, pp. 154–66. Cambridge: Cambridge University Press.

Hutcheon, L. (2006) *A Theory of Adaptation*. New York and London: Routledge.

Jenkins, H. (2006) *Convergence Culture: Where Old and New Media Collide*. New York and London: New York University Press.

Larson, R.D. (1995) *Films into Books: An Analytical Bibliography of Film Novelizations, Movie, and TV Tie-Ins*. Metuchen, NJ and London: The Scarecrow Press.

Leitch, T. (2007) *Film Adaptation and Its Discontents: From Gone with the Wind to The Passion of the Christ*. Baltimore, MD: The Johns Hopkins University Press.

Mathijs, E. and Sexton, J. (2011) *Cult Cinema*. Chichester: Wiley-Blackwell.

Miller, R. (2002) *Photoplay Editions: A Collector's Guide*. Jefferson: McFarland.

Naremore, J. (2000) 'Introduction: Film and the Reign of Adaptation', in J. Naremore (ed.) *Film Adaptation*, pp. 1–16. London: The Athlone Press.

Nicholls, P. and Lowe, N. (2011) 'Cinema', in J. Clute and D. Langford (eds) *SFE: The Encyclopedia of Science Fiction. Third Edition*, http://www.sf-encyclopedia.com/Entry/cinema (accessed October 2011).

Ruddick, N. (forthcoming) *Science Fiction Adapted to Film: Attack of the Mutant Parasites*. Canterbury: Gylphi.

Saint Jacques, J. (ed.) (2011) *Adaptation Theories*. Maastricht: Jan van Eyck Academie.

Sawyer, R.J. (2004) 'The Future Is Already Here: Is There a Place for Science Fiction in the Twenty-First Century?', in L. Anders (ed.) *Projections: Science Fiction in Literature and Film*, pp. 153–69. Austin, TX: MonkeyBrain Books.

Silverberg, R. (2004) 'The Way the Future Looks: *THX 1138* and *Blade Runner*', in L. Anders (ed.) *Projections: Science Fiction in Literature and Film*, pp. 171–7. Austin, TX: MonkeyBrain Books.

Stam, R. (2005) 'Introduction: The Theory and Practice of Adaptation', in R. Stam and A. Raengo (eds) *Literature and Film: A Guide to the Theory and Practice of Film Adaptation*, pp. 1–52. Oxford: Blackwell.

Stam, R. and Raengo, A. (eds) (2005) *Literature and Film: A Guide to the Theory and Practice of Film Adaptation*. Oxford: Blackwell.

Telotte, J.P. and Duchovnay, G. (eds) (2011) *Science Fiction Film, Television, and Adaptation: Across the Screens*. New York: Routledge.

Van Parys, T. (2011) 'The Study of Novelisation: A Typology and Secondary Bibliography', *Belphégor* 10 (2), http://etc.dal.ca/belphegor/vol10_no2/articles/10_02_paryst_noveli_fr.html (accessed October 2011).

Wadle, M. (1994) *The Movie Tie-In Book: A Collector's Guide to Paperback Movie Editions.* Coralville: Nostalgia.

Wood, R. (1986) *Hollywood from Vietnam to Reagan.* New York and Chichester: Columbia University Press.

Wright, P. and Short, S. (eds) (forthcoming) *When Worlds Collide: The Critical Companion to Science Fiction Film Adaptations.* Liverpool: Liverpool University Press.

Chapter 1

Science Fiction from Text to Screen
Adaptation, the Novum and Cinematic Estrangement

Peter Wright

Most science-fiction theorists – Darko Suvin (1979), Carl Freed-man (2000) and Istvan Csicsery-Ronay (2003) among them – have argued convincingly that sf is formally different from both mundane literature and fantastical genres reliant on the super- or supranatu-ral. Accordingly, it is not sufficient to rely solely on methodologies conventionally applied to mainstream or fantastic film adaptations; where relevant, theoretical approaches to print science fiction should inform the analysis of its rendering on screen. Only in this way can a critical discourse be developed that furthers the understanding of the adaptation processes involved. To date, few commentators have followed this line of reasoning. Hence, given that this is a preliminary venture, it is appropriate to consider the adaptation of two of sf's principal formal qualities: its deployment of novums or innovations within its story worlds and its estranging effect on the reader.

In his seminal *The Metamorphoses of Science Fiction*, Suvin argues that sf '*is distinguished by the narrative dominance or hegemony of a fic-tional "novum" (novelty, innovation) validated by cognitive logic*' (Suvin, 1979: 63). He suggests that the novum is 'so central and significant that it determines the whole narrative logic – or at least the overriding narrative logic' (Suvin, 1979: 70) of any sf narrative. Clearly, a novum could manifest in a variety of magnitudes, and in any number of ways, as 'a new locus, or an agent (character) with new powers transforming the old locus' (Suvin, 1979: 78–9), or a happening that alters the story world, or a totalized and/or totalizing technical innovation. Such novums would, therefore, include Isaac Asimov's positronic robots (in *I, Robot* [1950]) and other works), for example, or the dying sun of Gene Wolfe's four-volume *The Book of the New Sun* (1980–3), or H. G. Wells's titular time-travelling device in *The Time Machine* (1895). The 'totalized' novum, engendering an unfamiliar newness, is an essential element in Suvin's qualification of science fiction as the literature of 'cognitive estrangement': '*SF is* [...] *a literary genre whose necessary and sufficient conditions are the presence and interaction of estrangement and cognition, and whose main formal device is an imaginative framework alternative to the author's empirical environment*' (Suvin, 1979: 7–8). Although this definition has been revised and modified – most notably and usefully by Freedman in *Critical Theory and Science Fiction* (Freedman, 2000: 16–23) – it remains 'not only fundamentally sound but indispensable' (Freedman, 2000: 17).

Freedman clarifies Suvin's position by noting that 'science fiction is determined by the *dialectic* between estrangement and cognition' (Freedman, 2000: 16). Herein the novum can be the progenitor of both estrangement *and* cognition. Estrangement, Freedman makes clear, 'refers to the creation of an alternative world that, by refusing to take our mundane environment for granted, implicitly or explicitly performs an estranging critical interrogation of the latter.' The '*critical* nature of the interrogation is guaranteed by the operation of cognition, which enables the science-fictional text to account rationally for its imagined world and for the connections as well as the disconnections of the latter to our own empirical world' (Freedman, 2000: 16–17). Nevertheless, in much popular western sf (particularly in film and on television), one finds considerably more instances of *estrangement* than of *cognitive estrangement*, even if one broadens the scope of the term to accommodate critiques – feminist, postcolonial, queer – additional to Suvin's Marxist position. It is apparent that whilst sf literature and film both present estranging alternate worlds, they are less consistently engaged with 'activating the science fiction tendency' (Freedman, 2000: 22) towards cognitive reflection. As a consequence, and for the purpose of this essay, it is beneficial to separate *estrangement* from *cognition* to consider how sf's 'attitude of estrangement', what Suvin terms 'the *formal framework* of the genre' (Suvin, 1979: 7) is enunciated in sf cinema.

Before the enunciation of estrangement in film can be explored, however, it is necessary to consider how estranging effects are achieved in sf literature. Like the largely mimetic mystery genre, where information relating to story is often released gradually through plot, sf restricts information regarding story while *additionally* withholding information concerning a story world's reality, its history, social relations, et cetera. In effect, then, sf deploys both *epistemological estrangement* and *ontological estrangement*. Such estrangement arises from an asymmetry between the knowledge of the narrator and that of the reader, which leads to the incorporation of the reader into the process of textual reproduction. There are, in effect, moments of indeterminacy, Iserian gaps that engage the reader in Barthesian 'writerly' activity. As Samuel R. Delany points out, 'In a simple sense what science fiction does [...] is to take recognizable syntagms [strings of signs] and substitute in them, here and there, signifiers from a till then wholly unexpected paradigm [a whole class of signs that may stand for each other]' (Delany, 1978: 225–6, cited in Broderick, 1995: 34). Consequently, 'The reader's development of the missing paradigm may be idiosyncratic, but it remains limited by the syntagmatic aspects of the narrative' (MacLean, 1984: 171). The reading process, bounded by syntagmatic structures, ultimately leads to an understanding of how both story world and story structure work.

The reader's gradual comprehension of the principles governing sf's story worlds is examined in terms of the '*informativity* of the fictional world' by Peter Stockwell in *The Poetics of Science Fiction* (2000). Following Robert De Beaugrande's *Text, Discourse and Process: Toward a Multi-Disciplinary Science of Texts* (1980), Stockwell explains:

Working from the notion that readers bring certain real-world expectations to a reading, De Beaugrande [...] suggests that texts have
three orders of informativity (information-content matched against
the known 'facts' of the world). Occurrences in a text which are fully
expected when matched with the reader's world-knowledge are of
first-order informativity [...]. Unusual occurrences, with a middle order of probability, are classed as second-order *informativity*. Occurrences outside the expected range of probable options convey *third-
order informativity*; these are a serious challenge to a world-knowledge
which activates a motivation search to resolve ('downgrade') the discrepancy [...] (Stockwell, 2000: 164)

Clearly, as Stockwell points out, 'Science fiction often has third order occurrences that are downgradable by discoverable principles'
(Stockwell, 2000: 164). That is, anomalies (signifiers from Delany's
'unexpected paradigm', for example) are downgraded (possibly
through MacLean's 'syntagmatic aspects') by recognizing they were
part of a science-fictional story world wherein such anomalies are ex-
plicable. They move from third-order informativity to first-order informativity through contextualization. The 'discoverable principles'
usually result in the reader's reassessment of the contextual frame of
the story: 'the mental store of information about the "current context of reading"' (Stockwell, 2000: 13) is either replaced, modified,
repaired or switched. Most commonly, sf narratives rely upon frame
replacement (Philip K. Dick's *Ubik* [1969]) or frame modification
(the frame of Gene Wolfe's *The Book of the New Sun* [1980–3] is modified by the coda, *The Urth of the New Sun* [1987]). The principles by
which the reader experiences these replacements or modifications are
made available either *explicitly* through the diegesis – effectively resolved through the reconciliation of plot with story (*Ubik*) – or indicated *implicitly* through the text's linguistic, cultural, intertextual and
intratextual clues and cues (Wolfe's *Urth* cycle). Stockwell's redeploy-
ment of De Beaugrande's ideas provides a means for understanding
estrangement as *information rationing*. Moments of third-order informativity are moments of estrangement.

Arguably, such 'occurrences outside the expected range of probable options' which 'convey *third-order informativity*' are a feature

both within the diegesis as aspects of the contextual frame (narrative events, happenings or elements of setting, or unfamiliar agents or actants) and as linguistic elements of the text itself (which, of course, contribute to the unexpectedness of the diegesis). The reader can, therefore, be estranged narratively, conceptually and linguistically – although it should be acknowledged that all forms of literary estrangement derive from the text's existence as language. Estrangement as a consequence of formal textual innovation or experimentation is uncommon outside the British New Wave, perhaps unsurprisingly given sf's publishing history and status as a popular genre.

Since estrangement in sf literature is achieved through language, it is necessary to consider potentially estranging linguistic techniques. Stockwell notes that 'The vast majority of science fictional writing is not syntactically deviant or semantically challenging [...] Mostly, science fictional texture is about reporting a story, in a fairly plain manner' (Stockwell, 2000: 76). Nevertheless, he identifies a number of strategies that may produce instances of third-order informativity. These include the coining of neologisms through creation, borrowing, derivation, compounding, shortening and inflection (Stockwell, 2000: 118) and the deployment of neosemes (words demonstrating meaning shift) through broadening, narrowing, metaphor, metonymy and recontextualization – 'the source of most neosemy in science fiction' (Stockwell, 2000: 121).

Sf's linguistic ingenuity and its estranging potential are the factors largely perceived as distinguishing it from sf film (see Broderick, 1995: 111). Given that Hollywood cinema – the focus of this essay – is not a cinema of radical, formal estrangement, sf audiences are rarely exposed to departures from familiar stylistic or narrative conventions. Synchronous sound, continuity editing, cause and effect sequencing and unequivocal psychological motivations are rarely subverted. Plots and imagery are frequently derivative, even when sf film is not explicitly sourced from pre-sold properties. Indeed, historically, Hollywood cinema has avoided narratives that exhibit radical estranging effects, which are, in some ambiguous manner, 'untranslatable'. Nevertheless, estrangement is a factor in sf cinema. As Vivian Sobchack points out in *Screening Space: The American Science Fiction Film*, 'The visual surface of all sf film presents us with a confrontation between and mixture of those images to which we respond as "alien" and those we know to be familiar' (Sobchack, 1997: 87). Sobchack refers to images that 'evoke a sense of strangeness – a sense of wonder' or which are 'visually jolting' (Sobchack, 1997: 87). These may not, of course, be 'estranging'. However salient and incisive Sobchack's observations are, she does not consider fully the sources of estrangement occurring within sf cinema, and which are identified most clearly by an assessment of the enunciation of sf's literary estrangements in film.

There is a caveat, however. Just as the effect of estrangement in science-fiction literature is mitigated by its growing megatext, the effect of estrangement in sf film and sf film adaptation is undermined by generic verisimilitude, which informs sf's own cinematic megatext. Indeed, estrangement in sf cinema in general always exists in tension with generic verisimilitude. The icons of sf film and literature are well known to both reader and viewer. The future city, the robot, the alien, the wasteland and the spaceship, for example, have all had their estranging potential dispersed by overfamiliarity. Hence, achieving an estranging effect always depends upon novelty, upon Suvin's 'strange newness' or 'novum' that reinvigorates and, possibly, re-intellectualizes the reading and/or viewing experience. It marks the point at which the passive reader/viewer is activated, becomes aware and self-aware, and begins to question what he or she is reading or watching stylistically and/or intellectually. Estranging effects, therefore, are achieved in sf cinema when generic verisimilitude is transgressed, when diegetic absorption is interrupted, and/or when the non-quotidian element or elements of a narrative provoke a dislocation, repositioning the viewer as a questioning observer.

In terms of how sources of estrangement are communicated, Seymour Chatman's diagrammatic model of the cinematic narrator in *Coming to Terms* is invaluable (Figure 1).

The notion of the film narrator as the whole apparatus of film technique can be clarified by borrowing a term from Brian McFarlane's *Novel to Film: An Introduction to the Theory of Adaptation* (1996). McFarlane makes a distinction between 'Those elements of the original novel which are transferable because they are not tied to one or

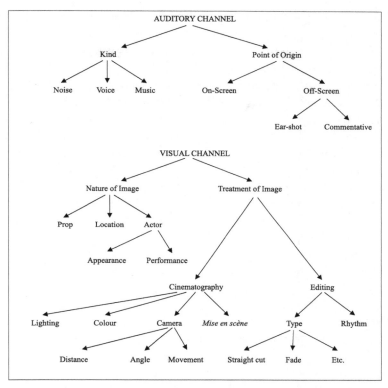

Figure 1. Seymour Chatman's diagrammatic model of the cinematic narrator in *Coming to Terms* (Chatman, 2000: 134–5).

other semiotic system – that is, essentially, *narrative*' (characters, plot, free direct speech, etc.) and 'those which involve intricate processes of adaptation because their effects are closely tied to the semiotic system on which they are manifested – that is, *enunciation*' (McFarlane, 1996: 20). Hence, it is useful to consider the film narrator as the process of enunciation, 'the whole expressive apparatus that governs the presentation – and reception – of the narrative' (McFarlane, 1996: 20). Clearly, the majority of sf's literary estrangement is not transferable because it is tied to 'one [...] semiotic system' (McFarlane, 1996: 20), as Stockwell indicates. Hence, literary estrangement must, in most cases, be subject to enunciation through the visual and/or auditory channels.

A notable exception is Stanley Kubrick's adaptation (1971) of Burgess's *A Clockwork Orange* (1962), in which the estranging Russian-inflected language of its youthful protagonists is *transferred* to the auditory channel. Although the linguistic sign system is verbalized, the correspondence between the signs and their phonetic equivalents is clear. Indeed, one could argue that the enunciation of the novel actually mitigates some of the source text's estrangement by pictorializing the unfamiliar signifiers's signifieds. In effect, the film's visual channel resolves the potential ambiguities of the auditory channel, providing a *mise-en-scène*-based context to supplement the linguistic context in which the neologisms are located on the soundtrack.

The language of *A Clockwork Orange* is an exception however. In most instances, literary estrangement requires cinematic enunciation. In order to assess the strategies employed for that enunciation, it is valuable to formulate a taxonomy for the sources of estrangement according to the likely magnitude or extent of the third-order informativity effect generated by each novum. This is, of course, a somewhat inexact exercise but it enables the articulation of the complexity of cinematic estrangement in a more coherent fashion. Hence, working from the concepts and observations of Suvin and Stockwell, it is possible to propose four types of estrangement before discussing how these might be enunciated in sf film adaptations:

1 Quaternary or Object-Based Estrangement
2 Tertiary or Subject-Based Estrangement
3 Secondary or Event-Based Estrangement
4 Primary or Spatially-Based Estrangement

The four sources of estrangement identified reflect an increasing complexity ranging from quaternary estrangement (or least complex) to primary estrangement (or most complex). The level of complexity is determined by the level of third-order informativity; in effect, how 'serious a challenge to world knowledge' (Stockwell, 2000: 164) each incidence of estrangement poses for the reader or spectator. Put simply, this is a measure of how much effort is required 'to resolve ("downgrade") the discrepancy' (Stockwell, 2000: 164) generated by the appearance of the estranging novum. The effort to resolve such discrepancies, to render them coherent and plausible, is what generates the reader/viewer interest observed by Sobchack in *Screening Space* (Sobchack, 1997: 43). The consequence of the resolution of estrangement, as Stockwell points out, is frame replacement or frame modification. This 'expansive' – and tentative – model, which commences with props before encompassing figures, events and narrative spaces, is arguably the first step towards understanding the principles governing the cinematic adaptation of literary science fiction's specific formal qualities. In taking this step, it indicates how science-fiction film adaptations are the texts *par excellence* for highlighting and assessing some of the conceptual and aesthetic differences between sf in print and sf on screen.

1 Quaternary or Object-Based Estrangement

Quaternary or object-based estrangement depends upon the introduction of a non-sentient physical novum or new object into a diegesis or story world or, alternatively, the introduction of a familiar object rendered strange. The object may be marked, appearing in a story world that is not radically estranging (one that is, perhaps, historically recognizable, contemporaneous, or displays distinct generic verisimilitude), or unmarked, forming part of a larger, more estranging story world. In literary sf, object-based estrangement, whether it is marked or unmarked, is invariably introduced using neologism or neosemy. Objects are identified by a signifier without a referent in the real world, or by a signifier that has undergone some form of neosemic shift (usually either broadening or narrowing). In either case, its third-order informativity is likely to be low; there will be little effort required to '"downgrade" [...] the discrepancy'. Sufficient clues will exist in its connotations or its grammatical context to resolve the mystery (e.g. William Gibson's 'slamhound' from *Count Zero* [1986] or Dick's 'mood-organ' from *Do Androids Dream of Electric Sheep?* [1968]).

Clearly, the cinematic enunciation of such object-based estrangement is largely dependent on the visual channel, although further estrangement could be achieved through the diegetic or non-diegetic auditory channels. Whatever the case, such enunciation is rarely concerned with fidelity, with establishing a visual parallel to the literary description provided in the source text. On occasion, this may be a consequence of there being an insufficiently explicit description in the source text from which to derive a cinematic design; more often than not, however, it is a result of constructing the object to complement a film's overall coherent visual design. Nevertheless, principles of visualization are found in sf film adaptations (and in sf film in general) that parallel sf literature's linguistic creativity. One finds estranging objects based on *visual* compounding, borrowing and derivation. They are a synthesis of the strange and the familiar, the estranging and the cognitive, though here cognition may be directed more towards understanding fictional function than reflecting on the spectator's socio-political context.

Two examples are instructive: H. G. Wells's compound creation, the Time Machine, in George Pal's 1960 adaptation, and Dick's Voigt-Kampff device from *Do Androids Dream of Electric Sheep?* in *Blade Runner* (Ridley Scott, 1982). Wells's description of the time machine is notoriously oblique: 'Parts were of nickel, parts of ivory, parts had certainly been filed or sawn out of rock crystal. The thing was generally complete, but the twisted crystalline bars lay unfinished [...] Quartz it seemed to be' (Wells, 1993: 11). Working from this minimal depiction, William Ferrari designed an archetypal Victorian device of brass rails, velvet, ebony and crystal, all shielded by an etched, vertically-set metallic parasol. In effect, the design is a visual compounding of bath-chair and roll cage; it is clearly a vehicle but one designed to move in dimensions other than the spatial. Its function is understood through connotation as well as explicit identification in the script. The strange and the familiar collide in its construction just as familiar materials form the unfamiliar device in the novel. More significantly perhaps, the machine connotes the Time Traveller's wealth; the design is sumptuous enough to identify his expedition as a luxurious middle-class venture and so provides juxtaposition with the gradual impoverishment of culture and civilization he experiences as he travels forward in time. He and his machine become increasingly anomalous and his wealth insignificant as his temporal perspective expands.

Like Wells's time machine, Dick's V-K device is described in indistinct terms: 'From his opened briefcase he fished out the Voigt-Kampff apparatus [...] and began to assemble the rather simple polygraphic instruments [...] a flat adhesive disc [...] a pencil-beam light' (Dick, 1972: 39–40). Syd Mead's design for the V-K machine is visually complex, incorporating a breather/bellows device, an interrogative opthalmoscope, and an oscillator. The viewer can determine the estranging machine's function from both design and context, yet its intricate enunciation works metonymically to convey the invasive, interrogating procedures required to distinguish replicant from human. The V-K's assessment of iris fluctuations not only connotes the powerful and determining gaze of the state, but also indicates the barely discernible differences existing between humanized replicant and robotic human. Visually, it also extends and confirms the relevance of the eye motif reoccurring throughout the film.

Such 'designed' estrangement points to a rare oversight in Sobchack's argument. She notes, quite correctly, that 'The major visual impulse in all SF films is to pictorialize the unfamiliar' (Sobchack, 1997: 88). However, she insists on separating 'alien' – more accurately estranging – images from 'familiar images', arguing that these are juxtaposed but rarely appear 'in the same frame' (Sobchack, 1997: 103). This is simply not the case. Not only do familiar and unfamiliar images exist in the same frame, they often exist in the same object or subject, thereby generating a recognition/misrecognition that provokes the estrangement. This becomes more apparent when tertiary or subject-based estrangement is considered.

2 Tertiary or Subject-Based Estrangement

Tertiary or subject-based estrangement develops from a novum with subjectivity and agency, a new sentience, which may be introduced into a story world similar to, or radically different from, the receiver's context. Such subject-based estrangement may derive from the presence and activities of altered humans, sentient machines or animals, or alien intelligences/species. The enunciation of its estranging qualities will depend on design (particularly in the case of non-human subjects) but will also derive from sound (effects and voice), actor and performance (Louis Gossett's performance as the alien Drac in Wolfgang Petersen's 1985 adaptation of Barry Longyear's 'Enemy Mine' [1979] is a good example). Given the homocentric nature of mainstream cinema, the subject is likely to be marked, whether the subject appears in the context of a familiar or an estranging story world. Four examples provide a sense of the range of third-order informativity available through subject-based estrangement. Each indicates a growing technical and cinematic complexity that requires greater downgrading.

Henry Kuttner and C. L. Moore's 'The Twonky' (1942) is a satiric story about a future human who travels back in time to manufacture the titular device, an artificially intelligent radio-gramophone that controls, then destroys, its owners. Arch Oboler's witless 1953 comic adaptation transforms the twonky into a capricious television set controlling its owner's life. It is unsurprising that Oboler, a successful radio dramatist, would effect this change and make television, America's newest mass-produced gadget and a threat to radio, the target of his satire. In the film, the twonky – a distinctly Suvinian novum – achieves its cognitively estranging effect by stressing television's negative influence on personal relationships, the performance of masculinity and freedom of choice.

Realized as a marionette-television, the twonky's visualization is less than impressive. Nevertheless, its twee design connotes the assumed innocuousness of the medium, which is then belied through actions with distinctly sinister possibilities. The lighting of its owner's pipe, for example, reveals that it is armed with a modest Wellsian heat-ray (Byron Haskin's *The War of the Worlds* was also released in 1953). As an example of designed estrangement, the twonky is crude at best, yet its palpable intelligence and its growing influence maintain its estranging qualities. Each newly disclosed ability requires the audience to re-evaluate the twonky and cognitively reflect on its metaphoric relationship to its own more prosaic television sets. This reflection is encouraged when one character speculates that the twonky is an Orwellian device from a future 'superstate' where every home has such a device to control and monitor the population. Accordingly, its enunciation is comparatively simple and, in terms of its informativity, its discrepancy is resolved thoroughly by direct exposition.

L. Q. Jones's 1975 adaptation of Harlan Ellison's 1968 novella 'A Boy and His Dog' is technically more complex, employing both sound and camera work cooperatively to enunciate the story's estranging opening lines: 'I was out with Blood, my dog. It was his week for annoying me; he kept calling me Albert. He thought that was pretty damned funny. Payson Terhune: ha ha' (Ellison, 1974: 9). The neosemic broadening of 'dog' to refer to a subject that has a sense of irony, and can both communicate *and* express a familiarity with American popular literature is the source of estrangement at this point in Ellison's narrative. To capture a similar disorientation in his adaptation, Jones opens on a desert landscape. The diegetic sound is layered: two male voices in conversation about 'solos' and 'roverpaks', the panting of a dog, the pinging of an echo-locator. One of the male protagonists moves into shot, then crawls forward into the medium distance. The film cuts to a pile of junk as the youthful protagonist seeks cover. He then closes on a 'solo' and incapacitates him. He waits – presumably – for the roverpak, guided by the other male's off-screen voice, which now seems to be telepathic communication since the off-screen male can sense concealed antagonists. At this point, a rather scruffy dog moves into shot and the off-screen voice speaks again. On this occasion, however, with no other subject available, the viewer is compelled to attribute the voice *to the dog*, an attribution proved correct in subsequent takes. The viewer understands retroactively that the pinging sonar echo denotes the dog's ability to scan telepathically for humans. This delayed identification of voice and talent with subject functions comparably with Ellison's gradual revelation of Blood's abilities in the novella's opening sentences. The film's third-order informativity parallels that of the story, requiring the receiver's patience to downgrade. The novella achieves this downgrading with a 300-word expository descriptive pause giving the history of Blood's sires and of Cold War genetic engineering. Jones's film is more economic, stripping down Blood's history to one simple line. In the midst of a spat, the dog's human companion, Vic (Don Johnson), snaps: 'And you can shove that part about how you lost the ability to hunt for food when you learned to talk.' This is pure exposition; one character is telling another character what he already knows. Jones's skill is in justifying Vic's outburst through the context of an angry exchange: the exposition is framed as the petulance of a horny teenager. Nevertheless, Vic's attitudes and Blood's presence – rather than the presence of the cinematically foregrounded wasteland – form part of an extensive ontologically-based estrangement developed through quaternary, tertiary, secondary and primary estrangement operating in concert.

In addition to neosemic broadening, neosemic recontextualization can also be a source of estrangement in literary sf. In Ray Bradbury's *Fahrenheit 451* (1953), 'fireman' is a compound word that has undergone such recontextualization. In Bradbury's novel, firemen no longer fight fires; they are the book-burning stormtroopers of an anti-intellectual totalitarian state. Bradbury estranges his reader with a typically lyrical description of fireman Montag burning books before returning to the 'fire station' to shower and rest. Truffaut's 1966 adaptation opens with a comparable visual recontextualization; the denotative and connotative signification of 'fireman' is transformed, resulting in estrangement. Truffaut enunciates this recontextualization by suggesting his firemen are nothing more than the emergency servicemen the audience assumes them to be. They seem, however, strangely diminutive; they are lessened in vitality and strength within the *mise-en-scène*. The fire-crew rides a miniature engine accompanied by a jaunty non-diegetic ensemble of xylophone and strings. It is only when the firemen search an apartment and torch the books they find that the audience recognizes the recontextualization and understands the reason behind the diminution of their equipment. They do not need fire-fighting equipment; they carry flamethrowers instead; nor do they need physical mass for their function as book-burners. Props, costume, characters' appearances and actors' performances all contribute to the film's third-order informativity, which helps form the larger ontologically-based estrangement – a new reality – that is gradually resolved as the plot develops.

In contrast, *Planet of the Apes* (1968), Franklin J. Schaffner's adaptation of Pierre Boulle's *Monkey Planet* (1963), provides one of sf cinema's most jarring instances of diegetic interruption and subject-based estrangement. When astronaut Ulysse Mérou lands on a planet orbiting Betelgeuse, he discovers a non-technological human culture preyed on by advanced apes. Boulle describes Mérou's first sight of the primates:

> I almost shouted out loud in amazement [...] stupefaction stifled all other sentiment when I saw this creature on the look-out [...] For it was a monkey, a large-sized gorilla [...] But an encounter with a gorilla on the planet Soror did not constitute the essential outlandishness of the event. This for me lay in the fact that the ape in question was correctly dressed, like a man of our world, and above all in the easy manner in which he wore his clothes. (Boulle, 1966: 41–2)

Although Mérou's incredulity and surprise substitutes for and somehow lessens the sense of estrangement the reader should experience – he becomes a surrogate rather than a conduit – Boulle's deferral of the ape's increasingly estranging characteristics is effective. Unable to replicate such a deferral in film, Schaffner employs a comparable technique through building intrigue by postponing a clear establishing shot of his antagonists and by fragmenting their activities. The audience hears the apes' hunting call, sees their beaters' flailing canes, their horses' stamping hooves, the volley of rifle-fire, until finally a medium long shot snatches at an ape-rider galloping passed the camera. Schaffner then cuts to a medium shot to identify the hunters. It is a further two minutes forty seconds before the first ape speaks. Foregrounding the film's satiric purpose, the ape photographer composes the hunters and says: 'Smile.'

The framing and representation of the subject enunciates the estranging scene variously. Primarily, the special effects make-up confronts the viewer with a truly innovative subject: a mounted, talking ape. Schaffner's decision to introduce the apes in this manner maximizes their third-order informativity. The audience faces a series of related questions: how did the apes learn to speak? How did they train the horses? How did they gain access or learn to manufacture projectile weapons and clothing? Why are they hunting humans? The estrangement – and the satire – is extended by such activities because hitherto the spectator has accepted them as limited to human beings. Estrangement occurs through analogies that will ultimately qualify the film as one of the best examples of cognitive estrangement in sf cinema. The questions posed – the film's third-order informativity – will not, of course, be fully resolved until the last scene when Taylor (Charlton Heston), Schaffner's version of Mérou, confronts his past on the shoreline. This deferral, which echoes but extends the deferral in the hunting sequence, ensures that the film's broader ontologically-based estrangement remains effective until the final, apocalyptic moment.

3 Secondary or Event-Based Estrangement

The estranging effects achieved in science-fiction cinema, as in sf literature, are the result of an additive process. In moving from quaternary estrangement to tertiary estrangement there was an increasing complexity in the range of enunciatory techniques employed. Secondary estrangement constitutes a further complication adding, as it does, narrative time into the development of the estranging effect. Secondary estrangement depends upon the introduction of events, customs or processes into a story world similar to, or different from, the receiver's context. It may derive from the enactment of agent-driven activities, or natural happenings, rituals, the functioning of bureaucracies and/or the processes of alien systems.

Clearly, it could be argued that the hunting scene from *Planet of the Apes* and the opening sequence of *A Boy and His Dog* can be considered as event-based estrangement. However, in both cases the narrative and visual emphasis is placed more upon subject-based estrangement, on the recontextualization of 'novums with agency'. Secondary estrangement occurs in cinematic sequences where greater visual emphasis is placed on the narrative event than on the participating subjects. Subjects will certainly constitute part of the event-based estrangement but it is the event itself that is the primary source of interruption in the viewer's diegetic absorption. The 'carousel' sequence from Michael Anderson's 1976 adaptation of William F. Nolan and George Clayton Johnson's *Logan's Run* (1967) provides a pertinent example. The sequence does not appear in the original novel; rather it transforms the chilling, understated oblivion of the novel's 'Sleepshops' into a cinematically spectacular, estranging ritual.

Although the film is prefaced by an introduction which explains that life in protagonist Logan's domed city 'must end at thirty unless reborn in the fiery ritual of carousel', the sequence remains estranging due to its enunciation. Initially, the neosemic recontextualization of 'carousel', with its connotations to children's merry-go-rounds, does not prepare the audience for the arena in which those who have reached 'last day' rise upward to a vast, descending crystal and explode. However, the round, circulating set denotes other forms of carousel: a slide projector's magazine or a rotating conveyor, both functional devices often part of a larger mechanical process. The focus of the sequence is not, however, on the set but on the ritual itself: on the noise of the crowd chanting 'Renew', the strangely synthesized score, the free floating motion of the subjects attired in skin-tight white and red flame-patterned body suits who wear hockey-masks, the circularity of movement that connotes entrapment, the intensely artificial lighting, the often distant camera that positions the audience objectively, as spectators of spectatorship. As the sequence unfolds, our sense of dislocation increases: what is the ritual for? How do these figures rise? What do the red and white crystals represent in the ritual? Are those bodies exploding as a consequence of renewal or are they purely denotative images? Following the introduction to Logan's city, part pleasure-garden, part shopping mall, with its 'sandmen', 'runners', 'seed mothers' and 'last days', the carousel affirms the unfamiliarity of an alien and alienating culture.

Event-based estrangement does not arise solely from unfamiliar rituals and processes, however. On many occasions it derives from an event occurring in a changed, though recognizable, quotidian world. Boris Sagal's 1971 *The Omega Man*, the second version of Richard Matheson's *I Am Legend* (1954), sees Neville (Charlton Heston) driving around an empty L.A. listening to an eight-track, presumably in the early hours of the morning. He passes down a litter-strewn street (a not uncommon sight in the 1970s) only to stop suddenly and machine gun a shadowy figure passing a window in an apartment block. The sequence is not in the novel but substitutes for the equally estranging ritual Matheson's Neville undertakes in securing his house against 'them'. Although the film's Neville will later undertake similar activities, the dramatic opening externalizes and visualizes the interiority of Neville's fears in the novel while arousing comparable questions in the audience: who is Neville shooting at/who are Matheson's 'they'?

Most sf films, and certainly many sf film adaptations, are structured narratively around a series of juxtapositions of event-based exposition and event-based estrangement. On occasion, the event-based exposition is also a source of further estrangement. During Neville's drive through the empty city, Sagal cuts to an elevated camera position on an apartment block roof. A slow pan across the terrace reveals a family of shrivelled corpses sat beneath a faded parasol or lying in a rotting swing-seat. The image is both expository and estranging. As it reveals more of the fictional world – the audience understands why the city is so quiet: its inhabitants are dead – the spectator is estranged by a lack of knowledge of the event that extinguished the population. Retroactively, through subsequent events, the viewer understands the relevance of the scene just as the relevance of carousel becomes clear as Logan begins to run. The audience learns that the stability of Logan's city is based upon lies that sustain and manage the oppression of the populace. The transcendental promise of carousel is nothing more than a convenient way of disposing of those over the age of 30 whilst providing a bread-and-circuses distraction for the masses, many of whom may rebel at the thought of compulsory euthanasia.

What such event-based estrangement demonstrates is that many sf films and sf film adaptations rely for their estrangement on restricted narration, on information rationing that ensures third-order informativity is not downgraded quickly or readily. The spectator is estranged because he or she does not understand completely how the story world functions; this incomplete understanding is a prime contributor to both ontological and epistemological estrangement. Ontological estrangement, however, is usually extended and developed through the narrative space or spaces of a particular text. The consideration of narrative space leads to the final level of estrangement: primary or spatially-based estrangement.

4 Primary or Spatially-Based Estrangement

Primary or spatially-based estrangement arises from the establishment and diegetic maintenance of a defamiliarizing place or places in which sources of quaternary, tertiary, and secondary estrangement can be situated. In the cinema, primary-based estrangement derives from the enunciation of visual space. Such spaces provide estranging performance areas for the location of further estrangement. Vivian Sobchack argues:

> Since it is usually not required to do anything but simply be, [the studio-created geography of science fiction] is able to achieve a visual power which can last, if not over-done and over-used, through an entire film, maintaining our responses to it as alien and wondrous. (Sobchack, 1997: 94)

Here, Sobchack is incorrect and, indeed, contradictory. The 'studio-created geography of science fiction' cinema is never created to 'simply *be*'. If it is 'maintaining our responses to it as alien', it is exerting an estranging effect that derives from its enunciation; it is equivalent to the designed estrangement observed in object-based and subject-based estrangement. In other words, an audience's responses are structured by art direction and design in the case of sets or by the cinematographic treatment of dressed or undressed locations. Sf film spaces are rarely denotative: they are not simply a site of action – of secondary estrangement – as they almost always signify something beyond themselves, often extending or rendering symbolically the narrative's themes.

Spatially-based estrangement in sf cinema is enunciated most simply by the cinematic treatment of an undressed location, a location filmed without additional props. It can be achieved through incongruity (an observation Sobchack makes with regard to what has been termed subject-based estrangement above), camera position or through diegetic or non-diegetic sound. In *The Omega Man*, for example, the estrangement derives initially from the spectral emptiness of the city, from the absence of human artefacts, particularly cars. Francis Lawrence's *I Am Legend* (2007) – which reflects the opening of Sagal's film – revises this emptiness with extensive use of CGI 'dressing'. Here, the estrangement derives from the wealth of abandoned human artefacts – from the sense of the city as 'relic' – juxtaposed with the absence of human subjects and the presence of non-urban animals like deer and lions. In effect, the denotation and connotations of 'city' have undergone sharp recontextualization.

In Schaffner's *Planet of the Apes*, Boulle's geographically and climatically unremarkable Soror are transformed into a barren wasteland very different from the temperate landscape Boulle describes. Although the Utah and Arizona locations are generally familiar, the film's atonal score and the use of extreme long shots recontextualizes the earthly landscape. As Sobchack observes of many of the 1950s desert-set sf films, 'what evokes awe and terror is the terrain of Earth itself [...] the spectator is forced to a recognition, however unconscious it may remain, of Man's precarious and puny stability, [...] his total isolation, the fragile quality of his body and his works' (Sobchack, 1997: 112). In this context, there is an implicit irony in Schaffner's film since the terrain of Earth, seemingly doubling for an alien world and accepted as such by the viewer as a consequence of plotting, sound and camera position, is substituting for an *actual* Earth millennia hence. As in many New Wave sf narratives, Earth *is* the alien world. Minimal dressing – quaternary estrangement – also enhances

Figure 2.   Planet of the Apes. Photo courtesy of 20th Century-Fox/Photofest.

the estranging power of the landscape. Importantly, Schaffner's treatment of location in *Planet of the Apes* ensures that the spectator becomes conscious of 'Man's precarious and puny stability' through the repeated use of long-shots – virtually a motif following the opening crash sequence – that foreground visually one of the key themes of the film and its social satire.

In sf cinema, primary or spatially-based estrangement is often achieved through the construction of sets. Set-design theory is a discontinuous discourse at best but in *Sets in Motion: Art Direction and Film Narrative*, Affron and Affron categorize five functions of the film set: 'Set as Denotation'; 'Set as Punctuation'; 'Set as Embellishment';

'Set as Artifice'; and, 'Set as Narrative' (Affron and Affron, 1995: 37–40). Sf cinema and sf film adaptations mainly employ 'Set as Artifice'; sets are 'Prominently featured, consciously foregrounded' and call attention to themselves 'as a consistently opaque object in pursuit of the "fiction effect"' (Affron and Affron, 1995: 39). Such sets transport the spectator into estranging environments. Most significantly, these sets are centralized, becoming integral to the viewer's cinematic experience and the narrative's diegesis:

> Sf film sets may also function as punctuation, entering into a dynamic with narrative that establishes not time, place, and mood alone but time, place, and mood as these centre on the specificity of plot, theme and, above all, character, as well as on the related specificities of class, gender, race and ethnicity. (Affron and Affron, 1995: 38)

Accordingly, they are able to 'accentuate the feelings or situation of the central protagonists' (Wright, 2007: 221) and achieve a kind of architectural pathetic fallacy. Given sf's analogical dimension, it is unsurprising that they also display a contiguous function as 'embellishment', where *décor* provides 'the powerful images that serve either to organize the narrative or as analogies to aspects of the narrative' (Affron and Affron, 1995: 38). In *Blade Runner*, Scott's richly textured enunciation of *Do Androids Dream of Electric Sheep?*, settings operate simultaneously as artifice (an estranging space), punctuation (the rain-drenched, decaying city reflects the melancholic, 'advanced decrepitude' of its replicants and rejects) and embellishment as the final scenes in the Bradbury Hotel chart Deckard's physical and empathic ascendancy.

Clearly, the degree of spatially-based estrangement the spectator experiences depends on the sets' visual similarities to the quotidian. The third-order informativity of *Blade Runner*'s L. A. in 2019, for example, is lower than visions of distant futures or alien worlds in Robert Zemeckis's 1997 adaptation of Sagan's *Contact* (1985) or David Lynch's *Dune* (1984) or Nathan Juran's *First Men in the Moon* (1964) or Michael Anderson's 1980 miniseries of Ray Bradbury's *The Martian Chronicles* (1950). In many instances, the sets of sf films and sf film adaptations are less estranging than the tertiary or secondary estranging elements that are foregrounded if not visually then certainly narratively. Indeed, the estranging potential of setting is often de-emphasized to prevent visual disorientation and maintain cinema's homocentric focus. Frequently, there are analogies with the quotidian available; even in a film as estranging as *Planet of the Apes,* the Gaudi-inspired 'Ape City' is still recognizable as a city. Nevertheless, locations and sets still retain a significant potential for exerting an estranging effect on the audience, for ensuring a third-order informativity that requires downgrading.

Although the taxonomy described above may risk obscuring possible intersections and overlaps between, for example, quaternary/object-based estrangement and tertiary/subject-based estrangement, it does provide a preliminary strategy for discussing how sf's literary estrangements are enunciated on screen. Each form of estrangement broadly accommodates its predecessor: object-based estrangement can form part of subject-based estrangement which, in turn, can contribute to event-based estrangement. All can be contained, though they may exhibit greater or lesser prominence in the cinematic frame, within a spatially-estranging location or set. This 'expansive' model, which commences with props before encompassing figures, events and narrative spaces, is arguably the first step towards understanding the principles governing the cinematic adaptation of science fiction's specific formal qualities.

References

Affron, C. and Affron, J. A. (1995) *Sets in Motion: Art Direction and Film Narrative.* Piscataway, NJ: Rutgers University Press.

Boulle, P. (1966) *Monkey Planet.* London: Penguin.

Broderick, D. (1995) *Reading by Starlight: Postmodern Science Fiction.* London and New York: Routledge.

Chatman, S. (2000) *Coming to Terms: The Rhetoric of Narrative in Fiction and Film.* Ithaca, NY: Cornell University Press.

Csicsery-Ronay, I. (2003) 'Marxist Theory and Science Fiction', in E. James and F. Mendlesohn (eds) *The Cambridge Companion to Science Fiction,* pp. 113–24. Cambridge: Cambridge University Press.

Delany, S. R. (1978) *The Jewel-Hinged Jaw: Notes on the Language of Science Fiction.* New York: Berkely Windhover.

Dick, P. K. (1972) *Do Androids Dream of Electric Sheep?* London: Panther Books.

Ellison, H. (1974) 'A Boy and His Dog', in M. Moorcock (ed.) *Best SF Stories from New Worlds 8*, pp. 9–47. London: Panther Books.

Freedman, C. (2000) *Critical Theory and Science Fiction*. Hanover, NH: Wesleyan University Press.

McFarlane, B. (1996) *Novel to Film: An Introduction to the Theory of Adaptation*. Oxford: Clarendon Press.

MacLean, M. (1984) 'Metamorphoses of the Signifier in 'Unnatural' Languages', *Science Fiction Studies* 11: 166–73.

Sobchack, V. (1997) *Screening Space: The American Science Fiction Film*. Piscataway, NJ: Rutgers University Press.

Stockwell, P. (2000) *The Poetics of Science Fiction*. Harlow: Pearson Education.

Suvin, D. (1979) *The Metamorphoses of Science Fiction*. New Haven, CT: Yale University Press.

Wells, H. G. (1993) *The Time Machine*. London: J. M. Dent.

Wright, A. (2007) *Telling Stories: Gender, Representation and the Appeal of the Screen Fairy Tale*, unpublished PhD thesis, Roehampton University.

Chapter 2

From Adaptation to Cinephilia
An Intertextual Odyssey

I.Q. Hunter

2001: A Space Odyssey (1968) is one of the few Stanley Kubrick films that is *not* an adaptation. The end credits on screen simply read, 'Based on a screenplay by Stanley Kubrick and Arthur C. Clarke', and no other source text is mentioned. But *2001* is nevertheless shadowed, and its enigmas potentially explained, by other texts, towards which viewers are directed extratextually; texts which, as with any adaptation, precede the film, complement it and perhaps even complete it, and which may also frame and influence the film's reception, for example by encouraging us to read it 'as' an adaptation. For viewers engaged in the longitudinal process of understanding *2001* or even, as cinephile cultists, acquiring an emotional investment in its production, meanings, authorship and 'secrets', these texts may become resources of additional knowledge and cultural capital that inform and modify their repeated encounters with the supreme masterpiece of sf cinema.

For example, 'everyone knows' that *2001*'s decisive, albeit unacknowledged, precursor was Clarke's 'The Sentinel' (1951) (originally published as 'The Sentinel of Eternity'), a short story about men discovering an alien object on the Moon and setting off a signalling device, which Clarke had offered to Kubrick in 1964 for adaptation.[1] Clarke's contract to work on *2001* included the sale of 'The Sentinel' and five other stories, with Clarke being paid specifically to write a treatment based on 'The Sentinel' (Clarke, 1972: 31–2; Lo Brutto, 1998: 263). This short story is reprinted as the film's source text in a number of satellite publications, such as Jerome Agel's *The Making of Kubrick's 2001* (1970: 15–23) and Clarke's *The Lost Worlds of 2001* (1972: 19–28), and in Piers Bizony's later *2001: Filming the Future*, which refers to it as 'the starting point' (Bizony, 1994: 75). Although *2001* drew thematically on other Clarke stories such as his novel *Childhood's End* (1953), also about an alien master race overseeing human development, it is 'The Sentinel' that is now discursively fixed as the film's true – 'if uncredited' – origin. This might be seen as a case of 'unacknowledged adaptation', where only extratextual knowledge of a film's sources, generated by discourses around the film or inter-textually signalled within it, primes audiences to approach it as an adaptation (or indeed remake or sequel or unauthorized version) – as with *Body Heat* (Lawrence Kasdan, 1981), for example, which riffs on *Double Indemnity* (Billy Wilder, 1944) and James M. Cain's original novel (1943) without acknowledging either text in the credits or ancillary materials. *2001* is – depending on the terms you wish to use – a massive expansion of 'The Sentinel', which is folded into the film's narratives along with other intertextual resources, or a realization of what 'The Sentinel' only hinted at. But so slight is 'The Sentinel' that it is pointless to judge the film (and comparative judgement seems the default option for adaptation studies) by its closeness to or betrayal of it; and indeed I am not aware of any critical articles that do so. Clarke commented:

> I am continually annoyed by careless references to 'The Sentinel' as 'the story on which *2001* is based'; it bears about as much relation to the movie as an acorn to the resultant full-grown oak. Considerably less, in fact, because ideas from several other stories were also incorporated. Even the elements that Stanley Kubrick and I did actually use were considerably modified. (McAleer, 1993: 193)

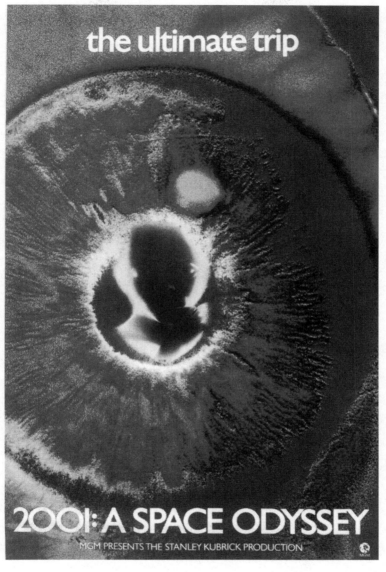

Figure 1. *2001: A Space Odyssey* poster. Photo courtesy of MGM/Photofest.

Nevertheless, that *2001* stands in some relation to 'The Sentinel' is an established 'fact' about the film, even though the story is not flagged up as a source text on screen. This is a different relationship of precedence and adaptation from the cases of Kubrick's *A Clockwork Orange* (1971), which he adapted quite closely from Anthony Burgess's 1962 novel, and *The Shining* (1980), which Kubrick and Diane Johnson adapted from Stephen King's 1977 novel, improving it immeasurably, much to King's chagrin. *2001* cannot be expected to adhere to the 'spirit' of the short story and most audiences – certainly when the film was first released – would not frame it as a conventional adaptation. But even if 'The Sentinel' is not the true begetter of the film, or at best one staging post in the film's thematic development, its subsequent pre-eminence in accounts of the film's origins sends out the message that *Clarke* was the key source and the film a continuation of Clarkean as much as Kubrickean themes.

Yet if *2001* cannot be regarded as an adaptation of 'The Sentinel', it is nevertheless haunted, as bona fide adaptations are haunted, by another identically titled text in the marketplace. There exists what might be called a 'parallel adaptation' – or even competitor adaptation – of the material and screenplay. This is the novelization by Clarke (1968) which was published a few months after the film's release, and which is itself positioned (as novelizations usually are) as an adaptation on the same terms as the film – 'based on the screenplay by Arthur C. Clarke and Stanley Kubrick' (Clarke, 1968: 3).[2] Thomas Van Parys describes this as an example of 'simultaneous novelization':

> Not to be confused with novelisations (partially) credited to the director or screenwriter but really written by a hired author only, these are collaborative efforts in that film and novelisation have mutually influenced each other, and illustrate the kind of symbiosis that texts in different media may reach. They are also part of a larger group of novelisations that have been developed simultaneously with the film, which dismisses from the outset any clear hierarchy. Other examples of 'simultaneous' novelisations are Thea von Harbou's *Metropolis* (1926), Graham Greene's novella *The Third Man* (1950), and Pier Paolo Pasolini's *Teorema* (1968). Often such novels enjoy the same respectability as the film; therefore it is telling that they are seldom

considered novelisations, and sometimes even mistaken for adapted novels instead. (Van Parys, 2011)

In an unusual process of script development, Clarke and Kubrick produced, rather than a screenplay, a jointly written 'long, novelistic treatment', *Journey beyond the Stars* (Kramer, 2010: 8); it was this extended screen treatment that was used to sell the project to MGM and became the basis for the screenplay (LoBrutto, 1998: 268). Clarke re-shaped *Journey beyond the Stars* as a novel by summer 1966 (Kramer, 2010: 42) but it was subsequently revised with input from Kubrick and both novel and screenplay were revised jointly right up to production:

> toward the end, both novel and screenplay were being written simultaneously, with feedback in both directions. Some parts of the novel had their final revisions after we had seen the rushes based on the screenplay based on the earlier versions of the novel ... and so on. (Clarke, 1972: 31)

Kubrick finally allowed the novel to be published in July 1968.

Novelizations are paradoxical texts with a long history. Though they might seem to be, like adaptations conventionally, follow-up texts, they are usually written at the same time as the film is produced and are sometimes available before the film. Rather than transcripts of the visuals of the film, they are imagined from a draft of the screenplay, and frequently include scenes missing from the final cut. In the days before video and DVD, novelizations were a way to pre- or re-experience a film outside the cinema, 'in line with the double goal of the novelization throughout its history, namely as promotional material before the film release as well as a prolongation of the movie experience to capitalize on its potential success' (Van Parys, 2009: 312).

Unlike most novelizations, that of *2001* has considerable authority as an 'authentic' treatment of the story material. It is not a secondary text, a mere spin-off or piece of hackwork, but a novel developed by Clarke, in consultation with Kubrick, which offers an alternative version of the narrative and considerably clarifies various plot points and dilemmas of interpretation. Not merely a written-up version of the screenplay, it is, like the film, the end product of a long process of textual elaboration. As such, it challenges the film's realization (or adaptation) of the screen treatment and screenplay and its deviations from the film might be regarded as corrections, by an expert sf writer, of its generically wayward mysticism and ambiguity. For one thing, the novel brings the material into line with the conventions of the commercial hard sf novel, Clarke's realm of creative authority. As Carrol L. Fry notes, 'Clarke wrote the story in genre-correct fashion' so as to 'transform visual poetry into prose' (Fry, 2003: 333). Michel Chion remarks, perhaps overstating the case a little, that the novel 'rather cleverly adopts an opposite position to the film. Probably in order to avoid being merely a written paraphrase of the film, it describes and explains everything much more explicitly, leaving nothing to interpretation' (Chion, 2001: 7). The novelization is at once a stand-alone text within Clarke's oeuvre; a double adaptation (of the screen treatment/ screenplay as well as the film, which it preceded rather than ekphrastically described); and, crucially, a handy primer and crib to a wholly unconventional film. Clarke said that the novel was 'an independent and self-contained work – even though it was created specifically for the movie' (Clarke, 1972: 30). But one can imagine a viewer in 1968 who has read the book feeling not only better equipped to negotiate the eccentricities of the narrative but also in a superior position vis-à-vis interpretation of it, just as someone familiar with the source text of an adaptation may feel better prepared to 'get' the adapted film. Like a running commentary, the novel of *2001* clarifies textual cruxes in the movie and offers straightforward factual explanations of its mysteries. The film and book might even be seen as necessary guides to each other (which harks back to the role of novelization in the silent era, when novelization 'functioned as announcement, explanation and completion of the silent film' [Van Parys, 2009: 307]). Indeed, this was quickly recognized shortly after publication – 'Since the motion picture has its baffling moments, a perusal of the book will help, and, indeed, the motion picture helps elucidate the book' (*Boston Globe*, quoted in Agel, 1970: 256).

There are numerous minor differences between novel and film, such as the astronauts' destination in the former being Saturn and not Jupiter (see *Wikipedia* for a comprehensive and otiose summary). Unlike the film, the novel provides detailed descriptions of prehistoric life, gives access to HAL's paranoid mind, and helpfully explains why Bowman ends up in a hotel room: 'So that was how this reception area had been prepared for him; his hosts had based their ideas of terrestrial living upon TV programmes. His feeling that he was inside a movie set was almost literally true' (Clarke, 1968: 217). These 'facts' do not belong to the film itself but certainly offer a different route into its meanings for viewers who approach it with knowledge gleaned from the novel. For example, building on the revelation, inaccessible in the film, that the spaceship which the ape's bone cuts to is a nuclear weapon, the book ends with the Star Child exploding other such weapons orbiting the Earth: 'He put forth his will, and the circling megatons flowered in a silent detonation that brought a brief, false dawn to half the sleeping globe' (Clarke, 1968: 223). As Kramer points out, this gives the novel an ambiguous ending, which could be read as the destruction of the earth. This was certainly not Kubrick's intention, though Clarke subsequently announced his ambivalence: 'despite his original intention to offer an optimistic ending, Clarke later acknowledged the validity of a pessimistic ending as well, thus affirming the fundamental ambiguity of the ending' (Kramer, 2010: 16; see Clarke, 1972: 239).

At the same time the novelization is certainly misleading as to the 'feel' – the all-important *experience* – of the film and its depiction of the future. For some critics (especially those aligned with sf literature) the novel was essential to a complete experience of the film:

> Audiences were mostly baffled; the final moments, especially, are entirely unintelligible without Clarke's text [...] Only with its belated appearance [...] was the tension resolved between Kubrick's allusive visual suggestion and Clarke's open rationalism. This peculiar symbiosis of novel and film remains key to the appreciation of both as finished texts; it is doubtful whether either work would seem as impressive without the other. (Nicholls et al., 2011)

Yet the novel's reductive factuality reduces the polysemic openness the film strives for. Rather than explain the film, the novel explains it away. The novel is also thematically distinct from the film. For example, describing the trip to the space station, the book states: 'no matter how many times you left Earth, D. Heywood Floyd told himself, the excitement never really palled' (Clarke, 1968: 39). In the book this sequence begins on Earth, delivers a good deal of information about the population explosion, food shortages, belligerency between thirty-eight nuclear powers (Clarke, 1968: 41), and then gives details of take-off and the 'extraordinary euphoria' of the experience of space flight (Clarke, 1968: 44). This is certainly in the keeping with the film's rapt depiction of technological mastery and shares some of the same details – the stewardess's Velcro slippers, for example, and later, in the trip to the Moon, the zero gravity toilet (though that is not a moment of comedy, as in the film). There is also a sense of the extraordinary ease and normality of the journey: 'He had made, utterly without incident and in little more than one day, the incredible journey of which men had dreamed for two thousand years. After a normal, routine flight, he had landed on the Moon' (Clarke, 1968: 59). In the film Floyd spends the entire trip to the station asleep and the film goes out of its way to suggest the boredom of the journey and the dull inability of humans like him to feel a sense of wonder. Rather than Clarke's optimism, *2001* is a study of violence, boredom, failed communication, and male inadequacy. Even as the film dazzles viewers with special effects, with a droll interest in convincing small details, paying as much attention to the returning of a floating pen to Floyd's pocket as to the docking of ship and station, it lulls us with visual redundancy so that the sequence, with the music in ironic counterpoint, courts tedium and banality and mere description. Meanwhile we have time to note the visual rhymes between the rotating phallic spaceships and pen (this is a film of sly homoeroticism), and the sexual implications of the docking (especially if we remember the aerial intercourse between refuelling planes at the start of Kubrick's *Dr Strangelove or: How I Learned to Stop Worrying and Love the Bomb* [1964]). The slow pace enables us to look closely, drift intertextually, and ponder symbolism and other repetitions, or simply revel in the special effects as we adjust to the film's curiously long rhythms of visual description.

The book fills in narrative gaps, but it describes a signifying universe absolutely different from the film. Kubrick hints at this:

> I think it gives you the opportunity of seeing two attempts in two different mediums, print and film, to express the same basic concept and story. [...] I think that the divergencies between the two works are interesting. Actually, it was an unprecedented situation for someone to do an essentially original literary work based on glimpses and segments of a film he had not seen in its entirety. (Gelmis, 2001: 96)

What are often held to be the surpassing advantages of the novel over film – interiority, access to consciousness, massive detail, and the use of an authorial voice to communicate psychological complexity and ideas – seem, in the novelization, merely conventional and deadening, precisely what you would expect from a genre writer trying to communicate a 'sense of wonder' by means of the usual formulae and novelistic techniques. Although the involvement of Clarke on board aligns 2001 with the 'ideas-driven' extrapolations of literary sf, Kubrick's method of visualizing ideas is predicated on a refusal not only of standard tropes of the sf genre, but of the novel itself. Rather as certain novels are said to be 'unadaptable', so 2001 is designed to be an unadaptable film.

This difference between film and novelization was intentional. As Peter Kramer has argued, Kubrick in his pre-release edit of the film got rid of most of the explanatory material in order to heighten the film's purely experiential qualities, the theme of communication through images, and its symbolism. While the film's grandeur and seriousness distance it from previous sf films, Kubrick also strove to distance the film comprehensively from both the novelization and written sf, and more fundamentally to distance cinema from print:

> the idea that the novel might be suitable for presenting explanations, while film would work better through a more open-ended narrative and ambiguous images, became ever more central for Kubrick's conception of the project. A kind of division of labour was slowly emerging whereby the film could afford to be mysterious because the novel would explain everything. (Kramer, 2010: 47–8)

Kubrick decided to drop the explanatory voiceovers a few weeks before release and put his faith in the power of the image.

Both film and novel are in a sense equally valid re-presentations of the material in the screenplay. Yet even if the novelization has its own integrity, it is the film that is generally seen as the superior if not necessarily the anterior text, neatly reversing the usual cultural assumption that novels are *a priori* superior to films. (There were some demurrals: Ray Bradbury said that Kubrick is 'a very bad writer who got in the way of Arthur C. Clarke, who is a wonderful writer' [Agel 1970: 299].) With *2001* what the film 'means' is therefore more likely now to be approached by seeing it as a Kubrick film, interpreted according to the evolving themes of his subsequent work. Like many 'art films', *2001* 'foregrounds the *author* as a structure in the film's system. [...] the author becomes a formal component, the overriding intelligence organizing the film for our comprehension' (Bordwell, 1979: 59). Audiences baffled by its sudden temporal shifts, languid pace, narrative ellipses and redundancies, and symbols can assume it all makes sense in the light of Kubrick's expressive intention. In 1968, the film more resembled the description of the monolith: its origin and purpose a total mystery (a comparison frequently made in the years since).

This is where the novelization came in. Looking beyond the film makes sense because *2001* *requires* interpretation. It forces viewers to augment narrative comprehensive with symbolic unpacking. Even the most casual viewers, not just film critics or academics who are professionally obliged to hunt for meaning, must do *something* with the jump cut from bone weapon to orbiting spaceship, the significance of the monolith, and the final image of the Star Child. These might be crudely described as 'WTF' moments, puzzles that engage the audience in a similar intellectual effort to the characters on screen – like dealing with images, pursuing clues, encountering symbols, and undergoing existential transformations. Kubrick did this throughout his films, not so much to create a puzzle story or even as a mark of authorship but to confront viewers with images that undercut the story world, pose an insoluble enigma or offer a baffling (non-)explanation: the orgy fantasy at the end of *A Clockwork Orange*, the photograph of the New Year's party at the end of *The Shining*, much of the dream narrative of *Eyes Wide Shut* (Stanley Kubrick, 1999). The novel of *2001* offered an authoritative gloss to a film whose opacity more or less required recourse to explanatory texts. The film's difficulty catered to late 1960s audiences increasingly attuned to what would become cult film reading practices – cult being 'a meta-genre that caters to intense, interpretative audience practices' (Gwenllian-Jones and Pearson, 2004: xvi). One of the key aspects of cult interpretation is watching and re-watching a film in order to unlock its mysteries, but with each re-viewing informed by extratextual information about the film – the sort of information that a skeleton key like *2001*'s novelization might provide. *2001* needs to be experienced (and mulled over) numerous times for its significance to emerge (this was also the case with Kubrick's *Barry Lyndon* [1975] and *The Shining*, which met with lukewarm critical reaction before achieving their classic status). Indeed there were a number of 'recant notices' of *2001* in which, unusually, critics took a second look at the film and revised their earlier judgements (*Variety*, 15 May 1968). The ideal viewer of *2001* would watch and re-watch the film, literally revisit it in optimum Cinerama viewing conditions, having used the intervening periods following up intertextual clues and reading up on the 'hip cosmological discourse surrounding the film' (Taylor, 1999: 133) – in other words, embarking on what we might now call a cult trajectory, a project of intertextual immersion that might last a lifetime. The 'experience' of *2001* went beyond simply watching it, although that was unusually important: the film was a 'purely' cinematic experience, and was framed as such when posters for the 1969 rerelease, repositioning the film as a hippie cult item, declared it as 'The ultimate trip' (Kaplan, 2007). You had to drop the film's acid in a cinema, not just read about it. For its 'young, quasi-"hippie" audience', as *Variety* put it, quoting a *New York Times* review, the film 'has broken loose from the novel and is exploring the possibilities of its own medium. "Space Odyssey" is poetry. It asks for groovin', not understanding' (*Variety*, 15 May 1968).

Each iteration of viewing would only be enhanced by preparatory extratextual exploration. Hence Clarke's advice: 'I always used to tell people, "Read the book, see the film and repeat the dose as often as necessary"' (McAleer, 1993: 223). But as well as reading the novel, interviews, sources such as 'The Sentinel', 'making of' books, Homer's *Odyssey*, Robert Ardrey (whose 'killer ape' theory influenced the 'Dawn of Man' sequence) and the Nietzsche of *Thus Spake Zarathustra* (1883–5), viewers might be inspired to dig Ligeti, Khachaturian and the two Strausses. Like many of Kubrick's films *2001* is a switchboard of cultural references, which reminds one of Clarke's description of the Star Gate: 'some kind of cosmic switching device […] a Grand Central Station of the Galaxy' (Clarke, 1968: 201) – sending the viewer hurtling through not just time and space but also new worlds of intertextuality. The ideal viewer, in other words, was (and remains) a *cultist*, who has a long-standing intellectual investment and emotional investment in the film, which would itself become an object of nostalgia and desire over a lifetime of educative re-viewings (see Mathijs, 2010). One cultist, Robert Castle goes so far as to say that:

> *2001: A Space Odyssey* (1968) has inhabited a large part of my life. […] How I have responded to the film reveals my growth as a thinker and critic, a growth I believe *2001* to be one of the causes. Not a dramatic growth that can be certified but one that effected an intellectual attention to the material/subject on the movie screen. Accomplishing this growth, in a sense, never ceased. Seeing and interpreting the film over the last 30 years has become analogous to the very process of change and growth happening in *2001*. (Castle, 2004)

With *2001* narrative comprehension ('Who or what is the baby?') has an unmistakeable edge of mysticism ('What does the baby *mean*?'), so that repeated viewings and 'deeper' interpretations are stages on a personal odyssey towards spiritual rebirth. Like other cult texts of the period, from John Fowles's novel *The Magus* (1966) to Carlos Castaneda, *El topo* (Alejandro Jodorowsky, 1970) and J. R. R. Tolkien's *The Lord of the Rings* (1954–5), *2001* is an auratic text containing, within the structure of a Hero's Journey, a mythic, grandiose and endlessly interpretable lexicon of Jungian imagery, through which audiences can imagine they reconnect with collective unconscious experience. Encountering the film – which is to say, *re*-encountering it – can be life-changing and transfiguring if the viewer is able to submit, to think and *to care*.

This notion of emotional investment in a film, obvious with cult films, emphasizes how much of our relationship with films is defined by what might be seen as intrinsic to adaptation – intertextual *dérives* across paratexts, pursuing allusions, comparisons, precursors, add-ons of all kinds. It is a relationship of *care* that takes place over *time*, from anticipation of the film to an embedded knowledge of it. Cultists care for texts in relationships of memory, nostalgia and anticipation; they have emotional investment in films, a sense even of ownership; they pursue the extratextual and seemingly irrelevant, specialize in breaking the boundaries of texts, and enthusiastically explore intertextual worlds. This dynamic relationship between a film and accompanying texts is, of course, always present, but it is most obviously so among audiences of adaptations (some of whose audiences may care passionately about the success and fidelity of an adaptation, and read the film always in terms of the book) and among cultists, who invest massively in the films they love and the significance they can wring from them. With adaptations, audiences may be invited to anticipate, view, recall, review and discuss films in relation to the original novel. With cultism, audiences acquire and are offered extratextual information and supplementary texts to extend and deepen their appreciation of films. The novelization of *2001* and books such as Agel's *The Making of Kubrick's 2001* and Clarke's *The Lost Worlds of 2001* performed this role for early cultists of *2001*, at the very start of the cult phenomenon.[3] Nowadays, the delivery of gap-filling 'textual expanders' to exploit fans and encourage word of mouth is standard industry practice: 'in a universe of converging media, reception is now definitively affiliated with multiple platforms of access and the associative intertextualities they inspire' (Klinger, 2010: 3). All interpretation of a film requires the film reader to work intertextually – aligning it with genre tropes, getting allusions (see Hills [2003: 180] for a discussion of how films, especially blockbusters, are characterized by 'intertextual stretching across culture' so that spectators 'become caught up in intertextual networks determined by marketing concerns'). Film viewing is not just attention paid to a single text but, for certain audiences and most emphatically with cult audiences and those for adaptations, always about shuttling between film and novel, original and new version, to the point where the borders of the text are ambiguous. The texts that frame and reframe the film, which determine the audience's relationship to it and invite different kinds of relationships to it (that of a fan, for example), are strictly speaking outside the film, and therefore secondary to it, but they nevertheless determine how we make sense of the film. They are rather like what Derrida calls 'parergons', frames that while outside the text define the text, not outside or inside but rather indeterminate – in other words, supplements that might be essential to the text itself:

> A parergon comes against, beside, and in addition to the *ergon*, the work done [*fait*], the fact [*le fait*], the work, but it does not fall to one side, it touches and cooperates within the operation, from a certain outside. Neither outside nor simply inside [...] It is first of all the on (the) bo(a)rd(er) [*Il est d'abord l'à-bord*]. (Derrida, 1987: 54)

Obviously most of the time we do not especially relate to films in this way, although the marketing departments may wish we did; but cult films and their fans are an example of how this experience functions, and therefore illuminate how this works in relation to adaptation.[4]

2001 is a marvellously bold and seemingly hermetic work of art and a work of precise cinematic machinery. But it is not a standalone object, or one whose meanings (thematic but also narrative) are to be discovered by textual explication of a single text. Rather than see the appearance of a film like *2001* as a simple textual event, one should regard it as the dominant text in a process of textual production that engages audiences – or at any rate audiences willing to be engaged – in an intertextual odyssey in search of the film's meaning – starting, perhaps, with the novelization. Yet *2001* is also, paradoxically, a film that seeks to escape its intertextual debts and connections. It is true that *2001* is an exceptionally intellectual film, which requires strenuous effort even to comprehend the narrative. But, inspired by the estranging formalism of art-house and underground cinema, it also aspires to the condition of 'pure cinema', communicating unparaphrasable visual and aural experiences as much as subtle and difficult meanings. The novelization, for neophyte cultists, offered some entry level introduction to the 'world' of *2001* but necessarily falls short in making sense of its leisurely camerawork, enhanced sense of duration and rhythm, and its immersion in abstractions beyond words. The film works on the emotions like music, even if it is the music of boredom and discomfort and incomprehension; and to that extent its meaning *is* the feeling the images and music evoke. *2001* is not least about the phenomenological experience of cinema itself, like a movie equivalent of a colour field painting (see Taylor [1999: 131–4] for a discussion of the film's reception in those terms by 'younger highbrow critics' such as Annette Michelson [1969], who 'positing the film as *essentially* cinematic [...] and the cinematic medium as essentially phenomenological' [Taylor, 1999: 133] could appropriate it as 'nothing less than the *ultimate* film' [Taylor, 1999: 132]). *2001* is 'Kubrick's reaffirmation', as Fredric Jameson said, 'of the *flatness* of the visual screen':

> The visual features of *2001* were, on the one hand, the screen as a surface to be inscribed, and on the other, the window-cockpit traveling across an expanse of landscapes. [...] we are spectators seated comfortably in the speeding vehicle of a movie theatre soaring into infinity. (Jameson, 1974)

In distancing the film from the novel, the visual from print, and celebrating the communicative power of the image in consort with music, Kubrick does more than claim the pre-eminence of the visual. He also offers, and thematically embeds in the experience of the film, the implication that cinema is an *evolution beyond* the novel, a uniquely, if ambivalently, powerful medium for triggering the unconsciousness, reproducing dream states, and altering consciousness as well as subliminally manipulating the viewer (an idea explored further and more acerbically in *A Clockwork Orange*). The distance between the film and its novelization is key to this, because Kubrick is that paradox – an auteur of adaptation who in *2001*, as in *A Clockwork Orange*, *The Shining* and *Eyes Wide Shut*, foregrounds the written text only to swerve emphatically away from it. He adapts so as to *trump* the original rather than to pay homage to or to respect its inviolable spirit. As

Thomas Leitch says, Kubrick 'earned his auteur status [...] by taking on authors directly in open warfare' (Leitch, 2007: 240). Because with *2001* there is no single originary text, the swerve away from the 'source', which is Kubrick's distinctive gesture of auteurist appropriation, is especially complex; numerous influences and anxieties must be confronted and overcome. In aiming to produce the consummate sf *film*, Kubrick must go beyond not only preceding sf cinema but also the literary sf tradition represented by Clarke and embodied in his novelization.

But if, for all Clarke's involvement, *2001* would ultimately be promoted and interpreted as a Kubrick film, it was the novelization that generated more direct textual offspring. Clarke went on to write three sequels (1982; 1988; 1997) without Kubrick's involvement (although Kubrick had shares in the property), one of which, *2010: Odyssey Two*, was adapted as a film, *2010* (Peter Hyams, 1984). Clarke brought the novel of *2010* into conformity with the film of *2001* (for example, the destination planet is Jupiter, as in the film), but the film of *2010* nevertheless hinges on a reference to a key moment at the end of the novelization of *2001* that is not present in the film – Bowman crying, 'Oh my God – *it's full of stars!*' (Clarke, 1968: 193). Hyams's film is therefore a sequel to the *2001* novelization as much as either an adaptation of Clarke's *2010* novel or a sequel to Kubrick's film – 'something much more complex than a straightforward sequel to the earlier novel – or the movie' (Clarke, 1982: 15). Although *2001* is invariably classed as a Kubrick film, his contribution to the *2001* 'universe' is dwarfed by Clarke's expansion (and ownership) of the material into a franchise over three decades. Even so, in returning the world of *2001* to that of literary sf, Clarke might be said to betray the spirit of Kubrick's extraordinary film as comprehensively as the generic ordinariness of Hyams's perfectly competent sequel / adaptation banalizes rather than enhances or retrospectively completes it.

Kubrick ensures that comparisons with such source or competitor texts demonstrate the inadequacy of words and the marvellous and troubling power of the visual, like music and often in combination with it, to possess, control, haunt, derange and unsettle. It was important to Kubrick that film should still be understood to be able to communicate ideas, and indeed a combination of intense visual experience and rigorous intellectual formalism is the most striking and characteristic quality of all his films. Kubrick said: 'Film operates on a level much closer to music and painting than to the printed word, and, of course, movies present an opportunity to convey complex concepts and abstractions without the traditional reliance on words' (Gelmis, 2001: 90). One of the clichés of opposing sf literature to sf cinema – usually as an indictment of sf cinema – is that the former is a medium of ideas while the latter 'expects much less intelligence in its audience' and 'with few exceptions, is no more sophisticated than was genre magazine SF in the 1930s' (Peter Nicholls, cited in Landon [1992: 4]. See Landon for a comprehensive discussion of the inadequacy of this dismissal). Kubrick was therefore engaged in a complex engagement with – and, crucially, disengagement from – a number of traditions and assumptions about sf, the relationship between sf film and sf genre writing, and the comparative abilities of cinema and literature, all of which determine his withdrawal of fidelity to the novelization. Simply put, the novelization of *2001* represents all that the film refuses and *transcends*. That is why Kubrick is so crucial to adaptation studies and its endless blasphemous refutations of the ineffable superiority of Word over Image. His films are *about* the evolution of image beyond word and of film beyond the novel. *2001* is a defining moment in, as well as a compelling allegory of, what Jameson calls the 'never-ending and unresolvable struggles for primacy' between literature and cinema (Jameson, 2011: 232).

Notes

1 For example, the entry for *2001* in the filmography of my *British Science Fiction Cinema* (1999) states that it was based on 'The Sentinel' (Hunter, 1999: 197). Strictly speaking, this was a mistake, but it merely reiterated common and uncontroversial knowledge.

2 On the cover of both the British Arrow paperback version and the American New English Library edition, the screenplay is credited to Stanley Kubrick and Arthur C. Clarke, giving priority to the director.

3 Speaking personally, I am obviously ambivalent and even hostile towards Clarke's novelization (for all its merits) and his sequels to *2001*. That is

because I am, like many cineastes, a Kubrick cultist, and Clarke, frankly, *gets in the way* of my confident attribution of intention and meaning solely to the director. This is clearly ridiculous. Film is a collaborative industry and although Kubrick had an exceptional measure of control over his films he usually co-wrote their scripts from previously published sources and relied upon the skills of numerous technicians to realize them. It is also ridiculous because the novelization offers another route into the *2001* universe, and, as I remark above, a cultist should generally welcome any opportunity to expand his recherché knowledge of a cult film and thereby enhance his cultural capital. I mention this only because, in my case, caring about the film for much of my life (and not especially caring for sf literature) leads me to distinguish radically between the film and the novel, which energizes (but hopefully does not determine) my analysis of Kubrick's agonistic style of adaptation. David Church has written about how Kubrick is a kind of gateway auteur for young, especially male, cinephiles – his films have clear signs of authorship, share themes that are attractively grand and pessimistic, and combine the thrills of pulp genre cinema with art cinema's stylistic flair and sense of a meticulously controlled authorial universe:

With a share in both popular and elite culture, the figure of Kubrick-as-auteur proves an especially 'safe' choice of filmmaker for young film buffs to idolize in cultish ways, helping to bridge the gap between those differing economic and cultural strata in the film buff's move from low/mass tastes to the high/elite tastes associated with a higher educational and/or economic level and a wider knowledge of world film. (Church, 2006)

Moreover, as Thomas Leitch remarks, Kubrick's auteurist persona as it developed in the 1960s of 'the last solitary romantic artist who embraced the technology of cinema only to recoil from its chilling institutional implications' was also 'perfectly calculated to appeal to the emerging academic field of film studies' (Leitch, 2007: 244). In practical terms, as an academic cultist, this makes it difficult for me to frame *2001* as anything else than a Kubrick film, with 'Kubrick' standing for a meta-frame of repetitions, self-references, echoes and thematic elaborations that confers retrospective coherence on his body of work. Clarke, unfortunately, interferes with that meta-frame. My concern for and even protectiveness of *2001* may be idiosyncratic but it is common enough in relation to adaptations generally. Viewers who care deeply about a novel care too about how faithfully and respectfully it is adapted, just as fans and cultists care about how the films they love are treated (or in the case of *Star Wars* [George Lucas, 1977] mistreated) when they are restored, re-released and re-edited (see Hunter, 2007 for a discussion of this in relation to *The Lord of the Rings*). Adaptation studies could learn a great deal from cult and fan studies about the importance of audiences' emotional investment not only in texts but also in the relationships between them, and how such bonds of caring are structured over time.

4 I should point out, though, that taking cultists as a guide to how audiences relate to texts is potentially as misleading as taking fans as 'ideal readers' with greater authority than other audiences. Fans and cultists may have too much investment in a text; and in any case, though much less often discussed, love and hate (the two poles of fandom) are extremes. Indifferent and bored audiences, rather than cultist audiences of passionately engaged fans, are the norm.

References

Agel, J. (ed.) (1970) *The Making of Kubrick's 2001*. New York: Signet.

Bizony, P. (1994) *2001: Filming the Future*. London: Aurum.

Bordwell, D. (1979) 'The Art Cinema as a Mode of Practice', *Film Criticism* 4: 59.

Castle, R. (2004) 'The Interpretative Odyssey of *2001*: Of Humanity and Hyperspace', *Bright Lights Film Journal* 46, http://www.brightlightsfilm.com/46/2001.php (accessed July 2011).

Chion, M. (2001) *Kubrick's Cinema Odyssey*, trans. C. Gorbman. London: BFI.

Church, D. (2006) 'The "Cult" of Kubrick', *Offscreen.com* 10 (5), http://www.offscreen.com/index.php/phile/essays/cult_kubrick/P1/ (accessed September 2011).

Clarke, A. C. (1968) *2001: A Space Odyssey*. London: Arrow.

Clarke, A. C. (1972) *The Lost Worlds of 2001*. London: Sidgwick and Jackson.

Clarke, A. C. (1982) *2010: Odyssey Two*. London: Granada.

Clarke, A. C. (1988) *Odyssey Three*. London: Grafton.

Clarke, A. C. (1997) *3001: The Final Odyssey*. London: HarperCollins.

Derrida, J. (1987) *The Truth in Painting*, trans. Geoff Bennington and Ian McLeod. Chicago, IL and London: University of Chicago Press.

Fry, C. L. (2003) 'From Technology to Transcendence: Humanity's Evolutionary Journey in *2001: A Space Odyssey*', *Extrapolation* 44 (3): 331–43.

Gelmis, J. (2001) 'The Film Director as Superstar: Stanley Kubrick', in G. D. Phillips (ed.) *Stanley Kubrick Interviews*, pp. 80–104. Jackson: University Press of Mississippi.

Gwenllian-Jones, S. and Pearson, R. (eds) (2004) *Cult Television*. Minneapolis: University of Minnesota Press.

Hills, M. (2003) '*Star Wars* in Fandom, Film Theory, and the Museum: The Cultural Status of the Cult Blockbuster', in J. Stringer (ed.) *Movie Blockbusters*, pp. 178–89. London and New York: Routledge.

Hunter, I.Q. (ed.) (1999) *British Science Fiction Cinema*. London and New York: Routledge.

Hunter, I.Q. (2007) 'Post-Classical Fantasy Cinema: *The Lord of the Rings*', in D. Cartmell and I. Whelehan (eds) *The Cambridge Companion to Literature on Screen*, pp. 154–66. Cambridge: Cambridge University Press.

Jameson, F. (1974) 'History and the Death Wish: *Zardoz* as Open Form', *Jump Cut* 3: 5–8, http://www.ejumpcut.org/archive/onlinessays/JC-03folder/ZardozJameson.html (accessed June 2011).

Jameson, F. (2011) 'Afterword: Adaptation as a Philosophical Problem', in C. MacCabe, K. Murray and R. Warner (eds) *True to the Spirit: Film Adaptation and the Question of Fidelity*, pp. 215–33. New York: Oxford University Press.

Kaplan, M. (2007) 'Kubrick: A Marketing Odyssey', *Guardian* (2 November).

Klinger, B. (2010) 'Becoming Cult: *The Big Lebowski*, Replay Culture and Male Fans', *Screen* 51 (1): 1–20.

Kramer, P. (2010) *2001: A Space Odyssey*. London: BFI/Palgrave Macmillan.

Landon, B. (1992) *The Aesthetics of Ambivalence: Rethinking Science Fiction Film in the Age of Electronic (Re)production*. Westport, CT and London: Greenwood Press.

Leitch, T. (2007) *Film Adaptation and Its Discontents: From Gone with the Wind to The Passion of the Christ*. Baltimore, MD: The Johns Hopkins University Press.

LoBrutto, V. (1998) *Stanley Kubrick: A Biography*. London: Faber and Faber.

McAleer, N. (1993) *Odyssey: The Authorised Biography of Arthur C. Clarke*. London: Victor Gollancz.

Mathijs, E. (2010) 'Television and the Yuletide Cult', *FlowTV* 11 (5), http://flowtv.org/2010/01/television-and-the-yuletide-cult-ernest-mathijs-the-university-of-british-columbia/ (accessed July 2011).

Michelson, A. (1969) 'Bodies in Space: Film as "Carnal Knowledge"', *Artforum* 7 (6): 54–63.

Nicholls, P., Brosnan, J. and Lowe, N. (2011) '*2001: A Space Odyssey*', in J. Clute and D. Langford (eds) *SFE: The Encyclopedia of Science Fiction. Third Edition*, http://www.sf-encyclopedia.com/Entry/2001_a_space_odyssey (accessed October 2011).

Taylor, G. (1999) *Artists in the Audience: Cults, Camp, and American Film Criticism*. Princeton, NJ: Princeton University Press.

Van Parys, T. (2009) 'The Commercial Novelization: Research, History, Differentiation', *Literature/Film Quarterly* 37 (4): 305–17.

Van Parys, T. (2011) 'The Study of Novelisation: A Typology and Secondary Bibliography', *Belphégor* 10 (2), http://etc.dal.ca/belphegor/vol10_no2/articles/10_02_paryst_noveli_fr.html (accessed September 2011).

PART II

THE ART FILM

Chapter 3

A Spatial Obsession
The Man Who Fell to Earth as Countercultural Science Fiction

Peter Verstraten

When Neil Badmington was screening a brief clip from *Invasion of the Body Snatchers* (Don Siegel, 1956) for an audience of undergraduate students, he was both struck by and prepared for the fact that they all laughed (Badmington, 2004). Way back in the 1950s, the film was seen as an indirect expression of genuine American paranoia for a far-away enemy, a popular preoccupation during the Cold War. *Invasion of the Body Snatchers* was deadly serious, because the fear of aliens was no laughing matter, as the studio executives believed. Even though Badmington admits that many of the science-fiction films of the 1950s bring a smile to his face too, his twenty-first century students burst into uncontrollable laughter when they are shown a fragment. For today's youngsters the suggestion of 'beware of the unknown' is apparently ridiculous. A relationship between human and alien that is based upon suspicion and hatred is perhaps 'laughably alien to the present', Badmington (2004: 2) concludes. At the end of the lecture, this conclusion was confirmed to him when he saw a student carrying a backpack that had the handwritten text 'Alien Love' on it, accompanying the face of an extraterrestrial.

Being attentive to signs of 'alien love', Badmington observes and discusses a multitude of examples, from children's toys to spiritual movements. He has his doubts, however, whether something has fundamentally changed, now that people seem to be inclined to cuddle the alien rather than fear the non-human Other. He notes a structural similarity between 'alien hatred' and 'alien love', since both concepts rely upon the same binary logic. In case of the first, we detest the aliens because they are utterly different from 'Us', while alien love presupposes that we are fond of the outsiders precisely because they are *not* like 'Us'. In the words of Badmington (2004: 152), '"we" love "them," quite simply, as a "them"'. Despite our warm feelings towards the aliens, we remain trapped in the 'continued reign of a human subject over its inhuman objects' (Badmington, 2004: 86). The widespread welcoming of aliens has not undermined so much as underlined the distinction between 'Us' and 'Them'. In order to neutralize the all too positive connotations of the term 'love', Badmington introduces the term that is also the title of his study, 'Alien Chic', out of deference to an essay by Tom Wolfe on 'Radical Chic' (see Wolfe, 1970).

The logical question crops up whether it is impossible to circumvent the dichotomy between aliens and humans. Badmington suggests a way out of the deadlock by following Jacques Derrida in stating that, on closer inspection, every opposition can be deconstructed and is contaminated by its supposed counterpart. He rereads *Invasion of the Body Snatchers* in order to illustrate that it is not a matter of 'human versus alien': even in a scenario of alien hatred, the term 'versus' is in crisis. Every close encounter with an alien confronts us with the Other within ourselves. I am in support of Badmington's argument, but its slight disadvantage is that in principle every film can be read as a potential critique of the human-alien dichotomy. As a consequence, one may lose sight of the differences between a science-fiction film by, say, Siegel, Franklin J. Schaffner or Steven Spielberg. The status of a film as an expression of contemporary fear, or a money-driven vehicle, or a critical revision may tend be ignored.

I aim to take a different route, starting from a remark Badmington makes in passing. He presumes that a turning point in the shift from fear to affection for the alien can be located somewhere between 1977 and 1982 (Badmington, 2004: 10). Stanley Kubrick's *2001: A Space Odyssey* (1968) can already be seen as a revision of invasion narratives, but with Spielberg's *Close Encounters of the Third Kind* (1977) and especially *E.T.: The Extra-Terrestrial* (1982) Alien Chic comes to predominate. Rather than these blockbusters (which were seminal for initiating a golden age of sf films), I shall highlight a 'countercultural' branch within the history of science-fiction cinema that has perhaps never been stronger than during these very same years. By discussing *The Man Who Fell to Earth* (Nicolas Roeg, 1976) as my key example, I will particularly situate a countercultural twist in the way the film version deviates from the literary source text, written by Walter Tevis in 1963.

Aliens R U.S.

There was a thirteen-year lapse between Tevis's book *The Man Who Fell to Earth* and Roeg's film adaptation. Science-fiction literature had evolved considerably in the meantime, while 1968 turned out to be a watershed in the history of sf cinema.[1] That year showed that sf cinema could offer not only exciting stories, but also serious, philosophical reflection. In her study *Screening Space*, Vivian Sobchack notes that while sf cinema emerged as a critically recognized genre in the 1950s, its status was still relatively low. Its audience remained predominantly juvenile, for, as Sobchack says, 'Most SF literature has been written for adults, while most, although certainly not all, SF films have been made for children and teenagers' (Sobchack, 1998: 25).

The history of sf cinema enters a new phase in 1968, thanks to the release of both *2001: A Space Odyssey* and Schaffner's *Planet of the Apes*. *2001* is of special interest because in this film the computer HAL 9000 is a scientific invention that is supposed to be free from any pathological motivations. The inhuman machine, however, turns out to express human emotions and cannot bear that it is not considered an infallible entity. From a narratological perspective we can observe a clear difference from sf from a decade earlier. The monster produced by science was always an 'It' – literally so in *Forbidden Planet* (Fred M. Wilcox, 1956), which features an 'Id' monster – a thing to be looked at. If 'It' was capable of the act of looking – a point-of-view shot of the creature was not uncommon as a special attraction – it was not capable of interpreting what it saw. Lacking a psyche, it was just a 'Thing' that roamed the earth. The creature was rarely an internal focalizer but merely an object to be destroyed. Its depersonalized nature was emphasized in titles as *The Thing from Another World* (Christian Nyby and Howard Hawks, 1951), *Them!* (Gordon Douglas, 1954) or *It Came from Beneath the Sea* (Robert Gordon, 1955). By contrast, HAL in *2001* is endowed with subjectivity, which is stressed in numerous point-of-view shots and by talent for lip-reading. The opposition between human and non-human is no longer as absolute as it used to be.

According to Sobchack, the space-time coordinates are shifting within the sf genre during this period. Space in sf films from the 1950s was inscribed as 'deep': those on a mission were thrilled to discover and conquer new territories. Any journey into unknown space was seen as a progressive step forward in time, as if one were sent into the future. After 1968, entering space is not an exciting enterprise anymore, as space becomes inescapably domestic. Time is static and seems in the grip of boredom. The future is expected to be even worse than the already grim present. Space and time become hollowed out in this phase, but the net result of this development is that sf gains in respectability. Its disenchanting tone matches with the bleak atmosphere in some American films that turned out to be unexpected box-office hits, such as *Bonnie and Clyde* (Arthur Penn, 1967), *Easy Rider* (Dennis Hopper, 1969) and *Five Easy Pieces* (Bob Rafelson, 1970).

After a period in which the film industry was in the grips of near bankruptcy, Hollywood regained its momentum in the mid-1970s and introduced new standards of production and strategies of marketing. Science-fiction cinema followed the new blockbuster formula and produced remarkably successful specimens, viz. *Star Wars* (George Lucas, 1977) and *Close Encounters of the Third Kind*. This type of sf derived from the narratives of B-movies from the 1950s and wrapped them up in the guise of a slick big-budget movie. What used to be mainly kids' stuff was now elevated into popular cinema for both adolescents and adults.

Owing to the input of Lucas and Spielberg the B-movie plots of sf films not only became commercially viable, but were also elevated to A-status. They used advanced special effects and a polished style that became parameters of what was termed high-concept cinema. However, the return to the plot structures of the movies of the 1950s did not involve a revival of the attitude towards technology, according to Sobchack (1988). In the 1950s, the characters were willing to marvel at all the new technology. By contrast, in the late 1970s blockbuster, we can speak of a lack of novelty. In these films, to quote Sobchack, 'the predominant emphasis is on mapping not the fearsome and wondrous "newness" of the new technology, but rather its awesome and wondrous familiarity' (Sobchack, 1988: 252). All the fascinating gadgets are accepted and experienced as consumable artifacts (Sobchack, 1988: 253). As a consequence, the space-time axis has undergone a shift as well. These films display a nostalgic tone for a lost childhood, which means that time has decelerated. Time is not strictly progressive as in the fifties, but it is headed towards both a past and the future. In turn, space is no longer as deep and three-dimensional as it was in 1950s sf. Sobchack contends that most sf films in this period use space as a surface for play and for intertextual allusions. She observes an increased awareness that the images we display are borrowed from a huge visual reservoir. No better example to illustrate this than John Carpenter's 1982 remake of *The Thing*.

This brief overview of the history of sf cinema is intended to point to a split that takes place in the mid-1970s. The mainstream variant I have just mentioned can be seen as a rupture with the preceding phase of bleak sf of *2001*, *The Andromeda Strain* (Robert Wise, 1971), *Silent Running* (Douglas Trumbull, 1971) and the strangely abstract *THX 1138* (George Lucas, 1971). Next to a mainstream variant we can detect countercultural tendencies within sf that are to be qualified as a continuation of the bleak trajectory with its hollowed-out time and space. I use the term 'countercultural' in a loose way to qualify a variety of sf films whose common denominator is that they deliberately transgress the regular conventions of the genre. These countercultural tendencies include films with a cultish appeal, such as the quite quirky *Dark Star* (John Carpenter, 1974) or the darkly humorous *Shivers* (David Cronenberg, 1975). In *Dark Star*, to mention one of its hilarious scenes, a crew member of a space ship tries to persuade a smart bomb not to explode, and in *Shivers*, a strain of parasites turns citizens into sex maniacs. Like *Shivers*, Donald Cammell's *Demon Seed* (1977) is a creepy cross between horror and sf. Symptomatic of the countercultural development is Philip Kaufman's 1978 remake of *Invasion of the Body Snatchers* because of the eerie twist at the end. Unlike Siegel's original, the final shot of Kaufman's film suggests that the main protagonist was only mimicking his human nature, hence collapsing any clear-cut distinction between human and alien. These countercultural tendencies within sf lead up to idiosyncratic movies like *Liquid Sky* (Slava Tsukerman, 1983), *Repo Man* (Alex Cox, 1984) and *The Brother from Another Planet* (John Sayles, 1984). From this list it may be observed that there is a sliding scale towards weirdness. The sf movies from the second half of the 1970s are modestly unorthodox compared to the outrageous, and sometimes downright comic, peripheral sf films from the early 1980s. *Repo Man* celebrates the anti-aesthetics of punk in an unconventional plot that centers on a car with a radioactive trunk; in *The Brother from Another Planet*, white guys are asked for their identity papers, but the taciturn, three-toed black alien is never requested to show his, and in the perversely bizarre *Liquid Sky* sexual difference is eradicated in order to celebrate, what Sobchack (1988: 297) has named, 'andr(oid)ogyny'.

For Sobchack, these three low-budget and marginal sf films from the 1980s are an appropriate antidote to the too idyllic embrace of the alien in the blockbuster sf film. In the films of Lucas and Spielberg, the non-human Other is idealized to such an extent that the alien is affirmed in its Otherness. Yoda in the *Star Wars* episode *The Empire Strikes Back* (Irvin Kershner, 1980) is just like us humans, only wiser and better. E.T. resembles us; he is cuter and more adorable. But humanity remains the yardstick of normality, and the alien is judged by its deviation from this standard, whether it is for the worse (as in the 1950s' invasion narratives) or for the better.

According to Sobchack, we should substitute our thinking in terms of 'resemblance' for one in terms of 'similitude'. Resemblance is based upon a similarity that is almost total, but not quite: the alien really looks like us, except for a tiny detail. This small difference may then be blown up to gigantic proportions in order to safeguard the distinction between Us and Them. In the case of similitude, difference and sameness become interchangeable. What is conventionally regarded as a difference is then self-evidently treated as 'sameness', as if an alien were an already fully accepted member of society. Sobchack coins this process 'Aliens R U.S.'. These sf movies presuppose a non-discernable similitude between human and non-human. The idea of 'aliens are us' can also be read reversibly as 'we are aliens' (Sobchack, 1988: 297). Sobchack argues that erasing the alien's alienness takes place mostly in marginal sf in the early 1980s. Here I want to position Roeg's *The Man Who Fell to Earth* as hovering between popular and marginal, between *E.T.* and *The Brother from Another Planet*.

Walter Tevis's Novel

Unlike Roeg's film, Walter Tevis's novel has no countercultural tendencies. Tevis was not a literary author, but rather a writer of pulp fiction, and the form and style of his novel are utterly conventional. In it Thomas Jerome Newton has arrived from outer space to examine whether the earth is a proper refuge for the less than 300 creatures on his dying home-planet Anthea. If so, then he will earn money to build a spaceship and transport them to earth. Within a few years Thomas gets incredibly rich thanks to the patents on some marvellous inventions. When he asks Professor Nathan Bryce for advice about materials that can take great heat, Bryce becomes curious about Thomas's background. Because of Thomas's peculiar appearance and his remarkable behaviour, Bryce begins to suspect that Thomas may come from another planet. His hunch is affirmed when he makes an X-ray recording of Thomas, noticing that he has 'impossible bones in an impossible body' (Tevis, 1979: 54). As Thomas himself tells Bryce later, when he finally reveals his background: 'There *is* nothing inside my bones. They are light and *empty*' (Tevis, 1979: 70).

Time and again, the word 'strange' is used to describe the impression Thomas makes upon those who have contact with him. The whole plot pivots around the question whether people will recognize that he is an alien, for Thomas is tall and very thin 'with wide eyes like a bird' (Tevis, 1979: 29). His body is almost without hair; his fingernails are fake; he has only four toes on each of his feet and he weighs very little, about ninety pounds: 'But for every difference there were many more things the same. He was human, but not, really, a man. But he could feel love, fear, and pain like any human being' (Tevis, 1979: 5–6).

Tevis's book is constantly concerned with marking both resemblance and difference. Rhetorically, the novel is structured around the formula of 'he is ... yet he is not ...'. Thomas is confident that he can look and act human enough to pass for one, but at the same time he is not human enough. Either he has shortcomings – his body is unfit to take an elevator – or he is better than men, and his technological inventions are a token of this superiority. When the secret services come to know about his existence, they consider him a threat to world peace, just in case he really is an invader from outer space. The services attempt to nullify any difference between Thomas and humans, in order to neutralize the danger he might pose to mankind. They adamantly want to prove that he is just a mutant with some physical deficiencies. During their investigations, they use X-rays on him, but since Thomas can see them he knows that they will have a devastating effect upon him. He shouts: '*I'm not a human being at all!*' (Tevis, 1979: 82), but since they continue the test, he temporarily loses his eyesight and becomes colour-blind. In a meeting with Nathan some years later, Thomas realizes that they have made him into an American, drawing an ironic conclusion: 'I worked very hard to become a human being [...] And of course, I succeeded' (Tevis, 1979: 90).

To some extent, *The Man Who Fell to Earth* reads like Badmington's 'worst nightmare'. The book is a typical example of alien versus human: how can we distinguish an extraterrestrial from a human? Can we spot its strange and extraordinary status? On top of that, humanity

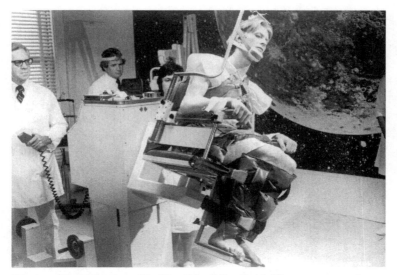

Figure 1. David Bowie in *The Man Who Fell to Earth.* Photo courtesy of Cinema 5/Photofest.

is posited as the desirable standard, the model that everyone wants to imitate. But at this point there is also a leeway for 'rereading the alien', as advocated by Badmington. Initially, Thomas avoids being exposed as an alien. His mimicry is successful, but it is always at risk. Whereas Thomas may fear that the differences are too obvious after all, humans will fear that the differences are too minimal. If an alien Other cannot be detected, the resemblance becomes uncanny: appearances cannot tell that he is not one of us. Badmington would celebrate such an uncanny experience as an encounter with 'the Other within'. By contrast, for the secret services such an encounter is their worst fear, so only two strategies are left for them. Either they exaggerate the differences so that no one could mistake the alien for human, or they neutralize the differences. In *The Man Who Fell to Earth*, the second trajectory is followed through in an aggressive attempt to humanize the alien. The novel ends on a wry tone, because Thomas has lost all appetite for his original plans and he cancels the idea to build a spaceship for the other Antheans. Humanity can still be upheld as a superior standard.

The novel conforms to Badmington's critical point that it is very hard to think beyond the notion of humanity. Although it briefly hints at a collapse of the boundaries between human and aliens, rendering the distinction between Us and Them practically negligible, at the end the boundaries are re-established to the advantage of Us, when Thomas, to his own dismay, has become a citizen of the US. In my reading of Roeg's film version of Tevis's novel, I will indicate that the movie is not just a regular adaptation, but that the film subjects the dichotomy between human and alien to a constant deferral.

Nicolas Roeg's Adaptation

If many of the characters in Nicolas Roeg's films are represented as disoriented, his movies have at the same time the habit of disorienting their spectators. In *Don't Look Now* (1973), John is not only lost among the streets and canals of Venice, but the twist is that he is also at a loss in terms of temporality. He is never aware that he has the ultimately fatal gift of seeing flash-forwards. In *Bad Timing: A Sensual Obsession* (1980), an inspector is trying to reconstruct the events of the night that a woman was badly injured. While doing so, we also see scenes from her relationship with her former boyfriend, without knowing to whom these flashbacks belong: to the woman on the operating table, her ex or the inspector trying to imagine the progress of the relationship. The viewer remains caught between story and scene, since it is not possible to put the chronology in order.

A play with temporality in *The Man Who Fell to Earth* is mainly limited to the fact that we see how all the characters grow significantly older, but Thomas seems to remain forever young in his appearance. More remarkable is the way the film disorients us spatially, because Roeg attempts to 'fracture the grammar' of film language, as his editor Graeme Clifford described their working method once.[2] At times there are fast zoom-ins and zoom-outs, uncommon superimpositions, parts of shots that are lit too brightly, or unstable point-of-view shots of Thomas. In the beginning of the film, when Thomas has just arrived on earth, the soundtrack is sinister, and it is cross-cut with the noise of a passing car that shocks the visitor. The most telling procedure to fracture the grammar is that the makers do not adhere to conventional rules of editing. A good example is the scene when Nathan is making love to a female student, while Thomas is attending a performance of kabuki theatre. We constantly go back and forth between the scenes so that we are encouraged to see parallels between them. Moreover, the soundtracks of both scenes intermingle and it seems as if Thomas is capable of overhearing the other scene. A similar principle reigns when Thomas is watching scenes from *The Third Man* (Carol Reed, 1949), and fragments of dialogue from this film return in a conversation between Nathan and Mary-Lou, which the viewing of *The Third Man* is cross-cut with.

Besides such cross-cutting, Roeg's film makes strange transitions between scenes. According to classical Hollywood convention, a new scene is introduced by way of an establishing shot so that we get to see how the characters are positioned within space. Only after such an introductory shot, might we see (medium) close-ups. If the characters start to walk around, we usually get a re-establishing shot so that we understand how they take up a new position towards one another. *The Man Who Fell to Earth* deviates from this convention at several occasions. In the case of one transition to another scene, there is a close-up of Thomas's feet, but only later do we understand that he is playing table tennis with Mary-Lou. We are surprised to learn that a time lapse has occurred, for Mary-Lou has aged visibly. At another occasion, there is an establishing shot, so that we expect that the camera will focus next upon the centralized characters in the shot, but instead in the next shot the camera shows two characters who were walking at the left of the frame. The most peculiar transition takes place when a man is thrown out of the window of a huge building. The next shot is taken from under water in a swimming pool, which we see a man fall into. At first we presume that this is the man who has been thrown out of the building, but it is simply another character from another scene.

The first meeting between Nathan and Thomas is unorthodox as well. Thomas walks to his door and says: 'Tomorrow, Mister Bryce.' Nathan asks who he is. 'Don't be suspicious,' Thomas says, but then he vanishes immediately, as if he were a hallucination. Or when

Thomas looks at a deserted landscape, he suddenly sees people who have visited that place in the past, and we get to see them as well. For us as spectators, watching *The Man Who Fell to Earth* means we have to be constantly on our guard. In this film, we are granted a perspective that expands beyond normal human vision.

The plot of both book and film hinges on ambiguity. On the one hand, the secret services take great pains to finally appropriate Thomas within a frame of humanity. Hence, the plot tips the scales in favour of humanity as an enforced yardstick. On the other hand, it is suggested that the outsider Thomas is a 'more human than human' character, with incredibly sharp sight. Tevis has not fully integrated this 'more human than human' quality due to his economic and workmanlike style of writing. By contrast, Roeg's adaptation is a terrific exercise in style. But his style is nevertheless functional, since we have to understand that Thomas, as a visitor from outer space, is not accustomed to the spatial conventions on Earth. Roeg's style therefore underscores Thomas's estranged vision. The defamiliarizing cuts in *The Man Who Fell to Earth* can be seen in parallel to Thomas's experience on planet Earth, confronting us with his 'more human than human' nature. The great achievement of Roeg's film is that we have to adopt an alien-ated way of seeing in order to enjoy the idiosyncratic stylistic principles of the adaptation. The film does not deviate from the storyline of the original book and is quite dystopian in the way humanity represses an alien. In Roeg's film, unlike Tevis's novel, this repressed returns on a formal level.

Conclusion

It was the popularity of Spielberg's sf films that led Badmington to suggest that Alien Chic began between 1977 and 1982. Alien contact in these films is represented as a 'remedy' for alienation: a close encounter is a solution to the chaos of family life, or an E.T. can assuage a boy's suffering after his parents' divorce.[3] The aliens in the popular sf of these years, according to Sobchack, are the improved counterparts of the imperfect humans. It troubles both Badmington and Sobchack that such films overshoot the mark. The blockbuster sf movies make too quick a transition from the hatred that motivated earlier invasion narratives to a loving embrace of the alien. The non-human Other is idealized to such an extent that the alien, in its turn, is affirmed in its Otherness. And due to this affirmation, an idea of humanity as the original model is maintained that still cherishes the opposition of human versus alien.

If Badmington's option is to search within the margins of conventional alien movies for a (posthumanist) alternative that contradicts the apparent dichotomy of the main story, Sobchack tries to formulate an alternative on the basis of totally marginal sf. According to her, we should substitute our thinking in terms of 'resemblance' for a 'similitude' that erases the alienation of the alien. The sf movies of the 1980s, she mentions, are utterly strange movies that, indeed, thanks to their bizarre assumptions, can overturn our notions of the distinction between humans and aliens. The drawback of movies that present strange things on an equal footing with 'normal' appearances is that nothing really is strange. These films may consist of strange juxtapositions and embrace all existence as 'wondrously e-stranged and alien-ated' (Sobchack, 1998: 227), but their transgressions are so hyperbolic that we appreciate them as bravura acts of imagination rather than as contributions to a critical debate. My position is to walk the middle ground between Badmington and Sobchack, and I am aware that this does not result into a straightforward solution, but into exposing a deadlock. Thanks to a correspondence between content and form/style, which is absent in the original novel, the film adaptation of *The Man Who Fell to Earth* confronts us with an unsolvable tension between 'aliens are just like us' and 'aliens R U. S.'. This confrontation makes us experience the alien as the Other within.

Notes

1 The development of sf writing is concisely documented by Brian McHale in his article 'POSTcyberMODERNpunkISM' (McHale, 1992). He describes an ever-tighter feedback loop between run-of-the-mill narratives and state-of-the-art fiction. According to him, literary sf has had a mediating role in lessening the divide between official high culture and

popular culture. Literary authors like William S. Burroughs, Italo Calvino and Thomas Pynchon drew on material from space operas and sf disaster movies, while some sf writers like J. G. Ballard and Philip J. Farmer adopted influences from mainstream models of (modernist) fiction. In the 1980s, the interaction between sf and postmodernist novels has become so intimate that McHale prefers to speak of a feedback loop of mutual influence.

2 Quoted in the documentary *Watching the Alien* (David Gregory, 2003).

3 Although I have emphasized the differences between *E.T.* and *The Man Who Fell to Earth*, Roz Kaveney has drawn an intriguing parallel between the two films. Both E.T. and Thomas are 'secular Christ figures who work miracles and undergo persecution; they are also saintly hippies threatened by the straight world – there is a sense in which all of the revisionist alien movies of the 1970s and 1980s are a rerun of the 1960s round of the culture wars in American society' (Kaveney, 2005: 40).

References

Badmington, N. (2004) *Alien Chic: Posthumanism and the Other Within*. New York: Routledge.

Kaveney, R. (2005) *From Alien to The Matrix: Reading Science Fiction Film*. London: I.B. Tauris.

McHale, B. (1992) 'POSTcyberMODERNpunkISM', in *Constructing Postmodernism*, pp. 225–42. New York: Routledge.

Sobchack, V. (1998) *Screening Space: The American Science Fiction Film*. New Brunswick, NJ: Rutgers University Press.

Tevis, W. (1963/1979) *The Man Who Fell to Earth*. Oxford: Oxford University Press.

Wolfe, T. (1970) *Radical Chic and Mau-Mauing the Flak Catchers*. New York: Farrar, Straus and Giroux.

Chapter 4

Unimportant Failures?
The Fall and Rise of *The Man Who Fell to Earth*

Andrew M. Butler

There is a moment in Walter Tevis's 1963 novel, *The Man Who Fell to Earth*, when we discover that one of its viewpoint characters, Nathan Bryce, is a science-fiction fan:

> He walked down town, hoping that there would be a science fiction movie – one with resurrected dinosaurs clomping around Manhattan in bird-brained wonder, or insectivorous invaders from Mars, come to destroy the whole damn world (and good riddance, too), so they could eat the bugs. (Tevis, 1976: 26–7)

Such a gesture is a risky one in a science-fiction novel as, while it might add to the sense of verisimilitude in that characters might do many things, including watching sf movies, it can draw attention to the novel's fictionality, and Tevis's (or Bryce's) rather camp vision of an sf movie might lead us to reject Tevis's own novel as camp. It is likely that the cinema-going is there as a device to ensure that Bryce is open to the concept of aliens, so that from the first he is willing to suspect that a reclusive inventor is not human. Indeed, Bryce theorizes that Newton is 'either the world's most original inventive genius, or an extra-terrestrial' (Tevis, 1976: 60). The first film adaptation of the novel, directed by Nicolas Roeg for British Lion in 1976, whilst not mentioning sf as such, does draw attention to the act of film-making within its diegesis, and the film in turn became a reference point in another sf novel, *VALIS* (1981) by Philip K. Dick. A film, which was a flop, has risen again. This chapter will examine some aspects of the fidelity of the film to the novel – in particular the theme of falling – and the impact of its director's auteurship upon that faithfulness. The foregrounding of the act of looking, within the cinematic apparatus, will be examined in relation to Laura Mulvey's description of Hollywood film as a purveyor of the male gaze, especially as Roeg challenges such mechanisms. His techniques, in turn, feed into *VALIS* for different purposes.

The Man Who Fell to Earth is the story of Thomas Jerome Newton, 'an alien visitor who comes to Earth on a mission to save his own planet but is corrupted by the influence of mankind' (Chapman, 1999: 137). He plans to save the people of Anthea, ideally by building a rescue ark. Anthean technology will uplift human technology, with human resources, but he also wants to warn the people of Earth about the apocalypse that it is heading for. This places him in a line of alien messiahs which dates back at least as far as *The Day the Earth Stood Still* (Robert Wise, 1951), a film which is almost an *ur*-text for this one. Hugh Ruppersberg, in his article on the alien messiah trope, notes that the film represents Newton's 'corruption by Earthly materialism' (Ruppersberg, 1990: 35), but arguably it is more pleasures than materialism which cause his fall, and his is very much a fall into vice.[1] The narrative also depicts the scientist Bryce and his attempts to investigate Newton, and his betrayal of Newton, and the life of Betty-Jo (Mary-Lou in the film).

Newton's assumed name – we never learn his Anthean one – is very suggestive. 'Thomas' is the apostle who doubted the reality of Christ's resurrection, and had to test the wound in Christ's side with a finger; later he was the sole apostle who witnessed the Annunciation of the Virgin Mary. He is the patron saint of architects and builders, appropriate for Newton's project. A Didymos Judas Thomas – possibly not the apostle Thomas – is the author of a gospel, or rather a collection of Christ's teachings, which was among the manuscripts found at Nag Hammadi in 1945; it was published in English in 1959. The names 'Didymos' and 'Thomas' both relate to words for twin, suggestive of Newton's dual nature and his status as *doppelgänger* of Bryce. Saint Thomas Aquinas was a thirteenth-century theologian, who both believed that divine revelation was necessary for humanity and that reason was a way to the knowledge of the truth. St Jerome was the patron saint of archivists, librarians, scholars and translators, having translated the Bible into Latin for the Vulgate; Newton is not described reading the Bible, but he is compared to Christ at various points, for example when he looks at a portrait – 'with its thinness and large piercing eyes it could have been the face of an Anthean' (Tevis, 1976: 20) – and his assimilation of knowledge about the Earth, via its media, is a form of archive. Finally, 'Newton' is a reference to the English scientist, Sir Isaac Newton, describer of calculus, optics and universal gravitation, who in popular legend theorized the rules of gravitation after an apple fell onto his head. The scientist motif is obvious, but this also points to the concept of falling, which is in the title of the book and film.

'Falling' has two distinct meanings – one literal, the other metaphorical – which can also operate in tandem. First, it refers to an object or person moving under the influence of gravity. Examples are the crash of Newton's spaceship to Earth, his fit in reaction to ascending in a lift for the first time, and his behaviour toward the end of the novel: 'It was only after he had fallen twice that they tested his eyes and discovered that he was blind' (Tevis, 1976: 155). There are other falls in the film, in the shape of the defenestration of patents lawyer Oliver Farnsworth (Buck Henry) and his lover Trevor (Rick Riccardo), which segues into the dive into a swimming pool of Peters (Bernie Casey), a CIA official. In the novel there is a reference (Tevis, 1976: 84) to Thomas Nashe's poem 'Adieu, Farewell, Earth's Bliss', which reads in part:

[...]
I am sick I must die –
    Lord have mercy on us.

Beauty is but a flower
Which wrinkles will devour;
Brightness falls from the air;
Queens have died young and fair;
Dust hath closed Helen's eye. (Nashe, 1952: 129–30)

As the poem is about the fact that everything will die and decay, this reference points to a more metaphorical meaning of falling, and is followed in the novel by Newton reflecting that he has 'an inability to withstand the bruises of the culture he had fallen into' (Tevis, 1976: 85). While 'fallen' is literal in this case, it has behind it the moral-tinged narratives of the Fall: the war in heaven between good and bad angels and the fall of Lucifer, the devil, for the sin of pride or hubris. In John Milton's *Paradise Lost* (1667), this is interwoven with the Fall in the Garden of Eden of Adam and Eve, a fall from innocence into experience, and a discovery of sexuality which led to their expulsion from paradise. It is perhaps a bit of a stretch to associate Betty-Jo/Mary-Lou with Eve, although there remains a residual distrust of women in too many narratives. In both cases, and especially with Lucifer, the fall is associated with overreaching imposed limitations.

This overreaching is at the heart of one of the most significant intertexts for the novel and film: the myth of Icarus. Icarus was the son of Daedalus, and both had been imprisoned by King Minos in Crete, after Daedalus had fashioned the labyrinth. Daedalus made two sets of wings out of wax and feathers, to enable an escape, and warned Icarus not to fly too close to the sun. Icarus ignored this advice, the wax melted, the wings failed, and he plummeted into the sea where he drowned. This legend has proved an inspiration for a number of artists – most notably the Flemish painter Pieter Brueghel the Elder, whose *Landscape with the Fall of Icarus* (c. 1558) in turn was partly the inspiration for a 1938 poem by W. H. Auden about a number of Brueghel paintings. In his meditation on the mundane locations for pain and suffering, Auden describes:

In Breughel's *Icarus*, for instance: how everything turns away
Quite leisurely from the disaster; (Auden, 1977: 237)

A ploughman going about his everyday work is in the foreground of the Brueghel painting; in the background a number of boats are visible. In the bottom right there is a leg of someone – presumably Icarus – disappearing into the sea. Auden speculates if the ploughman is aware of the fall – there is a shepherd to his right who is looking upwards into the sky and has seen something or someone, presumably Daedalus flying – but in this fixed instant the plougher is not responding to the accident and is getting on with his life:

> [...] the ploughman may
> Have heard the splash, the forsaken cry,
> But for him it was not an important failure; the sun shone
> As it had to on the white legs disappearing into the green
> Water (Auden, 1977: 237)

Life goes on, the poem says, even in the midst of suffering and death.

Both the painting and poem are given prominent positions in the book and film. The subdivisions of the novel include 'Icarus Descending' and 'Icarus Drowning'; Bryce also quotes the poem and has a copy of the painting on the wall in his research complex apartment. In the film, the painting and the poem appear in a coffee-table book of art-inspired poetry given as a present to Bryce, and it is this book which first draws his attention to WE (World Enterprises), the corporation established by Newton to manufacture and sell new technology in an attempt to raise money for his mission. This mission remains shadier in the film than it does in the book: 'The film does not provide the detailed background to Newton's mission' (Leach, 1978: 372), although we are shown pictures of parched landscapes and dying aliens, with an ambivalent chronological status (which I will discuss further later). The gift is linked to an early sex scene between Bryce and a young lover, Elaine, dismissed by John Brosnan, along with similar sequences, as 'some of the longest and most boring sex scenes ever filmed' (Brosnan, 1978: 241). It begins with her taking photographs of him (with a WE camera), and becomes intercut with a scene of Newton watching Kabuki dancers. The editing seems to be suggesting that Newton is aware of Bryce – and maybe even vice versa – and is a significant set piece in the early part of the film that draws attention to photography, direction and control of the gaze. At times this threatens to be chaotic, especially by the editing standards of the 1970s. Leach even argues that 'Brueghel gives us a vision of impending chaos, Roeg gives us clutter' (Leach, 1978: 373), having suggested that 'Since the film medium is not a conceptual medium the visual details tend to drown out the ideas' (Leach, 1978: 372). Leach implies here that books are superior to films.

It has become a truism of adaptations that the f-word – sometimes 'faithfulness', sometimes 'fidelity' – is a dead end: the fact that a character scratches his nose in a book, but his ear in a film, is often neither here nor there. Yet the original text – which need not be granted a greater degree of authenticity merely through earlier production – is inevitably an uncanny ghost for the reader who comes to a film adaptation. Criticism which focuses on policing transitions between media takes us back to the debate about cinema as a unique medium versus cinema as a populist presentation of literature, most fruitfully identified by the *Cahiers du cinéma* critics of the 1950s as the division between the *auteur* and the *metteur en scène*, the cinematic artist and the technician for hire. They were reacting against the 1940s and 1950s *cinéma de qualité* directors, such as Claude Autant-Lara, who made literary and literal adaptations which the *Cahiers* critics derided as *cinéma de papa*. In the view of many of the *Cahiers* critics, John Huston's faithful renderings of classics could be dismissed, while Alfred Hitchcock's films should be celebrated, even though with odd exceptions they were adaptations of novels, short stories and plays. Huston subsumed his own messages to be faithful to the literary sources, while Hitchcock, as auteur, found a way to express his worldview through adaptation, his unfaithful versions also being critiques of their sources. We come to his adaptations of Daphne Du Maurier materials – *Jamaica Inn* (novel 1936; film 1939), *Rebecca* (novel 1938; film 1940) and *The Birds* (short story 1952; film 1963) – through the prism of his other films, and the same is true of Roeg.

After his debut, *Performance* (Donald Cammell and Nicolas Roeg, 1970), Roeg filmed two adaptations: *Walkabout* (1971) – based on James Vance Marshall's 1959 novel – and *Don't Look Now* (1973) – from a short story by Daphne Du Maurier (1971). In his early films,

Roeg had already developed an identifiable style, in large part defined by his editing techniques. Mainstream Hollywood films almost always deploy the technique of continuity editing, which comprises an establishing shot of a scene, a limited number of camera angles positioned on one side of or along an imaginary line running through the scene, and a series of shots matched to eyelines. This is an attempt at a kind of psychological realism, suturing together shots from different takes, perhaps taken on different days or on different locations, into the illusion of a continuous four-dimensional whole which is consistent in space and time. Because we have been trained by Hollywood to decode this construction, it is frequently invisible, not drawing attention to itself, unlike the Soviet dialectical montage of Sergei Eisenstein. One of the functions of continuity editing is to facilitate audience identification with the characters on screen, to immerse themselves in the diegesis; dialectical editing often has an estranging purpose, a cinematic equivalent to the *Verfremdungseffekt* of Bertolt Brecht, with a political agenda to make the audience think rather than emote. If Leach is correct in arguing that cinema is visual rather than conceptual, this is potentially problematic.

Roeg tended to a dialectical style which might be tagged discontinuity editing, reminiscent of the work of Eisenstein, but not as rigorously pursued. Eisenstein wanted each shot to contradict rather than confirm the previous one – upwards followed by downwards, light by dark, fullness by emptiness, vertical by horizontal – with meaning to be located in the continual play of thesis and antithesis of a series of cells. Roeg's editing style is an open one, which eschews linearity: there is neither one continuous thread of chronology, nor is he bound by the barriers of a single location. The sex scene between Bryce and Elaine cuts together different stages of love-making, as well as events outside of it, and is clearly a variation on a scene in *Don't Look Now*, between John and Christine, which juxtaposes the foreplay, the act and the aftermath in a single sequence. The estrangement overrides what might have been a soft-porn titillation. The collapse of chronology in the sequence is symptomatic of the structure of the film itself, where John is haunted by memories of his drowned daughter and inexplicably sees his wife in Venice, when she is clearly still in England.

Figure 1. The Man Who Fell to Earth. Photo courtesy of Cinema 5/Photofest.

The audience can conclude that he is having a vision of his wife in the future at his funeral. Such prolepsis and analepsis is used in *The Man Who Fell to Earth* to depict a group of aliens on a desert world, which we take to be Newton's family – although it is not certain whether these are memories, events which are taking place or are imagined as taking place at the same time as the events in the film on Earth, or whether these are fantasies or foretelling of his return to Anthea. It has been suggested that 'The planet from which Newton comes in the film is not another world one hundred million miles away but the earth itself in its future' (Leach, 1978: 376) and that these shots 'could be visions of a hallucinating genius' (Peary, 1983: 82). The Man Who Fell may just be a man who fell.

In Roeg's previous films, the discontinuity editing had differing purposes. In *Performance* it was attached to the characters' use of drugs, and the increasing disorientation of London gangster Chas (James Fox) in the drug-addled world of Turner (Mick Jagger). In *Walkabout,* where it is not clear whether the ending is a real or fantasized future, the editing serves as a technologized approach to the representation of the aboriginal dreamtime. Finally, in *Don't Look Now*, it both portrays the guilt and grief of the Baxters after the death of their daughter, and gives a sense of the supernatural menace which may or may not be operating in England and Venice. John Walker argues that the editing encourages us to ask if 'what is seen is reality or fantasy or a visual equivalent of the protagonists' state of mind' (Walker, 1985: 96) and there is a long tradition of film theorizing – dating back at least as far as Hugo Münsterberg in 1916 – which equates camerawork and editing with the way that human consciousness works, complete with desires, memories, anticipations and daydreams as well as every day (albeit dramatic) experiences. If continuity editing represents the workings of a 'normalized' consciousness, Roeg's discontinuity editing represents the abnormal.

In 'Visual Pleasure and Narrative Cinema' (1975), Laura Mulvey argues that continuity editing within Hollywood cinema constructed a heteronormative, male gaze. She draws on the ideas of Sigmund Freud and Jacques Lacan, who see scopophilia as a means of disavowing castration. Freud's 1922 'The Medusa's Head' unpacks the 'turning to stone'/'making rock-hard' metaphor of the Medusa not so much as a moment of castration anxiety (being faced with snakes; literal petrification as unmanning) but rather as the reassurance through an erection that the observer is still a man. Mulvey argues that Freud associates scopophilia with 'taking other people as objects, subjecting them to a controlling and curious gaze' (Mulvey, 1989: 16). There is a power imbalance between the person who looks and the person who is being looked at, especially if she does not know that she is being looked at, and the person who is doing the looking is often willing the object of his gaze to perform certain actions. This desiring gaze is encouraged in cinema, with attractive diegetic females to be looked at projected for our pleasure. The mechanics of the editing encourage an identification with the male protagonist, which reinforces the desire since the protagonist also desires the (female) object of the spectator's gaze. Taboos against homosexuality discourage the audiences from desiring the protagonist – the viewer instead wishes to be him – and the female viewer is either partially excluded from the process or 'cross-dresses' for the duration of the film. It is worth noting that Mulvey is calling for a kind of cinema which works against these mechanisms even as she describes them. There are at least three functional gazes at work in the film: that of the characters within the diegesis, of the camera and crew outside of the diegesis and of the audience in the auditorium. That Newton's first big invention is a special kind of colour camera draws attention within the diegesis to the act of spectatorship, reminding us that this is just a film. That the photographs being taken are part of the sex play of Bryce and Elaine makes a link with the sexualizing of looking, but with two important quibbles: first, both parties are fully aware of their scopophilia, removing the nonconsensual aspect which might locate this as a perversion (Freud, 1991a: 358; 1991b: 70), and second, it is Elaine who is taking pictures of Bryce. This objectification of a man – an aggressively heterosexual man – is abnormal to say the least. Since this sequence is intercut with Newton's own spectatorship of Kabuki theatre, and Newton seems to be aware of the intercourse, it could be argued that Bryce and Elaine are passive, unaware objects of a controlling and curious gaze.

The desire between Bryce and various co-ed students – blurring boundaries of age and the teacher-pupil relationships – is one of a series of non-normative sexual conjunctions in the film, which also includes the interracial relationship between the African American Peters and his Caucasian wife, the homosexual partnership between Farnsworth and Trevor, and finally Newton and Mary-Lou. In part, such relationships – Bryce/Elaine's now being perhaps the most scandalous – are there as a means of showing the social progress of the 15 or so years of screen time, but they have a mutually reinforcing normalization impact on each crossed taboo. Some critics have complained that sexuality is something which Roeg has imposed onto the material. Leach for example argues that 'sexuality never becomes a major issue in the novel' (Leach, 1978: 376). On the other hand, Newton's sexuality is repeatedly speculated about, by Betty-Jo, for example: 'maybe he was queer – anyone who sat around reading all the time and looked like he did [...] But he didn't talk like a queer' (Tevis, 1976: 57). Bryce has similar thoughts: 'his way of walking [...] reminded Bryce of the first homosexual he had ever seen [...] Newton did not walk like that' (Tevis, 1976: 77), which is a literally queer

way of putting it, as it seems to suggest that Newton does not do what
Bryce has been reminded of.

Newton has learned about Earth by watching television, although
'he had known that seeing [humans] would not be the same as watching them on television' (Tevis, 1976: 9). Given the significance of
Newton's names, it is surely no accident that the patents lawyer who
he consults is called Farnsworth, which is a reference to Philo Farnsworth (1906–71), a pioneer of early television (and the character's
increasingly thick pebble glasses also draw attention to the act of
looking through his growing blindness). In the film, Newton seems
to withdraw into watching an ever increasing number of televisions,
his retreat into commercial visual culture mirrored by his descent into
gin drinking. Glimpses of films such as *The Third Man* (Carol Reed,
1949) and *Billy Budd* (Peter Ustinov, 1962), as well as various westerns, Elvis movies and many other films, point towards a number of
potential intertexts, endlessly multiplying: surveillance, ambivalent
sexuality, the mythic history of America and pop musicians as spectacle. Bowie as rock idol, who in his persona had been flirting with
bisexuality or even homosexuality, demands to be looked at; here we
are entranced by looking at him looking. Adam Roberts has noted
that the film offers 'a commentary upon the strange cultural explosion
of pop music and the status of pop stars of the late 1960s and early
1970s' (Roberts, 2009: 158), a commentary which had begun with
the casting of Mick Jagger as the *doppelgänger* for James Fox in *Performance*. The striptease Newton performs for Mary-Lou, with Newton stripping down to an alien identity, reverses the order of the male
gaze: if he is the object of the gaze, then at this point we cannot help
but look, as he removes his false eyes to reveal his true self.

But what the characters do not realize is that Newton is under
surveillance from the start. A shadowy figure has seen the descent
of Newton's ship, and forces move against Newton as he prepares
to launch his spaceship. Whereas in the book there is a sense that
Bryant's curiosity has left Newton exposed, in the film his cards are
marked from the start. Surveilling which can spot a tiny spaceship in
a small desert town is clearly panoptic in scope, and suggests a wider
network of monitoring, controlled by the government, the mob or

even big business. Whoever it is, the shadowy figure has heard the forsaken cry, and if he has turned away, it has only been to inform his superiors. In the process of interrogation, Newton's eyes are X-rayed; in the book this blinds him, while in the film it fixes him in his human identity, and he starts wearing sunglasses to hide his eyes. Blinding, for Freud, is a symbolic castration; certainly Newton has been neutralized and can now be left to his own devices, though not the high-tech ones he has been marketing through World Enterprises. Such surveillance is archetypal of the 1970s, whether in the fictional form of *The Anderson Tapes* (Sidney Lumet, 1971) or the real life Watergate scandal, in which President Richard Nixon bugged his own conversations.

With the assassination of Farnsworth and Trevor, only Bryce and Mary-Lou are left to bear witness to Newton's mission, brought together in a strange affair by their shared encounter with the alien, Bryce acting as substitute lover in place of Newton. At times they deny that they have known Newton, like Peter of Christ; at other times they deny that they have seen each other. At the end of the novel, Newton releases a book of poems, *The Visitor*, and hopes that they will be broadcast on the radio and may be picked up on Anthea. A waiter says 'I'm afraid that fellow needs help' (Tevis, 1976: 170), and thus the figure who had once claimed 'I came to save you [...] I came to save them all' (Tevis, 1976: 165) can hardly save himself. In the film there is a sense that Newton has had enough: more in keeping with the age, he has managed to release a record, which again through radio play could carry a message to his family, but his time has passed. His mission has been a failure, and whether it was important or not seems irrelevant to him; the people of Earth have turned 'quite leisurely away' from him, rather than run in panic. In both book and film, he has overreached by trying to save everyone. Icarus has fallen and drowned. Leach claims that 'The film eliminates the Messianic aspects of the novel' (Leach, 1978: 373), but this seems too sweeping a statement, especially in the film's allusion to *The Day the Earth Stood Still*.

The story of the adaptation of *The Man Who Fell to Earth* does not stop there: as I write, a musical version and a remake are reported to be in the works. A TV movie remake already exists, directed by Bobby Roth, with Newton – now John Dory (Lewis Smith) – getting involved with a single mother, the significantly named Eva Milton (Beverly D'Angelo), and her street punkish kid Billy (Wil Wheaton). Dory's attempts to get home are frustrated as much because it was intended to be a series as because of a need for narrative closure. The whole feels much more pedestrian than Roeg's vision. More interesting is Philip K. Dick's astonishing semi-autobiographical novel, *VALIS*, in which Horselover Fat, the friend of the character Phil Dick, has had a series of mystical encounters with what he takes to be God, but may be some alien force. A mutual friend, Kevin, introduces them to an sf film, *Valis*, which describes a similar mystical encounter, and which in structure is clearly an analogue of *The Man Who Fell to Earth*. Dick, as Phil, writes that 'on the surface the film made no sense whatsoever. Unless you ferreted out the subliminal and marginal clues and assembled them all together you arrived at nothing' (Dick, 1987: 158). The film is made by a version of Bowie – here called Eric Lampton, a name that nods at Clapton, or Mother Goose – and Brent Mini, a version of Brian Eno. When they visit the Lamptons, and their mysterious daughter, Sophia (supposedly the Messiah), they learn that Fat and Dick are the same person, the psyche split by the traumatic theophany. Phil Dick is not entirely convinced the Lamptons are on the level, and, while his alter ego Horselover scours the world for more evidence, he awaits further messages from somewhere out there about salvation, transformed into a small-scale version of Newton, watching a single rather than multiple televisions.

As the real world Philip K. Dick wrote this novel, he drew upon his own apparent encounter with the infinite – a series of mystical visions in the early Spring of 1974 (Butler, 2007: 16), which were to obsess him for the rest of his life, as he sought explanations for them. At times Dick thought that it was God who had spoken to him, the Prophet Elijah or Holy Wisdom, Sophia, or his dead sister, Jane, or the late Bishop of California, James Pike, who had been a friend; alternatively it might have been scientists in Leningrad experimenting with telepathy or aliens making first contact. Or perhaps it was just the drugs and exhaustion. Like Bryce, he could read the encounter with the transcendent in science-fictional terms; like Newton, his messiah could no more save herself than save the world. Although some of Dick and Fat's theophanies were auditory, the emphasis is put on the gaze – pink lights, the film *Valis* and so forth. At the end of the novel we learn from (fictional) Phil that: 'My search kept me at home; I sat before the TV set in my living room. I sat; I waited; I watched; I kept myself awake. As we had been told, originally, long ago, to do; I kept my commission' (Dick, 1987: 228). Between Horselover and Phil, there a division into looking *for* and looking *at*, an active seeking out and a passive waiting for an arrival, the latter perhaps echoing the ending of a more ambivalent adaptation about first contact, *The Thing* (Christian Nyby, 1951) – based on John W. Campbell's 'Who Goes There?' (1938) as by Don A. Stuart – which ended with a warning to 'Keep watching the skies!'. In *VALIS*, as in *The Man Who Fell to Earth*, there is no salvation, perhaps due to a failure of imagination to imagine it, but all these texts hold out the hope that there may be a saviour, which seems to be at the least not unimportant.

Note

1   For more on the role of Newton as messiah, in relation to Levinasian ethics, see my chapter '*The Man Who Fell to Earth*: The Messiah and the Amphicatastrophe', in M. P. Berman and R. Dalvi (eds) *Heroes, Monsters and Values: Science Fiction Films of the 1970s* (Newcastle: Cambridge Scholars Press, 2011).

References

Auden, W. H. (1977) *The English Auden*. Ed. Edward Mendelson. London and Boston: Faber & Faber.

Brosnan, J. (1978) *Future Tense: The Cinema of Science Fiction*. New York: St Martin's.

Butler, A. M. (2007) *Philip K. Dick*. Harpenden: Pocket Essentials.

Chapman, J. (1999) '"A Bit of the Old Ultra-Violence": *A Clockwork Orange*', in I.Q. Hunter (ed.) *British Science Fiction Cinema*, pp. 125–37. London: Routledge.

Dick, P. K. (1987) *VALIS*. Worcester Park, Surrey: Kerosina.

Freud, S. (1955) 'Medusa's Head', in J. Strachey (ed.) *The Standard Edition of the Complete Psychological Works of Sigmund Freud*, pp. 273–4. London: Hogarth Press.

Freud, S. (1991a) *Introductory Lectures on Psychoanalysis*. Harmondsworth: Penguin.

Freud, S. (1991b) *On Sexuality*. Harmondsworth: Penguin.

Leach, J. (1978) '*The Man Who Fell to Earth*: Adaptation by Omission', *Literature/Film Quarterly* 6 (4): 371–9.

Mulvey, L. (1989) 'Visual Pleasure and Narrative Cinema', in *Visual and Other Pleasures*, pp. 14–26. London: Macmillan.

Nashe, T. (1952) 'Adieu, Farewell Earth's Bliss', in K. Muir (ed.) *Elizabethan Lyrics: A Critical Anthology*, pp. 129–31. London: Harrap.

Peary, D. (1983) *Cult Movies 2*. New York: Delta Publishing.

Roberts, A. (2009) '[Review:] *The Man Who Fell to Earth*', *Science Fiction Film and Television* 1 (1): 155–9.

Ruppersberg, H. (1990) 'The Alien Messiah', in A. Kuhn (ed.) *Alien Zone: Cultural Theory and Contemporary Science Fiction Cinema*, pp. 32–8. London and New York: Verso.

Tevis, W. (1976) *The Man Who Fell to Earth*. London: Pan.

Walker, J. (1985) *The Once & Future Film: British Cinema in the Seventies and Eighties*. London: Methuen.

Chapter 5

Solaris – Lem/Tarkovsky/Soderbergh
Adaptations in Space

Teresa Forde

The relationship between adaptations of a text often emphasize a hierarchy of recognition based on specific discriminating factors. At the extreme, one version is privileged above all else. However, occasionally, each version is recognized for what it brings to the whole and is appreciated for the specificity of its contribution. Three science-fiction texts with such an interrelationship tell of the experiences of the fictional planet Solaris: Stanislaw Lem's novel *Solaris* (1961) and its two most famous film adaptations, Andrei Tarkovsky's *Solyaris* (1972) and Steven Soderbergh's *Solaris* (2002). These texts each hold a separate status in the world of science-fiction film and literature, yet audiences and critics are often drawn to discuss them relationally and want to 'experience' all three – as though an engagement with all of the texts will provide some kind of deeper understanding, appreciation or satisfaction.[1] The adaptations were produced consecutively but are not necessarily viewed or read in such a chronological manner, as engagement with each version can rest on such criteria as the order in which the viewer or reader encounters the texts and the moment when one reads or watches them. The audience's search for and experience of versions of *Solaris* builds memories that provide the viewer/reader with a process of textual layering and enable a set of distinctions to be made between the texts as well as a recognition of their contribution to the whole of *Solaris* as a 'metatext'. In this way, the concept of adaptation is embedded within the notion of inter-textuality; it is a process of inscribing the film or novel into having an intertextual and, more widely, metatextual presence. In addition, the process of adaptation may implicate genre precepts, knowledge and authorial intent alongside viewer/reader responses as a way of expressing recognition, appreciation and discrimination between and across the texts.

Solaris illustrates the science-fictional trope of an alien encoun-ter, with all three texts essentially telling the same story. Solaris is an ocean planet that has an effect upon astronauts who go to investigate it. Hovering above the planet in their spaceship, the crew witness what appear to be hallucinations of people and places from their own lives and memories, emerging from their subconscious and taking shape in front of their eyes. However, these apparent apparitions are solid and physically present and are, in a sense, given life because they are part of the astronauts' memories. Also, *Solaris* contains supernatural elements, particularly in the manifestation of 'nimoids', *doppelgänger* figures from the subconscious which seem to haunt the astronauts and, ultimately, test their grip on reality. As the planet (re)constructs people based upon the astronauts' emotions and memories it can re-produce people who have died and those who have had a close emo-tional connection to the crew on board the spaceship. Due to their unusual behaviour, Chris Kelvin is sent to find out what is happening to the crew who are investigating the planet, although ultimately he becomes affected by the planet himself. Chris's dead wife appears to him a number of times. This manifestation of his former wife, Rheya/ Hari (depending upon which version or translation used), seems to have no personal memory of her own, only remembering what Chris recalls, since it is his mind that is being used to (re-)create her pres-ence. Eventually Rheya/Hari becomes aware of her 'living' status as she realizes who she is (not) and that she exists because he wills her

Figure 1. Natalya Bondarchuk and Donatas Banionis in *Solaris*. Photo courtesy of The Criterion Collection/Photofest.

to do so. Each text ends differently, in ways that exemplify the preoccupation of each version with the enigmatic quality of Solaris.

To understand the readings of *Solaris*, it is first of all necessary to consider in what ways the authors and readers/viewers relate to adapted texts and how multiple adaptations can be conceptualized. For Roland Barthes, 'the reader is the space on which all the quotations that make up a writing are inscribed'; the reader holds together 'all the traces by which the written text is constituted' (Barthes, 1977: 148). Simultaneously Barthes signals the death of the author and the importance of the reader as a vessel or nexus for textual dynamics, recognizing that the meaning of multiple texts is located in the reader or viewer. However, the author, as well as the reader/viewer, comes into play in the adaptations of *Solaris*. As Marko Juvan recognizes in his account of Jonathan Culler's development of intertextuality, 'presuppositions are a significant phenomenon of "intersubjective knowledge." On the one hand they oblige author and reader to interpret a text but on the other they fix the text among other writings and discursive practices that articulate the culture' (Juvan, 2009: 117). Therefore, the texts are situated within their own context as well as relationally.

As *Solaris* explores ideas about human existence, it is ripe for comparison in both its subject matter and narrative construction. The subject matter of an alien world, physical apparitions emerging from characters' memories and the striking endings to all versions of *Solaris* encourage a dialogue about what the texts achieve and how they achieve it, even though the three texts represent different modes of sf: Lem's novel is a hard science-fiction novella which questions the purpose of scientific exploration; Tarkovsky's film is an example of metaphysical and poetic art cinema drawing upon, and maybe struggling with, the science-fiction genre; Soderbergh's film is a Hollywood version presenting both science-fiction discourse and art cinema to a potentially wider audience. To a degree, the texts can be seen as palimpsests on their predecessors, layering and adapting onto each other. As an example of such textual layering, in an account of adaptation as archive, Desirée Jung explores the complicated relationship between all three versions: 'Regardless of being closer to Lem's novel, except for its portrait of Rheya and Kris' relationship in a true Hollywood fashion, Soderbergh's film seems to have been marked by the trace, or the ghost and signature of Tarkovsky' (Jung, 2004). Jung's account draws upon the notion of the Derridean archive, which reveals a secret through its textual traces so that the adaptive link becomes one of tracing meaning. She argues that the 'desire to discover the secret of Solaris increases the abyss of supplements, of film adaptations as a type of archive'. Therefore, the attempt to discover each version and its relationship to the others, is both driven by and culminates in some form of investigation of its secret meaning(s). Specifically, the uncovering of archival traces is central to both an ephemeral search for a 'secret' to the meaning of the texts and the distinctive subject matter of the *Solaris* texts themselves, whether it is in considering the limits of human knowledge, metaphysical questions of life or the power of romantic love.

As well as recognizing the relevance of authorial influence and commentary, we can foreground the reader/viewer as an interpreter of adaptation and a centre for textual interpretation. In his discussion of intertextuality, Mikhail Iampolski draws upon Eisenstein's idea of a third text arising from the relationship between and juxtaposition of two texts and the reader/viewer (Iampolski, 1998: 242). This third text, as an invisible text, lies in the act of comprehension by the reader/viewer, producing a speculative, almost mystical, response to the meaning between texts. Departing from his earlier 'montage of attractions', where meaning is constructed by the viewer in the 'space' between two juxtaposed images on screen, Eisenstein identifies the third text as the process by which meaning is made as a 'point of trans-formation' (Iampolski, 1998: 248). Developing this transformative quality, Iampolski identifies the process of intertextuality, 'which is particularly active in moments of narrative rupture, where the linear logic of the story breaks down, provides cinematic language with a certain corporeality, […] its hieroglyphic quality […], remaining opaque to the end' (Iampolski, 1998: 248). The presence of meaning as a puzzle is presented in the corporeal nature, or the weight, of the images constructed by the text. Extending this account of intertextu-ality allows for the third text to become an 'invisible intertext', which is not only located within the viewer but, by extension, in the viewer's memories. The *Solaris* texts conjure a response from the viewer or reader that places them at the centre of negotiating a 'reading'. Due to the nature of these texts being speculative science fiction, this ne-gotiation is encouraged by the self-reflexive strategies, which call into question narrative logic, character motivation and the question of what it is to be human.

The three versions adopt different textual strategies. The novel is structured as a first-person narrative presented by Chris, which ini-tially captures his experience of arriving on the planet: 'Now I had the sensation of falling, even with my eyes closed' (Lem, 2003: 3). Chris begins to experience first sightings of the visitors on the craft and eventually encounters his own visitor, Rheya. In addition, Lem constructs a self-reflexive early chapter within the novel, entitled 'The Solarists', on the history of the study of Solaris. Known as Solaristics, this study came to prominence and then lost its glory due – in no small part – to the inability of humans to understand the planet. Due to its inscrutability, Solaristics goes out of fashion until its cause is taken up again by the next generation. As one scientist jokes: 'How do you expect to communicate with the ocean when you can't even understand one another?' (Lem, 2003: 23). Such a remark on the futility of human enquiry provides commentary both on scientific study and the construction of the novel itself. Its self-reflexive nature forewarns the reader that no knowledge will be gained about Solaris. This self-reflexiveness is echoed in the statement on the futility of scientific exploration to establish first contact:

> We are searching for an ideal image of our own world: we go in quest of a planet, of a civilisation superior to our own but developed on the basis of a prototype of our primeval past. At the same time, there is something inside us which we don't like to face up to, from which we try to protect ourselves, but which nevertheless remains, since we don't leave Earth in a state of primal innocence. (Lem, 2003: 72)

After being visited by a simulacrum of his dead wife, Chris decides to stay on the planet and continue his investigations of Solaris in a kind of sublime purgatory:

> I hoped for nothing. And yet I lived in expectation. Since she had gone, that was all that remained. I did not know what achievements, what mockery, even what tortures still awaited me. I knew nothing, and I persisted in the faith that the time of cruel miracles was not past. (Lem, 2003: 204)

Therefore Chris recognizes his own limitations in his ability to comprehend Solaris but still wishes to suffer, to experience, to dream. Lem's novel is part of a tradition of 'hard' sf literature emerging from Soviet-influenced Polish science fiction. However, Lem's portrayal of the study of the planet is both enigmatic and playful, countering the boundaries of hard science-fiction realism in its rather speculative tone. Chris is left to finally and infinitely explore his relationship with the planet within a hermeneutic bubble as he places his arm in and out of the planet's surface. He does not seem to discover anything or find any profound answers, but merely experiences his world and his relationship to it.

Initially, in his film version, Tarkovsky envisaged a popular sf film intended for the Soviet market. Maya Turovskaya comments upon the traditionally low status of sf and horror genres and the extent to which this has implications for envisioning *Solaris* as a science-fiction film. Consequently, Turovskaya sees the film as surpassing its genre limitations and becoming part of Tarkovsky's oeuvre – a goal that she identifies as emulating Boris Pasternak's auteurist aim with the novel: 'The *unchanging subject* of that one great film that he continued to make was the striving for the absolute' (Turovskaya, 1989: 100–1). In this interpretation of the film as part of an ongoing struggle for some form of perfect state, Chris is viewed as a martyr who undergoes a 'moral transformation' (Tarkovsky, cited in Turovskaya, 1989: 59) through his experience of the planet and his struggle for redemption in life. The refocus, or reaccentuation, on Chris's struggle establishes an emotional response both from the director and the viewers. Tarkovsky states:

> I have noticed from my own work that if the external, emotional structure of images in the film is built on the author's own memories, on a link between his own life and the fabric of the film, then the audience will feel the emotional effect. (Tarkovsky, cited in Turovskaya, 1989: 59–60)

Therefore, in Turovskaya's account, Tarkovsky the auteur has explored and exceeded the realm of science fiction in order to undertake his ongoing voyage of self-exploration. Although Tarkovsky's version of *Solaris* is embedded within the tropes of science fiction as a structuring principle, in the end Tarkovsky felt that this genre mode was too restrictive and may not have spoken to audiences in a way that allowed them to connect with the film. In other words, this implies that the stipulations of the science-fiction genre may be a barrier to individual viewers' mediation of the film and 'get in the way' of its speculative qualities.

One of the benefits of choosing science fiction as a film genre within film is the possibility, budget allowing, of constructing a 'cinema of attractions' as a dazzling spectacle to amaze audiences.[2] Perhaps with this in mind, Lem was dissatisfied with Tarkovsky's version, particularly with what he perceived to be the lack of a rendering of the ocean planet within the film, although Lem also claimed that he had not watched the whole film, and thus did not see Tarkovsky's vision of the planet in the final scenes as the camera pans out into space. Science fiction often offers a vision of the future or a spectacular wonder to contemplate. The continuing emphasis on image within science fiction is an extension of the return to early cinema and the recognition of a cinema of attractions, which 'exceeds the logic of narrative and exaggerates the poetics of spectacle' (Bukatman, 1999: 255), celebrates image beyond narrative and, one could say, lends it weight. Equally, the European art film has traditionally been associated with experimentation, use of alternative visual codes, exploration of cinematic space and providing ambiguity rather than resolution. This approach to image and effect links Tarkovsky's *Solaris* to the recognized tradition of art cinema, which often privileges image over narrative. Lem also criticized Tarkovsky's vision of the voyage to the planet. Instead of providing the anticipated view of the planet as Chris ends his space journey, the viewer is presented with the arrival to the planet as a fast-paced car drive through Tokyo streets. This re-interpretation of space travel seems to be a 'love it or hate it' sequence as it certainly does not depict a typical voyage into outer space, but instead displaces this trip onto the modern cityscape. However, Lem equally avoids 'facing' the vision of the planet in his novel: although Chris explains that 'I did not want to miss anything there was to be seen' (Lem, 2003: 3), he laments on arrival that 'I had missed the precious moment that the planet first came into view' (Lem, 2003: 2). So it seems as though Lem wishes Tarkovsky to insert that 'missed' experience of the first sighting into his film, perhaps as a cinematic possibility that could not be expressed in the novel. So, as part of his criticism of Tarkovsky's film, Lem chides Tarkovsky for not showing the planet or, one might say, for not providing the sublime spectacle that cinema is capable of in a way that is not possible with the written word. However, as well as portraying the alien ocean, Tarkovsky encapsulates the strange and wondrous scenes of earth both prior to and as part of the planet's projection. The opening images of the film involve reeds swaying in the water in closely-cropped frames, which provide both a contemplative and defamiliarizing image and make the earth appear as mystical and intriguing as any far-off enigmatic ocean planet. Lem identifies the planet with earthly qualities: 'the noise which followed reminded me irresistibly of earth: [...] the moaning of the wind' (Lem, 2003: 4). Thus, the strange world is compared to what is familiar on earth in both the novel and the film.

In exploring the relationship between individuals and social space, Westwood and Williams recognize the way in which nostalgia functions as an 'intimate knowledge of place that generates a sense of belonging', and such a sense can haunt one's memory (Westwood and Williams, 1997: 12). This sense of belonging explores not so much the idea that home is left behind but that it has become displaced, so the exploration of home becomes intrinsic due to its absence. Within Tarkovsky's *Solaris*, in the library housing Brueghel's painting *The Hunters in the Snow*, Tarkovsky uses slow panning shots of the landscape within the painting to articulate his wife's comprehension of his past. As her eyes scan the painting her looking and comprehension, as evoked through Chris's memories, become intrinsically embedded within a communion of memory between the two of them. As she scans the painting she simultaneously incorporates the memories of Chris's home movies into a collage of his past experiences and her constructed consciousness. Nostalgia in this context refers specifically to the longing for home. In this regard, the ending of the film is particularly over-determined, which Tarkovsky recognized himself. Chris finds himself back near the shore of his family's homestead, although he would not have been able to actually return there; he sees his father through the window of the dacha while it is raining inside the house. Water is often a redemptive motif in Tarkovsky's films, and his father comes out and Chris falls to his knees to hug him; the camera pans out to show that the dacha is on an island in the middle of the Solaris sea. Where Lem takes Chris right into the heart of Solaris, Tarkovsky seems to leave Chris in a simulation of his earthbound life. Indeed, the director seems to almost try to get himself away from the scene through the extreme reversing camera dolly shot he uses to draw back from the planet into space. Although Stanislaw Lem worked early on with Tarkovsky on his screenplay, Tarkovsky's film departs from Lem's novel in both tone and focus as it shifts from hard science fiction to soft science fiction and, some would argue, beyond science fiction completely.

Soderbergh's version of *Solaris* draws upon both Lem's novel and Fridrikh Gorenshtein and Andrei Tarkovsky's script. So both Tarkovsky and Soderbergh recognize Lem's novel as the 'source' of their adaptations, as they return to the novel while intrinsically changing it. As hard sf, Lem's novel intends to provide a cognitive exploration into human scientific enquiry. In response to the versions by Tarkovsky and Soderbergh, Lem has argued:

> I only wanted to create a vision of a human encounter with something that certainly exists, in a mighty manner perhaps, but cannot be reduced to human concepts, ideas or images. This is why the book was entitled Solaris and not Love in Outer Space. (Lem, 2002)

Indeed, Soderbergh has described his version as not really being 'hard' science fiction. In his review of the film, Matthew Turner touches on the largely unsuccessful attempt to promote *Solaris* in the USA as 'a fast-moving "love-story in space" kind of thing' (Turner, 2003). The paraphernalia of a space station is extremely pared down to provide sleek and futuristic steel and glass surfaces. However, the *mise-en-scène* makes this future scenario more similar to scenes from *Gattaca* (Andrew Niccol, 1997) than an action-packed guns and gadgets affair. Instead the emphasis is upon the relationships between the characters and the way in which the *mise-en-scène* captures both the layered nature of these relationships and their effect upon Chris's mental state. The way in which the *mise-en-scène* enables a representation of the character's psyche influences our understanding of Chris's emotional state. This approach to the *mise-en-scène* can also be seen to give the film a particularly 'art-house' look and to eschew the spectacle of dazzling special effects in favour of the appreciation of set design, establishing a filmic differentiation based upon a sense of 'taste'. The colour palette works well with the lighting in creating subtle tones and changing the atmosphere of the film, providing meaning even when the characters do not convey a lot of information about how they feel. The soundtrack contains eerie noises and hints at what may be unseen, providing a suitable adjunct to the sparse and strange setting. The music swells when Rheya appears and the potential for a romantic liaison is made possible. Lem rejected the concentration upon the two main characters and the conversion into a love story in favour of a focus on ideas of scientific progress. Tarkovsky eschewed hard sf to provide a more poetic feel. In relation to the other two versions, Soderbergh seeks to walk a tightrope between hard and soft sf, incorporating scientific speculation on the Higgs boson theory into his predominant treatise of romantic love. However, whether as hard or soft sf, *Solaris* provides an ideal vehicle for speculative fiction.

The effect of the planet Solaris on the crew is like a psychotic encounter in the sense that 'long or intense experience with computer-mediated electronic communication is associated with a certain fluidity of identity' (Poster, 1996: 200). Interaction with the planet can cause a sense of dislocation and daydreaming, of losing time or elongating it. Ultimately, Chris appears to be in such a state of psychosis. Soderbergh's film can be most easily understood in the context of other contemporary films, such as Michel Gondry's *Eternal Sunshine of the Spotless Mind* (2004), which explores memory and desire through the trials of romantic love. In these films, the impossibility to start again is made possible by way of a science-fiction philosophy being re-accentuated as romantic love. Soderbergh draws upon Dylan Thomas's 'And death shall have no dominion' to express his simulated idyll. Also, Soderbergh can be compared to Danny Boyle in his genre-hopping approach, which means that he focuses on a different genre for each film he directs and adapts his own style to that genre.

The vision of Chris's wife pervades all three versions of *Solaris*. As she 'returns' from the dead, Rheya/Hari invokes the monstrous, the horrific, that by which we are fascinated with but also appalled. For Rosi Braidotti, the monster often functions as a warning evoking horror, fascination, aberration and adoration (Braidotti, 1996). Monsters represent the uncontrollable elements of what is deemed to be natural life and in this context that which cannot be contained. As Braidotti has recognized, the monster raises the question of 'what constitutes an object of scientific enquiry' (Braidotti, 1996: 137). Clearly, Rheya/Hari is presented as an enigma. As such, she presents the way in which the feminine is a 'nonthematizable materiality' (Butler, 1993: 43). Her corporeal presence is completely disturbing in all three texts and she is an enigma that cannot be decoded. Rheya/

Hari becomes representative of Solaris itself. According to Elizabeth Grosz, the concept of the volatile body provides a physical manifestation to its meaning: 'The body is not simply a sign to be read, a symptom to be deciphered, but also a force to be reckoned with' (Grosz, 1994: 120). Therefore Rheya/Hari's presence evokes interpretations of and within the texts. She is also a mediating figure who expresses Chris's memories and desire whilst equally fulfilling some of the recognizable features of the *femme fatale* as a potentially deadly yet alluring vision.

The relationship between the three versions is established by both authorial referencing and viewer or reader recognition. In terms of novel and film adaptation, Robert Stam and Alessandra Raengo recognize that the transition of novel to film has traditionally been seen as a move to an 'inescapable materiality' where the corporeal nature of film, its physicality, is viewed as 'obscene' (Stam and Raengo, 2005: 3). The obscene nature of the scene is a negative criticism, which clearly privileges the written word over the physical image on screen. Instead, Stam and Raengo prefer to describe adaptation from novel to film as a form of mutation as such adaptations can enable a text to adapt and survive. A more optimistic vision is also expressed by Mikhail Bakhtin, who establishes the chronotope as a historical and visceral paradigm of the 'textual rendering of time and space' (Bakhtin, 1990: 27). Bakhtin applies this rendering process to literature but we could say that film, too, forms the textual site where time 'thickens, takes flesh, becomes artistically visible' (Bakhtin, 1990: 45). The rendering of time and space realigns us with a sense of history where adaptation is part of a process of constructing meaning. In these terms the chronotope accounts for the ways in which each adaptation re-accentuates the past and produces meaning, for the chronotope incorporates the notion of intertextuality, genre, reader/viewer and author:

> Thus the chronotope, functioning as the primary means for materializing time in space, emerges as a center for concretizing representation, as a force giving body to the entire novel. All the novel's abstract elements – philosophical and social generalizations, ideas, analyses of cause and effect – gravitate toward the chronotope and through

it take on flesh and blood, permitting the imaging power of art to do its work. Such is the representational significance of the chronotope. (Bakhtin, 1990: 250)

The chronotope can be found within different narratives and can link texts in its formation of themes. Initially, it seems that Bakhtin's definition of the adventure chronotope – which is 'characterized by a *technical, abstract connection between space and time*, by the *reversibility* of moments in a temporal sequence, and by their *interchangeability* in space' (Bakhtin, 1990: 100) – is most relevant to *Solaris*. However, what all the texts of *Solaris* invoke or explore most clearly is the chronotope of the idyll – 'where the world of the characters is static and hermetic, the hero is wholly engrossed in the "little world" (*mirok*) of his own home, his countryside and his country' (Clark, 2002: 280) – which is potentially both a thwarting and redemptive state. *Solaris* is open to a speculation that exceeds the boundaries of each of its versions.

The story of *Solaris* encapsulates a sense of 'mystification' and enacts a form of memory work, both for the characters within the texts and for the viewers and readers who interact with them. Annette Kuhn argues:

> for the practitioner of memory work, it is not merely a question of *what* we choose to keep in our 'memory boxes' – which particular traces of our pasts we lovingly or not so lovingly preserve – but of what we do with them, *how* we use these relics to make memories, and how we then make use of the stories they generate to give deeper meaning to, and if necessary to change, our lives today. (Kuhn 2002: 158)

In terms of adaptation and the relationship between specific texts, the 'question arises whether intertextuality ceases to work if the reader is unfamiliar with the intertexts involved' (Riffaterre, 1990: 73). This question is twofold: it asks whether there is a need to be familiar with the adaptive links and whether that knowledge contributes to the understanding of either text. As Linda Hutcheon (2006: 6) recognizes, 'there must be something particularly appealing about adaptations *as adaptations*'. This appeal can refer to the recognition of a text as an adaptation as well as to the nature of a text that causes it to be chosen to be adapted or to be adaptable. In relation to *Solaris*, Hutcheon's recognition of the appeal of adaptation is highly evident as responses to the relationship between the novel and the two films range from privileging one particular text relationally to evaluating and appreciating all three texts according to different criteria. To indicate the interest in the relationship between the three versions, the *Facebook* page for Solaris is entitled 'Solaris – Lem/Tarkovsky/Soderbergh'. Many reviewers have felt the need to engage with all three versions of *Solaris*. One IMDb user says: 'Since I had just read Lem's novel Solaris and had in the past seen the 1972 Russian movie Solyaris, I was interested in seeing the new Solaris' (Knouse, 2003). Others begin with what they perceive to be the most noted version: '*Solaris* was Andrei Tarkovsky's 1972 adaptation of the Stanislaw Lem novel which Stephen Soderburgh [sic] remade in 2002' (*Cinematheque*, 2010). In this response Soderbergh's version is deemed to be a 'remake' of Tarkovsky's film, which is the privileged text as it holds together the other two references. This comment continues: 'They say that imitation is the highest form of flattery. If that's the case than [sic] Stephen Soderburgh [sic] has a bit of a crush on Andrei Tarkovsky'. Here the implication is that Soderbergh is basing his film on Tarkovsky's version, and it can certainly be argued that some of the visual elements in Tarkovsky's film are traceable in Soderbergh's later offering. Equally, the polarity between a hard science-fiction novel and Soderbergh's romantic story is expressed in Gary Wolf's article 'Solaris, Rediscovered: SOLARIS 2.0': 'Stanislaw Lem made hard science and deep philosophy into some of the greatest science fiction you've never seen. Now his classic Solaris is getting the Hollywood treatment' (Wolf, 2002). Thus, different versions of *Solaris* are privileged in an ongoing circulation of discussion about the three texts and a fascination with the issue of adaptation. The three texts of *Solaris* form a kind of triumvirate where Tarkovsky's film is most often recognized as a classic by those who are interested in metaphysical art films or soft science fiction. In contrast, Lem's novel is appreciated as a classic by those who privilege hard science fiction of a literary tradition and Soderbergh's version is appreciated for its accessibility and arthouse style.

The work of memory enables Solaris, the ocean planet, to shape people from characters' memories, posing the dilemma of what to do with these manifestations, while the narrative rests on what Chris remembers and forgets. Equally, the viewer or reader becomes the third text who negotiates and remembers the work of *Solaris*. Each version of *Solaris* has a different ending: for Lem, Kris is a true scientist who wishes to stay on the vessel to try to learn more about the planet and maybe see Rheya again; for Tarkovsky, Chris immerses himself in the planet and seems to come back to 'earth' and to a simulacrum of home; for Soderbergh, Chris is happy to spend his time living with Rheya in a simulated home in domestic bliss. The chronotopic structure of the idyll, however problematic as a resolution, encourages the juxtaposition of all three versions as adaptations of each other. In invoking these memories of *Solaris* we also encounter the secrets that 'haunt our memory-stories, giving them pattern and shape' (Kuhn, 2002: 2). In the study of *Solaris*, audience and readers draw upon their own experience and invoke the third text, the 'invisible intertext', which exists in our memories. Just as Chris and Hari hover in the room of Brueghel paintings in the library during Tarkovsky's key film sequence, our experience of these adaptations of *Solaris* 'hovers' in the adaptation of memories and texts.

Notes

1 There is yet another potential adaptation which could be included in this study, namely the television film 'inspired by' Lem's novel, *Solaris* (Boris Nirenburg, 1968). It is not part of the circulation of texts which these audiences and critics have included, or would have been able to access, as its status as a film broadcast on Soviet television would possibly preclude it from this 'canon'.

2 The cinema of attractions refers to the emphasis upon spectacle and display (as opposed to narrative and diegetic realism) that was found within early cinema. It has also been used to describe the visual and performative strategies of musicals and comedies as well as the emphasis upon spectacle over story in blockbusters and, specifically, the science-fiction film genre with its interest in speculative fiction, new worlds, aliens and scenes of wonder (see Bukatman, 1999; Gunning, 1986).

References

Anon. (2010) 'Red Corner/Blue Corner – Solaris v Solaris', *Cinematheque*, http://cinematheque.leithermagazine.com/2010/05/02/red-corner-blue-corner-%E2%80%93-solaris-v-solaris/ (accessed November 2010).

Bakhtin, M. M. (1990) *The Dialogic Imagination: Four Essays*. Austin: University of Texas Press.

Barthes, R. (1977) *Image, Music, Text*. London: Fontana.

Braidotti, R. (1996) 'Signs of Wonder and Traces of Doubt: On Teratology and Embodied Differences', in N. Lykke and R. Braidotti (eds) *Between Monsters, Goddesses and Cyborgs: Feminist Confrontations with Science, Medicine and Cyberspace*, pp. 135–52. London: Zed Books.

Bukatman, S. (1999) 'The Artificial Infinite: On Special Effects and the Sublime', in A. Kuhn (ed.) *Alien Zone II: The Spaces of Science Fiction Cinema*, pp. 249–75. London: Verso.

Butler, J. (1993) *Bodies that Matter: On the Discursive Limits of Sex*. London: Routledge.

Clark, K. (2002) 'M. M. Bakhtin and "World Literature"', *JNT: Journal of Narrative Theory* 32 (3): 266–92.

Grosz, E. (1994) *Volatile Bodies: Towards a Corporeal Feminism*. Bloomington: Indiana University Press.

Gunning, T. (1986) 'The Cinema of Attraction: Early Film, Its Spectator and the Avant-Garde', *Wide Angle* 8 (3–4): 63–70.

Hutcheon, L. (2006) *A Theory of Adaptation*. London: Routledge.

Iampolski, M. (1998) *The Memory of Tiresias: Intertextuality and Film*. London: University of California Press.

Jung, D. (2004) 'Adaptation Fever: On *Solaris*', *The Film Journal*, http://www.thefilmjournal.com/issue9/adaptation.html (accessed November 2010).

Juvan, M. (2009) *History and Poetics of Intertextuality*. West Lafayette: Purdue University Press.

Knouse, C. (2003) 'Disappointing if you've read the book; baffling if you haven't', *IMDb user reviews for Solaris*, http://www.imdb.com/title/tt0307479/usercomments (accessed November 2010).

Kuhn, A. (2002) *Family Secrets: Acts of Memory and Imagination*. London: Verso.

Lem, S. (2002) 'The Solaris Station', *LEM.PL: Stanislaw – Lem The Official Site*, http://english.lem.pl/index.php/arround-lem/adaptations/soderbergh/147-the-solaris-station (accessed November 2010).

Lem, S. (2003) *Solaris*. London: Faber & Faber.

Poster, M. (1996) 'Postmodern Virtualities', in G. Robertson et al. (eds) *FutureNatural: Nature, Science, Culture*, pp. 183–201. London: Routledge.

Riffaterre, M. (1990) 'Compulsory Reader Response: The Intertextual Drive', in M. Worton and J. Still (eds) *Intertextuality: Theories and Practices*. Manchester: Manchester University Press.

Stam, R. and Raengo, A. (eds) (2005) *Literature and Film: A Guide to the Theory and Practice of Film Adaptation*. London: Blackwell.

Turner, M. (2003) 'Solaris (2003): The ViewLondon Review', http://www.viewlondon.co.uk/films/solaris-2003-film-review-3794.html (accessed November 2010).

Turovskaya, M. (1989) *Tarkovsky: Cinema as Poetry*. London: Faber & Faber.

Westwood, S. and Williams, J. (eds) (1997) *Imagining Cities: Scripts, Signs, Memories*. London: Routledge.

Wolf, G. (2002) 'Solaris, Rediscovered: SOLARIS 2.0', *Wired* 10 (12), http://www.wired.com/wired/archive/10.12/solaris.html (accessed November 2010).

CHAPTER 6

DEGENRIFICATION IN ANDREI TARKOVSKY'S *STALKER*
THE SCIENCE-FICTION NOVEL TRANSFORMED
INTO ART-FILM PARABLE

Jamie Sherry

For Tzvetan Todorov, the preoccupation with the structural elements that comprise texts became a 'vain if not anachronistic pastime' due to the established techniques of modernist and experimental writers and directors, in which genres constantly 'seem to be coming undone' (Todorov, 1990: 13). Further to this, prescriptive classifications of genre theory are at odds with the more fluid, open understanding of how texts interrelate, long unravelled by figures in the fields of post-structuralism and deconstruction. For Foucault, the route into understanding the aesthetic, social and psychological impulse to form taxonomies can be found in the shifting history of scientific discourse – in particular, natural history. Foucault shows how arbitrary forms of classification for life have changed radically over time as 'up to the end of the eighteenth century [...] life does not exist: only living beings'. Foucault goes on to show the weakness of these organizations as 'a category of classification, relative, like all the other categories, to the criteria one adopts' as well as being 'subject to certain imprecisions as soon as the question of deciding its frontiers arises' (Foucault, 1970:

160). For Robert Stam, it is not just an issue of imprecision, but also of relevance as he asks whether genres are 'really "out there" in the world, or are they merely the constructions of analysts?' and whether there is 'a finite taxonomy of genres or are they in principle infinite?' (Stam, 2000: 14).

While genre theory is an increasingly complex field of study, prone to attacks regarding its understanding of transcultural and historical readings, it is a useful discourse to adopt for the purposes of illuminating adaptation studies. Not only do both fields employ similar language (and a self-reflexive discourse on its own usefulness and validity) but genre theory also strengthens adaptation studies' increasing preoccupation with the notion of reception and audience response. This connection between an adaptation's texts and audience can be interrogated by studying genre. For Annette Kuhn, the genre film 'will provide the security of generic conventions whilst promising the pleasure, and limiting the risk, of the new, the unexpected', and in doing so create 'a kind of contract between the film industry and cinema audiences' (Kuhn, 1990: 1).

Both genre theory and adaptation theory share an anxiety over the chronology of seniority and the linking of low-status secondary texts and concepts to their high-status forebears. Film-genre theory lies within, and is inherited from, a long tradition of literary genre theory. Similarly, adaptation theory has been overshadowed by the sense that adapted films are derived from literature, and are therefore historically tethered to a formal tradition from which it cannot liberate itself. This political view of historical dominance is for Robert Stam 'a priori valorization of historical anteriority and seniority' in which it is assumed that 'older arts are necessarily better arts' (Stam, 2004: 4).

The defining point at which genre and adaptation meet, in terms of critical discourse, is a problematic issue. There is a long-held presumption that issues of equivalence will dominate the transference of a novel into film. It is assumed that the adaptation of genre fiction involves the creation of a unified text that adapts not just the literary narrative into a cinematic narrative, but also adapts the chosen literary genre into its equivalent cinematic genre. This medium specificity often dictates the *direction* of adaptations. Features of literature are amplified and condensed in order to foreground elements of the text that can be transferred into known film narratives and genres. In other words, despite the pitfalls of medium specificity, in which it is assumed that a narrative can only be presented adequately in its original medium, the dominant genre of a piece of literature will dictate and control the choice of its destination genre.

It is from this position of displaced genre routes that Andrei Tarkovsky's *Stalker* (1979), adapted from the science-fiction novel *Roadside Picnic* (1971) by Arkady and Boris Strugatsky, can be examined. Tarkovsky's film has entered into the pantheon of films that are regarded as having a deviant relationship with the texts that they are adapted from. Rather than creating a critical remoteness from their source material, these films become tethered to their sources because of their very act of self-conscious distancing. The inherent radicalism of post-modernist and experimental fiction allows, or even demands, transformative adaptation techniques (as found in such films as David Cronenberg's *Naked Lunch* [1991], *Crash* [1996] and Michael Winterbottom's *A Cock and Bull Story* [2005]). In contrast, the adaptation of genre fiction and mainstream literature is compromised by the expectation of equivalence between the two media – particularly in genres where there is a clear conversion from literature to film.

Due to the economic and industrial demands of film-making, the adaptation of literature often produces an amplification of equivalent genre characteristics. However, the reverse of this, the adapting of popular fiction into a non-mainstream genre art-film, is far less common. The long and difficult production of the *Stalker* screenplay uncovers a progressive act of genre reductionism that is authored and sanctioned by the Strugatsky brothers under the supervision of an uncredited Tarkovsky. In this process is revealed a distinctive rupture of the fetishistic demands of literary authenticity or genre expectation.

For Kuhn, 'perhaps more interesting, and probably more important, than what a film genre *is* is the question of what, in cultural terms, it *does* – its "cultural instrumentality"' (Kuhn, 1990: 1). Despite the canonical science-fiction pedigree of the Strugatskys's source novel, and the director's previous foray into the genre with the adaptation of

Stanislaw Lem's space-epic *Solaris* (1972), it is necessary to explore how and why Tarkovsky's *Stalker* eventually subverts and discards the majority of the sf conventions contained in the original story, and how this impacts on the sf genre as a whole. The source material ultimately serves as a catalyst for Tarkovsky to explore his themes of time, space, memory, faith and nature. The resultant film, an art-film parable in which jaded protagonists move through a profoundly psychogeographical landscape, is also a map of the radical adaptation process.

The Strugatsky brothers are considered to be the most widely read Soviet science-fiction writers, and the short novel *Roadside Picnic* is arguably their most well-known work. The brothers are honourable members of the Mark Twain Society due to their outstanding contribution to sf literature, and have been awarded the John W. Campbell Award for the best science-fiction novel of 1977 published in English. *Roadside Picnic* is regarded as a seminal piece of sf, from two writers firmly placed within their chosen world of sf literature.

The narrative of *Roadside Picnic* takes place after an alien visitation to Earth, the life forms leaving behind distinct areas characterized by a baffling array of unexplainable and highly deadly phenomena, as well as many mysterious artefacts deemed to be the detritus of their incomprehensibly advanced technology. The areas are designated as 'Zones', and start to attract a sub-culture of stalkers – people willing to brave the deadly anomalies contained within the Zone for profit. The novel concerns the illegal activities of one such stalker, Redrick 'Red' Schuhart, set in an imagined future Canada. Schuhart, a hardboiled-detective-style character, routinely evades the law and authorities in order to enter the Zone to find alien objects to sell to his black-market contacts. The novel's title is derived from the notion that the alien's visitation was merely a 'roadside picnic' – the artefacts left behind metaphorically representing the kind of litter left behind for scavenging animals. In contrast to the majority of 'alien-visitation' narratives, we do not see the extra-terrestrials interact with humans, either to befriend or kill them.

The clear sf genre characteristics of the novel offer the text the possibility of a smooth journey to film, thanks to an equivalent sf film genre. However, Tarkovsky's film sees the Strugatskys' novel transformed into a metaphysical allegory and moral fable. The demands of medium specificity are largely ignored in favour of a more aesthetic and *auteured* form of adaptation. Instead of finding solutions to the *problems* of literary adaptation, Tarkovsky and the Strugatsky brothers transform the novel into a newly authored piece of cinema. In Tarkovsky's adaptation the novel's characters are excised completely, replacing them with three archetype protagonists. They are the Writer, representing intuition and imagination, the Professor, representing rationalism and scientific objectivity, and the Stalker, a central metaphor for humanity's struggle with faith. The Stalker leads the two men through the Zone seemingly according to random rules due to the shifting and metamorphosing dangers that lurk there, but which we do not witness. Rather than being a barren land filled with an array of baffling, fantastical and deadly phenomena, Tarkovsky's Zone is a kind of quiet and tranquil Oz. The film stock shifts from a depressing sepia brown to vivid colour as the men enter the Zone, the landscape free from people, but otherwise entirely normal, and characterized by beautifully lush and green vegetation. Inverting the terrible sense of menace and deadly traps in the novel, Tarkovsky creates a Zone that is for the Stalker entirely utopian.

In many ways, Tarkovsky's treatment of the novel mirrors his previous approach to the filming of his sf film adaptation *Solaris*. As Vida T. Johnson and Graham Petrie point out, even when operating 'within the fairly safe and popular science fiction genre' Tarkovsky also 'retarded the action with his long takes and slow camera movements', as well as making sure that he 'subordinated the plot (where almost nothing *happens*) to his philosophical ruminations, once again frustrating the genre expectations of both viewers and critics' (Johnson and Petrie, 1994: 15). In *Stalker* there is a distinctive break from the demands of literary authenticity, a violent rupture, combined with visual set-pieces that are designed with exquisite attention to detail, fetishizing the scope of the camera eye, producing something that in isolation has more in common with avant-garde and experimental film, or the overt abstractions of his previous film *Mirror* (1975).

Rejecting Eisensteinian 'montage of atttractions' as an evocation of older Soviet propagandist methodology, Tarkovsky ultimately wished *Stalker* to be filmed in one long take. *Stalker* ostensibly focuses on the movement of characters through the landscape, the sparse narrative driving the men forward towards their final geographical goal. Yet the film is also endowed with a self-awareness of its dichotomous stillness, a negation of the animus of the moving image. Mark Le Fanu comments on the interaction this causes with the actors, as Tarkovsky 'takes his time, almost uniquely in modern cinema, to look at men's faces inquisitively' (Le Fanu, 1987: 93). Mark Riley takes this further, examining the way in which Tarkovsky's 'extended close-up of the stalker's face in the zone resists the anticipation of a profound oration in favour of a study of vulnerability' so that the character's face 'reflects the stratification of the landscape' (Riley, 2008: 59). Here, Riley is informed by the Deleuzian concept of 'landscapity'; as Deleuze writes in *A Thousand Plateaus*, the 'close-up in film treats the face as a landscape: that is the definition of film, black hole and white wall, screen and camera' (Deleuze and Guatarri, 1996: 172). In her introduction to the printed edition of Tarkovsky's collected screenplays, Natasha Synessios remarks that the director 'also believed that the talented writer possessed psychological insight and was therefore capable of introducing concrete elements to a character's underlying state of mind, which in turn would come to bear upon the *mise-en-scène*' – something that was 'of paramount importance to him in attempting a visual depiction of a character's inner world' (Synessios, 1999: xvi). For Maya Turovskaya, 'the world of Stalker in its ordinariness, with its laconic, pared-down simplicity' becomes a zone which is 'reduced to such a tense singularity that it almost ceases to be an "external" world, appearing instead as a landscape of the soul' (Turovskaya, 1989: 108).

The typical critical response to radicalized forms of adaptation is to situate the director as desecrator of the text, committing aesthetic acts of burglary in their adaptation, or as auteur, the single-minded artist who uses the source material merely as a starting point. In the case of *Stalker*, these proffered opinions are problematic. While Tarkovsky is in every sense an archetypal auteur, the production history

Figure 1. Aleksandr Kajdanovsky in *Stalker*. Photo courtesy of Media Transactions/Photofest.

of the *Stalker* screenplay, and the acts of degenrification, are unusually authored by the Strugatsky brothers themselves, albeit under the supervision of the director. Tarkovsky had experienced a difficult relationship with sf during his time on *Solaris*, Natasha Synessios observing that he 'had waged a losing battle with the genre of science fiction, exacerbated by Lem's approach and his unwillingness to permit a "Tarkovskian" adaptation of his story' (Synessios, 1999: 133). Despite this, Tarkovsky's relationship with the screenwriting process throughout all his films, and in *Stalker*, was clearly collaborative, occasionally the entire responsibility placed in the hands of his co-writers, while for others he was overbearing and wilfully rewrote sections of the script. The development of the *Stalker* screenplay is a long and complicated one, with the Strugatsky brothers working on multiple revisions of the story. While the initial treatments and outlines demanded by the Moscow-based producers Mosfilm clearly display a breakage from the novel, there is still a sense of the story being explicitly sf in tone and content. On the first occasion that the film went into production, it was discovered half-way through filming that the Mosfilm developers had accidentally destroyed all of the film stock used for shooting. While this massively set back the project, it also gave Tarkovsky the perfect opportunity to rethink the entire story. However, the writing of the screenplay for the second *Stalker* project became a torturously difficult process for the Strugatsky brothers. They were asked persistently by Tarkovsky to redraft and change submitted scripts, with little direction or specific advice as to what the specific narrative problems entailed. As Arkady Strugatsky states:

> I would revise it. I attempt to catch the tone and intention as I understand it. 'It's even worse now. Revise it.' I sigh and trudge along to the typewriter. [...] He reads and rereads for a long time, his moustache bristling. Then he says hesitantly: 'Well, it'll do for the time being. At least we have something to start on ... And then rewrite this dialogue.' [...] 'What don't you like in the dialogue?' 'I don't know, just revise it. Have it ready by tomorrow night.' This was how we worked on a screenplay which had long been accepted and approved at all official levels.
> 'What should Stalker be like in the new screenplay?'
> 'I don't know, you're the author not I.' (Strugatsky, 1990: 260)

It was at this point, after numerous redrafts of the screenplay, that the writers finally came to the conclusion that the degenrification of the narrative, and the stripping away of sf elements, could aid its adaptation:

> On a sudden urge I asked:
> 'Listen, Andrei, what do you need the science fiction in the film for? Let's throw it out.'
> He smirked: just like a cat that has eaten its owner's parrot.
> 'There! *You* suggested it, not I! I've wanted it for a long time, only was afraid of suggesting it, so you wouldn't take offence.' (Strugatsky, 1990: 260)

On reading this first draft of the degenrified script, Tarkovsky remarked to the Strugatsky brothers that for 'the first time in my life I have my own screenplay' (Strugatsky, 1990: 261). In this drawn-out process of degenrification, Tarkovsky's *Stalker* becomes untethered from its explicit sf origins, becoming a metaphysical and symbolic parable regarding faith and memory, utilizing the distinctive auteurist practices that dominate his *oeuvre* before and after.

While it is rare for the author(s) of a novel to radically adapt their work into film, it is of particular relevance in the case of *Stalker*. The Strugatsky brothers are received and read as sf authors – writers clearly working within and conforming to sf genre conventions in their books. This amputation of genre elements during the adaptation process is all the more remarkable given the typically protective ownership that authors usually display towards their cherished novels (as seen in the problems Tarkovsky experienced with Stanislaw Lem in the adaptation of *Solaris*). Turovskaya sees the change as a profound shift in the whole narratological perspective of the story. For her, 'it is not only the fantasy of science fiction and special effects that are vanquished, but also the everyday verisimilitude round which the original science-fiction story was built' (Turovskaya, 1989: 110). This shift has an ironic element to it: the sf elements of the source novel are spectacular, visual, cinematic; the existential preoccupations of the characters in *Stalker* are literary, wordy, inward-looking, and concerned with ideas rather than spectacle. Turovskaya continues:

> Monochromatic images, flowing occasionally into colour. Nothing which even remotely resembles the future. The Stalker's wretched dwelling, with its one metal bed shared by the whole family [...] Even the notorious booby-traps, the famous 'wonders' of the Zone that stand like milestones on the journey, show no signs of the marvellous, let alone anything 'sci-fi' in their manifestations, but suggest rather a moribund monotony. (Turovskaya, 1989: 111)

The multifarious reasons why *Stalker* is ultimately considered an art-film are obviously more complex than simply the fact that its narrative structure, tone and pro-filmic tropes are self-consciously artistic and cinematic. From his masterwork *Andrei Rublev* (1966), through to his final film *Sacrifice* (1984), Tarkovsky's films were continuously bestowed with auteurist 'art-film' status by critics. The metaphysical questions that Tarkovsky poses in his films, alongside his characters' search for meaning, philosophical grapplings with the notion of nature and religion, marked him out as an iconic writer and director. While the film is believed to contain many symbols for Tarkovsky's own beliefs, the director rejected all forms of metaphorical inference and the notion that his films could be decoded. However, it is assumed that the film explores Tarkovsky's own personal debates with faith, religion and the notion of a God; his status and sense of his own environment as someone confined to, and exiled from, the Soviet Union.

In more general studies of adaptation and adaptation theory, the notion of a textual and medium-specific value system tends to dwell on the perspective of film as a 'parasite' and 'predator'. Robert Stam offers a variety of conceptual reasons for the hierarchical privileging of literature over film, explaining the 'source of the hostility' as a 'subliminal form of class prejudice'. He goes on to extrapolate the reasons for this hostility to film, evoking Bourdieu's notion of 'cultural capital':

> The cinema, perhaps unconsciously, is seen as degraded by the company it keeps – the great unwashed popular mass audience, with its lower-class origins in 'vulgar' spectacles like sideshows and carnivals. Through a class-based dichotomy, literature pays indirect, and begrudging, homage to film's popularity, while film pays homage to literature's prestige. Adaptations, in this view, are the inevitably 'dumbed down' versions of their source novels [...] The frequent charge against adaptations that they have 'vulgarized' [...] bears the etymological traces of this prejudice [...] (Stam, 2004: 7)

While the prestige of literature is deployed as a method to critique adaptations (as discussed in the ongoing fidelity debate), *Stalker* offers a quite different response. The critical discourse surrounding the aesthetic status and worthiness of *Stalker* tends to be situated at a very specific political and value-based vantage point. In particular, *Stalker* is consistently regarded as a text that has usurped and transcended its source material not just in terms of narrative content, but also its status as mainstream genre fiction. In a reversal of Stam's position on the traditional relationship of film and literature, *Stalker* becomes framed as an art-film of significant aesthetic and artistic merit. Employing Stam's language, we can see that in the removing of elements, characteristics and tropes of the sf genre, Tarkovsky's film has gained prestige by distancing itself from the 'vulgar spectacle' of sf literature. While the Strugatsky brothers' novel is examined for its sf qualities and as a critique of the perils of East European black-market profiteering, a variety of more 'worthy' interpretations are attached to Tarkovsky's film. Peter Green describes the main character as a 'Charon ferrying tourists across the Styx, through the various circles of hell' or as an 'apostle, a Christ-like figure, a guide to paradise?', as well as citing 'parallels to Dante's Divine Comedy' (Green, 1993: 94–5). Green's book is emblematic of the kind of fannish discourses on Tarkovsky, and *Stalker* specifically, regarding its shedding of science-fiction elements. For Green 'the real world of the Zone that Tarkovsky evokes [...] is far more frightening than any science fiction scenario' (Green, 1993: 97) while the director 'sheds the props of science fiction to create a work relevant to our own spiritual situation, a statement of the condition humaine' (Green, 1993: 95). For critics such as Green, the problem of adapting mainstream fiction for Tarkovsky comes in the detaching of its classic genre conventions – and replacing them with the high-art film tropes that mark the director out as an artist, and auteur.

In her book on the relationship of sf to post-modern fiction, Barbara Puschmann-Nalenz critiques the self-reflexivity of writers such as William S. Burroughs, J. G. Ballard, Thomas Pynchon and Kurt Vonnegut and their techniques for employing the aesthetic devices of sf (contributing to the notion of a 'literary' sf). Puschmann-Nalenz describes how the 'more demanding and intricate products of SF are postmodernizing' (Puschmann-Nalenz, 1992: 226). Her enquiry into the 'science fictionalization of postmodernism' and the 'postmodernization of science fiction' makes clear that these texts do not necessarily usurp or subvert the genre, but rather change and reshape our perception of what sf is and what it can be. Therefore, Tarkovsky's *Stalker*, rather than dispensing with sf, can be seen to exist in a long tradition of sf texts that push the boundaries of the genre, and in doing so adjust our definitions of science fiction. Continuing this argument,

Vivian Sobchack states that 'the most simultaneously catastrophic and progressive SF films are those that I have identified as marginal' (Sobchack, 1987: 302). She goes on to uncover the meaning these marginal films can have for our understanding of genre:

> Indeed, marginal SF films tend to be generically 'dissolute' as well as culturally 'deconstructive.' That is, while their subversion of the boundaries between inner city/outer space [...] 'deconstructs' the hierarchical relations that ground capitalist notions of power, desire, and value, this subversion also 'dissolves' the very structure and notion of the film genre as a bounded category of texts valuing the marked and hierarchical difference between signs of 'science' and signs of 'fiction.' (Sobchack, 1987: 302)

The formal attempts by Tarkovsky and the Strugatskys to degenrify the novel during adaptation are to some extent thwarted because of its association with the science-fiction genre. Instead of breaking free from its status as a science-fiction film, *Stalker* becomes part of the corpus of texts that form the genre. In their critical examination of Tarkovsky's cinema, Johnson and Petrie, while recognizing the overt rejection of sf in *Stalker*, also try to re-examine the presumptions of these omissions, and the critical assumption that it is not a sf film. In their view, although Tarkovsky 'attempted – as with *Solaris* – to downplay the science fiction element of *Stalker*, it has much more in common with the Strugatskys' *Roadside Picnic* than the convoluted history of its script might suggest.' For Johnson and Petrie, whilst 'Tarkovsky turned the original story into something very different and deeply personal' he can also be seen to have absorbed 'rather more of the original and was less cavalier in the process of adaptation that he liked to assert for public consumption' (Johnson and Petrie, 1994: 140).

Therefore, *Stalker* can be seen to be contemporaneously realigned with the sf genre, not just because of the subsequent body of work that has extended the boundaries of what can be classified as sf, but also because of the film's status within that discourse. For Todorov, it is the subversion of these genre elements that ultimately form our understanding of it:

The fact that a work 'disobeys' its genre does not mean that the genre does not exist. It is tempting to say 'quite the contrary,' for two reasons. First because, in order to exist as such, the transgression requires a law – precisely the one that is to be violated. We go even further and observe that the norm becomes visible – comes into existence – owing only to its transgressions. (Todorov, 1990: 14)

It is in the pushing back of the boundaries of a taxonomy, in transgressing the very rules that it uses to categorize, that ultimately lead *Stalker* to be reappraised as a science-fiction film.

Further to this, if, as Sobchack suggests, the genre of science fiction can become 'dissolute' or even dissolve, can this be seen as a destructive or creative act? Can the boundaries of a genre as critically *understood* as sf become informed by those films which operate on the margins of genre? It appears that despite the actions of the Strugatskys and Tarkovsky the genre credentials for *Stalker* could transcend the authorial mission statement for the film, becoming a marginal sf film within a family of similarly art-film influenced cinema. Despite its resistance to the genre, *Stalker* can be seen to exist in a tradition of highly cinematic, often dystopian, sf art films, influenced by the existential loneliness and poetics of *La jetée* (Chris Marker, 1962), *Alphaville* (Jean-Luc Godard, 1965), *Fahrenheit 451* (François Truffaut, 1966), *2001: A Space Odyssey* (Stanley Kubrick, 1968), *THX 1138* (George Lucas, 1971), *Silent Running* (Douglas Trumbull, 1972), *Zardoz* (John Boorman, 1974), and *The Man Who Fell to Earth* (Nicolas Roeg, 1976). This sub-genre of sf then contributes to a subsequent corpus of films in this tradition, that recently include *Children of Men* (Alfonso Cuarón, 2006), *The Fountain* (Darren Aronofsky, 2006), *Sunshine* (Danny Boyle, 2007), *Moon* (Duncan Jones, 2009) and *The Road* (John Hillcoat, 2009), the last of which is explicitly indebted to Tarkovsky's oeuvre.

Beyond cinematic texts only, the fragmentation of a hypotext, as it is dispersed intertextually through culture, is of particular importance in the study of adaptations. But in the case of *Stalker* it takes on a different perspective entirely, as events conspire to relocate the film *back* into the realms of sf. *Stalker* has gained a speculative status in part due to what many see as its prescience in the foreshadowing of apocalyptic ecological disaster. In 1986, seven years after the completion of *Stalker*, the Chernobyl Nuclear Plant explosion caused a depopulation and militarization of the local area, officially referred to as the Zone of alienation, but known by locals as 'The Zone'. Those employed to enter the site to clean it up at the time were referred to as 'Stalkers'. The eeriness of the juxtaposition of these ghost towns, in which abandoned concrete buildings and huts mix with thriving plant life, becomes an unavoidable semiotic reference point to *Stalker*. As Turovskaya states, before the Chernobyl disaster 'the word "zone" had for many Russians an association with the camps and Siberia; but in 1986 it was to acquire' the literal definition that *Stalker* holds for the Zone, the 'site of a catastrophe' (Turovskaya, 1989: 111).

As portrayed in Tarkovsky's Zone, the local area around Chernobyl, despite the effects of radiation, and most likely due to depopulation, has become a thriving nature reserve for plants, trees and wild animals, which thrive in the human-free environment. More recently the area has seen people, with increasing regularity, illegally entering this ravaged and extremely dangerous area to find artefacts discarded after the accident. A further intertextual reference point in the reading of Tarkovsky's film is the 2007 released PC game *S.T.A.L.K.E.R. – Shadow of Chernobyl*. Ostensibly a first-person shooting game with dystopian science-fiction themes, the game actually becomes a curious post-modern fusion of Tarkovksy's film, with reintroduced elements of *Roadside Picnic*.

Taking place after an assumed second Chernobyl accident, players must navigate their Stalker through a very recognizable Zone to ultimately reach a wish-granting monolith. The gap between speculative fiction and the non-fiction event is eroded in this complex marriage of both texts, and the environmental devastation that both book and film are deemed to predict. This symbolic tethering of Tarkovsky's film to the Chernobyl accident endows the film retroactively with speculative and dystopian science-fiction characteristics that could not be predicted, and cannot be controlled by Tarkovsky. The *S.T.A.L.K.E.R.* computer game also reworks and repositions Tarkovsky's film, endowing it with sf tropes by proxy and by association. Through this we see that the notion of genre is again not controlled by the author, but rather by a discerning audience influenced by history, the shifting characteristics of genre and a text's changing reception based on intertextual references. For Linda Hutcheon the stickiness of the source and adapted text is based in the experiential reading of the film. She states that 'adaptation as adaptation involves, for its knowing audience, an interpretive doubling, a conceptual flipping back and forth between the work we know and the work we are experiencing' (Hutcheon, 2006: 139). For the majority of audience members, this 'flipping back and forth' grounds *Stalker* as birthed from the sf genre and arguably prevents the film from fully escaping its origins. But the reference point of the original novel is clearly only one influence amongst many that intertextually weave their way into our readings of adaptations.

Science fiction, arguably more than any other genre, has undergone the greatest hybridization and proliferation of sub-genres, in part due its self-conscious deployment in a variety of post-modernist literature and film texts. In response to this stratification of the genre's use comes a stratification of its meaning and reception. These responses have begun to form a corpus of films that deviate from classical notions of what adaptation is or should be. In genre theory, and as we have seen in the case of Tarkovsky's *Stalker*, it is the playful deconstruction of these taxonomies that can inform new understandings of such concepts as genre and adaptation. In our understanding of the dynamics of adaptation, it can be concluded that our readings of texts through subsequent 'simulacra' copies create new source material as it becomes repositioned through the prism of its filmic form. Therefore, while literature appears as a finite object, with only its subsequent adaptations offering new avenues for analysis, it can be seen as a fluid concept controlled and informed by these adaptations. They exist in a state of flux, in line with Rick Altman's view of genre as a permanently fluctuating concept. For Altman, 'film genres are perpetually caught up in the process of becoming' (Altman, 1999: 140), in keeping with all texts – both literary and cinematic.

References

Altman, R. (1999) *Film/Genre*. London: BFI.

Bordwell, D. (1986) *Narration in the Fiction Film*. London and New York: Routledge.

Bourdieu, P. (1984) *Distinction: A Social Critique of the Judgement of Taste*. London and New York: Routledge.

Cohen, R. (1986) 'History and Genre', *New Literary History* 17 (2): 202–12.

Deleuze, G. and Guattari, F. (1996) *A Thousand Plateaus: Capitalism & Schizophrenia*. London: Continuum.

Foucault, M. (1970) *The Order of Things*. London: Routledge.

Geraghty, C. (2008) *Now a Major Motion Picture: Film Adaptations of Literature and Drama*. Lanham: Rowman & Littlefield.

Green, P. (1993) *Andrei Tarkovsky: The Winding Quest*. Basingstoke: Macmillan Press.

Hutcheon, L. (2006) *A Theory of Adaptation*. London: Routledge.

Johnson, V. T. and Petrie, G. (1994) *The Films of Andrei Tarkovsky – A Visual Fugue*. Bloomington and Indianapolis: Indiana University Press.

Kuhn, A. (1990) 'Introduction: Cultural Theory and Science Fiction Cinema', in A. Kuhn (ed.) *Alien Zone: Cultural Theory and Contemporary Science Fiction Cinema*, pp. 1–12. London: Verso.

Le Fanu, M. (1987) *The Cinema of Andrei Tarkovsky*. London: BFI Publishing.

Puschmann-Nalenz, B. (1992) *Science Fiction and Postmodern Fiction: A Genre Study*. New York: Peter Lang.

Stam, R. (2000) *Film Theory: An Introduction*. Malden and Oxford: Blackwell.

Stam, R. (2004) 'Introduction: The Theory and Practice of Adaptation', in R. Stam and A. Raengo (eds) *Literature and Film: A Guide to the Theory and Practice of Film Adaptation*, pp. 1–52. Oxford: Blackwell.

Riley, M. (2008) 'Disorientation, Duration and Tarkovsky', in I. Buchanan and P. MacCormack (eds) *Deleuze and the Schizoanalysis of Cinema*, pp. 58–75. London and New York: Continuum.

Sobchack, V. (1987) *Screening Space: The American Science Fiction Film*. New York: Ungar Publishing Company.

Strugatsky, A. (1990) 'As I Saw Him', in M. Tarkovskaya (ed.) *About Andrei Tarkovsky: Memoirs and Biographies*, pp. 257–62. Moscow: Progress Publishers.

Synessios, N. (1999) 'Introduction', in A. Tarkovsky, *Collected Screenplays*, pp. ix-xxv. Trans. W. Powell and N. Synessios. London: Faber & Faber.

Todorov, T. (1990) *Genres in Discourse*. Cambridge: Cambridge University Press.

Turovskaya, M. (1989) *Tarkovsky: Cinema as Poetry*. London and Boston: Faber & Faber.

Part III

Nation, Politics and Gender

CHAPTER 7

DESCENT RAMP
REVISITING J. G. BALLARD'S *CRASH*
AND ITS FILM ADAPTATION BY DAVID CRONENBERG

Nicholas Ruddick

CANNES – Fasten your seat belts.
David Cronenberg's *Crash* is bearing the flag for Canadian film here
and it's got more sex, nudity and kinkiness than all the European and
Scandinavian pictures combined.
Kinda makes a Canadian in Cannes feel downright cool [...]
One of the most exciting things about the movie for Torontonians,
much more than the sex, is suburban Toronto appearing as itself [...]
But the focus on busy superhighways, underpasses, ramps and ga-
rages, along with the steely gray shades of concrete and sky make
the GTA [the Greater Toronto Area] seem awfully dismal. (Gerstel,
1996: C1)

In *Crash* (1973), J. G. Ballard deliberately produced a novel that resembles violent hard-core pornography. David Cronenberg in his
film of the same title (1996) with equal deliberation took up the challenge of adapting Ballard's renegade scenario to a popular audiovisual
medium. While both works generated reams of controversy on their
respective appearances, Ballard and Cronenberg expressed mutual
admiration. The novelist referred to the film adaptation as 'a master-

piece', affirming that his novel, which he once thought of as unfilmable, had been completed, even superseded by Cronenberg's remediation (Grünberg, 1996b: 31; Sinclair, 1999: 10–11). Meanwhile, the director spoke of his film as 'a lovely fusion of me and Ballard. We're so amazingly in synch' (Rodley, 1996: 8). History seems to have vindicated both author and auteur. For at least a decade both works have apparently enjoyed canonical status in their respective media: the back-cover blurb of the current standard Picador paperback edition of the novel (2001) refers to it as 'a classic work of cutting-edge fiction', while Cronenberg's film is the subject of a book-length study (1999) by Iain Sinclair in the British Film Institute's BFI Modern Classics series. I am not convinced, however, that the matter of the two *Crash*es' compatibility and reputation has been quite so comfortably settled. Now that the author is dead and 'J. G. Ballard' is a term in literary history, it may be time to revisit novel and film in the hope of attaining whatever evaluative clarity might be afforded by retrospect.

On the main theoretical questions raised by novel-to-film adaptation, I neither believe that fidelity to a source text is an essential criterion of a film's aesthetic success, nor do I feel that a film is fated always to simplify the novel from which it is adapted. That said, the function of adaptation studies remains unclear to me unless its critical praxis allows works in different media that are causally and closely related to be considered aesthetically comparable. Ballard's and Cronenberg's *Crash* do not share a title by coincidence, nor are they as incommensurable as ballet and architecture (see Bluestone, 1957/1968: 5–6). No one ever claimed the Johnson Wax Building owed its existence to *Swan Lake*, while Cronenberg's film publicly acknowledges Ballard's novel as its source text, and if it had not, there would have been a universal cry of plagiarism when it first appeared. An artist cannot appropriate the title of a renowned existing work without invoking the spirit of comparison – not even if, like Borges's 'Pierre Menard' (1939), he claims to have totally supplanted the original.

I consider *Crash* one of the most important novels of the last century. That Cronenberg evidently arrived at a similar evaluation (see Hultkrans, 1997: 80) encourages me to weigh his adaptation here against its source text with the question in mind: 'did he do it justice?' I will conclude that Cronenberg adapted Ballard's novel intelligently and produced a striking and timely film that neither exploits nor betrays its source text. Cronenberg's reading of *Crash* is no wilful misunderstanding or distortion as was Jean Baudrillard's (Ruddick, 1992: 356). En route, however, I will argue that Cronenberg's film is not only quite different thematically and generically from Ballard's novel, but also that it is a more modest achievement. It amounts to an audiovisual supplement rather than a complement to its source text, and – with due respect to Ballard – it is very far from being a completion or replacement of his novel.

In my view, one way of measuring the different impact of the two *Crash*es is via the geographical specificities of their respective urban settings. The manner in which each of these settings is rendered has major generic, semantic and aesthetic consequences. Ballard's London is proleptic; his descriptive mode is surrealistic; the tone of his narrative is apocalyptic; its emotional keynote is disgust. This is a scenario of bodily fluids spilled and mingled with pornographic excess; and one of his main authorial aims is cautionary (Hultkrans, 1997: 78), or better, admonitory, a word evoking a prophetic, futuristic dynamic: this near-future man-made disaster area is western civilization as it will become if certain present trends are allowed to continue unabated. In generic terms, *Crash* is a speculative, future-oriented fiction with a strong dystopian element – in short, it is a science-fiction novel. Though there is no futuristic technology in its 'novum', there is a metastasizing excess of the existing kind. Heightening a realistic, even naturalistic rendering of the present urban scene, Ballard brings into being a fantastic, horrific near-future London.[1]

Cronenberg, by contrast, explicitly rejected the necessity of remediating the moral dimension of the novel: 'I'm trying to be experimental, but not cautionary' (Hultkrans 1997: 118). In his film, dread is passé, the disaster a *fait accompli*, as Ballard himself noted: 'les personnages acceptent dès le début cet univers. Ce qui reste latent dans le roman devient manifeste dans le film' [the characters from the start accept this universe. What remains latent in the novel becomes manifest in the film] (Grünberg, 1996b: 31). Cronenberg's scenario, transposed to Toronto and the consensus reality of 1996, celebrates the sexual perversity lurking inside the upmarket high-rise condos and beneath the overpasses of the concrete built environment. Cronenberg's tone is deadpan, his emotional keynote a deliberately disingenuous detachment suggesting but never affirming a satirical intention. His film is neatly structured as a soft-porn screwball romance in which two photogenic but slightly sinister yuppies spice up their marriage by going slumming on the wrong side of the expressway. The affect denied by the plot's remorseless sexual serialism is cleverly displaced into the 'bruise colours' of the cinematography and brilliantly echoed in the stark, glacial soundtrack by Howard Shore, so what might have been farcical becomes invested with a certain ironic portentousness. In summary, then, while Ballard's *Crash* is a science-fiction novel in a dark fantastic mode, Cronenberg's *Crash* is a work of contemporary quasi-documentary realism – as the director himself has noted (see Bouquet, 1996: 24; Camblor, 1999: 12; Grünberg, 1996a: 27).

This generic difference ought to be more obvious, but it was obscured by the eagerness of the older Ballard to repudiate his science-fictional affiliations, and by the willingness of his supporters, especially after the success of his autobiographical novel *Empire of the Sun* (1984), to claim him for the literary mainstream. Briefly, after the rise of the 'sci-fi' cinematic blockbuster, science fiction as genre and institution seemed no longer receptive to literary experimentation. Ballard noted that *Star Wars* (1977) and its ilk 'exist in a kind of timeless continuum that has nothing to do with the future', while in good earlier science-fiction movies 'the future *seized* your imagination by the throat' (Vale and Juno, 1984: 17). In Ballard's 1974 introduction to the first French edition of his novel, science fiction represented 'the main literary tradition of the 20th century [...] – a tradition of imaginative response to science and technology' linking H. G. Wells, Aldous Huxley and William Burroughs (Ballard, 1975: 46). But by the time this introduction was recycled for the 1995 Vintage edition of *Crash*, all references to science fiction were omitted and the novel was promoted as a classic of avant-garde literary fiction.

Ballard's *Crash* is set in west London in a non-specific near future, when London (i.e. Heathrow) Airport has swollen in size and the motorways feeding it have multiplied in number and complexity.

The interlinked villages that formerly dotted the exurban landscape and whose names bear witness to a long history of settlement have been overlaid with, and their ancient patterns erased by, multi-storey car parks and 24-hour gas stations. Ballard the author lived for most of his writing life in the outer London suburb of Shepperton, about four miles south of Heathrow Airport. In the 1960s, urban planners intended to encircle London with four concentric Ringways, all of which would be connected to each other and central London by radial motorways. Of these Ringways, only one, the M25 orbital, was actually completed (in 1986). However, one of the spokes – the M3 – was being driven through Shepperton while Ballard was composing *Crash*. An ongoing unstoppable process of dehumanizing (because dehistoricizing) transformation of a familiar locale underlies and propels the novel's plot; it is entirely absent from the film.

In Ballard's *Crash*, London Airport and its service areas, fed by endlessly proliferating Ringways and spokes, now cover a vast expanse of west London. Central London, meanwhile, is not mentioned in the novel and the characters never venture farther than Earls Court for the motor show (Ballard, 2001: 174). The great city's once enormous cultural presence has now receded into irrelevance. Indeed, in *Crash* a superhighway, 'Western Avenue' (Ballard, 2001: 18, 47, *passim*), linking the Airport to the Ringway system, has usurped the role of the city itself as natural focus of the action. An actual road called Western Avenue, also known as the A40, runs parallel to and about five miles north of the Heathrow perimeter. From this fact one may infer that Ballard in 1973 aimed to appal his many readers familiar with the terrain by depicting his 'London Airport' as a monstrous devourer of the urban fabric. But Ballard's 'Western Avenue' also has an eschatological connotation, hinting that western civilization is on a sunset, death-bound trajectory (cf. German *Abendland* [literally, 'evening land'], i.e. western, occidental). The narrator's references to the Airport's 'Oceanic Terminal' (the former name of Heathrow's Terminal 3) augment the apocalyptic mood (Ballard, 2001: 9, 107, 144).

Its setting, then, marks Ballard's *Crash* as a futuristic fiction with a strong dystopian element. London is no longer present as a great metropolis with all the cultural weight of its 2000-year-old history; it has become a 'distant bulk' shielded from the main characters by an 'elegant' motorway access spur (Ballard, 2001: 48). London's natural features such as the Thames are never mentioned; we hear merely of artificial reservoirs. Ballard the narrator, emerging from hospital, notes that his life 'was now bounded by a continuous artificial horizon' (Ballard, 2001: 53). Indeed, London Airport (significantly, its acronym is 'LA') is referred to figuratively as an 'overlit metropolis' (Ballard, 2001: 92), by which phrase the narrative also suggests that 'LA' and its hinterland serve as a film set on which motorists can act out and record their deepest fantasies.

Moreover, while the narrator has been recuperating in hospital after his car crash, another half-mile has been added to the motorway system: the vast energies of civilization are being deployed to bury a world city under concrete and asphalt. The narrator tells us that the flyovers 'overlaid one another like copulating giants' (Ballard, 2001: 76). His imagery here is not of cancerous metastasis but of progenitiveness; but it is concrete and steel, not organic life, that is multiplying. It is the existence of this awesome, brutal setting, the envisioned culmination of a process already under way in 1970, which the novel interrogates. *Why* are such energies being expended on erasing the natural and historic landscape? If it is so that cars can go faster – then to where? Why? And with what consequences? The London area in *Crash* has become a pastiche of 1960s Los Angeles, a vast, denatured, centreless dream factory enslaved to the automobile. But while Los Angeles was built largely over a natural desert, in *Crash* an artificial desert is being built over London.

William Beard remarks on how the 'contextless and unifocused characters and settings' in Cronenberg's screenplay are effectively recreated in his film (Beard, 2001: 382). Of Cronenberg's transposition of the action from London to Toronto, Iain Sinclair notes that the Canadian metropolis is a 'subtopian nowhere' whose very anonymity made it perfect in Ballard's eyes as it stripped the film of the novel's 'autobiographical specifics' (Sinclair, 1999: 87–8). Chris Rodley (1996: 7) muses, 'Toronto, that most archetypal of North American cities. The perfect quasi-sci-fi backdrop. Nowhere. No time. A brilliant solution to the novel's *sense* of America'. Murray Forman claims that Cronenberg's film is 'largely devoid of explicit topographical and cultural references' (Forman, 2001: 114). In my view, however, the director's use of his home town was deliberate and affirmative: Cronenberg chose Toronto because it is Toronto, not because it might be anywhere. His use of realistic, recognizable Toronto settings filmed in available light forecloses exploitation of the futuristic, dystopian, admonitory thrust of Ballard's novel. But Cronenberg has other fish to fry.

In his film, Cronenberg deliberately provides enough topographical details for the viewer to recognize or discern that the setting can be nowhere else but Toronto, Ontario, Canada in the present day. The film's opening shot features an orange and white monoplane with the registration prefix 'C' for Canada painted prominently on its fuselage. The first shot of traffic seen from the Ballard's high-rise balcony, and the establishing shot as James Ballard (James Spader) and his wife Catherine (Deborah Kara Unger) return from the hospital, are both instantly recognizable to anyone familiar with Canada's largest city as the Macdonald-Cartier Freeway – locally referred to as 'the 401'. This highway, 18 lanes wide near Pearson Airport, is among the busiest in North America.

Later on, the view of the airport apron from the multi-storey car park shows a taxiing plane with Air Canada livery. Several cars in the film have licence plates clearly bearing the banal slogan, 'Ontario: Yours to Discover'. Just before Vaughan (Elias Koteas) shows Ballard the James Dean death crash photos, a sign indicates Lake Shore Boulevard, the road that runs beneath the elevated Gardiner Expressway through west-central Toronto. A distinctive Beck Taxi from the largest fleet in Toronto appears in the car-wash scene. And even more distinctively, one of Toronto's quaint electric streetcars trundles past outside as the scene in the automobile showroom concludes. Cronenberg, that quintessentially Canadian filmmaker, has discreetly contextualized the film in his own home town in the present.[2] But to what end?

A Toronto setting was undoubtedly economically expedient for a director who lived in the city and who 'literally shot the whole movie within half a mile of my house' (Rodley, 1996: 11). Moreover, parts of Toronto in 1994 probably did bring to Cronenberg's mind Ballard's dreadful near-future London. However, Cronenberg need have included no specifically Torontonian visual references had he wished simply to depict a dehistoricized airport-centred megalopolis. Indeed, Cronenberg's screenplay omitted references to specific places. His process of adaptive distillation from novel via screenplay to film involved removing London references from the text, and then including visual Toronto references during shooting and editing.

Critics have noted that Unger plays Catharine Ballard as a 'mannequin' or 'living sex-doll', whereas her husband, Spader, 'represents blank yuppiedom par excellence' (Beard, 2001: 389; Brottman and Sharrett, 2002: 127; Springer, 2001: 209). However, to my knowledge no one has remarked that this pair have a specifically Canadian resonance prepared for by the film's topographical detailing. Facially, Spader and Unger are strongly reminiscent of the serial rapist and murderer Paul Bernardo and his blonde wife and partner in crime Karla Homolka. This couple, among Canada's most notorious criminals, resembled stereotypical southern Ontario young professionals. However, these 'Ken and Barbie Killers', as the tabloids referred to them, filmed themselves sodomizing, torturing and murdering schoolgirls, until their capture, trial and conviction between 1993 and 1995. Unger's high-cheekboned, unsmiling Catherine seems 'harder' than her softer-featured husband, as it also seemed with Homolka and Bernardo.

May Cronenberg not be suggesting through these topical visual allusions that female desire, even when couched as passivity or masochism, is the more ruthless? While Beard (2001: 409) feels that 'the issue of the hurtfulness to females of male sexual desire is not far from the film's imagination', I would suggest that Cronenberg, presenting Catherine as a passive-aggressive femme fatale, invests female sexuality with the greater destructive power. As a Canadian, he could not be unaware that Homolka, claiming to be a victim of Bernardo, had arranged a plea bargain that saw her released early from jail. When videotapes subsequently revealed her willing participation in his crimes, she became for the Canadian public an even more notorious embodiment of evil than her husband. But the ambiguity of Cronen-

of us are barely conscious combatants. It notes with horror the radical and rapid dehistoricization of London, a world city embodying the best of civilization, by the automobile. It probes the significance of the hypertrophy of transportation systems, noting for example how ever-open airport terminals fed by never-sleeping expressways prefigure the globalization of death-fixated forms of human desire. The novel's depiction of Vaughan's attempts to fuse in automotive death with a female celebrity makes *Crash* perhaps the chief document of resort if we are to make sense of the mass hysteria caused by the 1997 fatal car crash of Princess Diana and the bizarre reversion of millions of people to primitive or childish forms of behaviour in its wake.

Cronenberg's *Crash*, on the other hand, is a serious and reasonably effective exploration of the erotics of automotive technology, while keeping within the bounds of what is acceptable in mass-market film. Cronenberg understands that Ballard's densely literary text resists effective remediation, so he makes a wise move in the opposite direction, distilling the novel's plot and dialogue (see Grünberg, 1996a: 28; Rodley, 1996: 8) so as to maintain close control over a potentially explosive scenario and to suggest the flattening of his protagonists' identities. When he occasionally missteps, as with the 'completely tokenistic' lesbian sex scene between Catherine Ballard and Helen Remington (Creed, 1998: 178), it is perhaps because he is trying to 'counterbalance' and so partially defuse the transgressive effect of the (not very graphic) sex scene between James and Vaughan (Grundmann, 1996: 27). Otherwise, his film has an admirable coherence that I would attribute to a reticently expressed but clear topical purpose: to suggest that Canada's white-bread metropolis has a hidden streak of sexual deviance and is thus weirder and cooler than anyone expects. But while he achieves his aim (*Crash* is a *very* cool, *very* Canadian film) (see Beard, 1994: 118; Rosenbaum, 1997: 5), Cronenberg fails to engage with the larger moral implications of his insights; his film is therefore a narrower, less daring artistic achievement than its source text. As Harpold judiciously puts it, 'Cronenberg's project since *Shivers*, "to show the unshowable, to speak the unspeakable", runs up in *Crash* against a guiderail of sexual abjection that it never quite crosses' (Harpold, 1997: 4). Ballard's *Crash* is what his fictional alter ego refers to as a 'long punitive expedition into my own nervous system' (Ballard, 2001: 193); Cronenberg's *Crash* takes a descent ramp into the shadows under the Gardiner Expressway.

Notes

1 Angela Carter noted: 'Naturalism need not affirm the status quo, but when it doesn't, as in Zola, when it becomes a form of heightened realism, it's amazing how Gothic it gets' (Carter, 1975: 133).

2 Sinclair, unaware of their local signification, over-interprets signs in Cronenberg's film. Catherine Ballard's Mazda's Ontario registration plate is QRC 509; Sinclair reads the letters as ORC and takes this as a 'Blakeian allusion' (Sinclair, 1999: 69).

3 The city acquired this nickname in the nineteenth century for its self-righteous conservatism.

4 The sex scenes are surely intended to be erotic, however. Cronenberg, who bravely confessed that he was aghast to discover that he was turned on by Ballard's novel (see Camblor, 1999: 6) surely would not wish to be 'defended' by critics (e.g. see Craven, 2000: 206; Ebert, 1997: 1) claiming that his film was not intended to arouse.

References

Ballard, J. G. (1974/1975) 'Some Words about *Crash!* 1. Introduction to the French Edition of *Crash!*', *Foundation* 9: 45–8.

Ballard, J. G. (1973/2001) *Crash*. New York: Picador.

Beard, W. (2001) *The Artist as Monster: The Cinema of David Cronenberg*. Toronto: University of Toronto Press.

Beard, W. (1994) 'The Canadianness of David Cronenberg', *Mosaic* 27 (2): 113–33.

Bluestone, G. (1957/1968) *Novels into Film*. Berkeley: University of California Press.

Bouquet, S. (1996) 'Sweet Movie', *Cahiers du cinéma* 504: 24–5.

Brottman, M. and Sharrett, C. (2002) 'The End of the Road: David Cronenberg's *Crash* and the Fading of the West', *Literature/Film Quarterly* 30 (2): 126–32.

Camblor, M. (1999) 'Death Drive's Joy Ride: David Cronenberg's *Crash*', *Other Voices* 1 (3), http://www.othervoices.org/1.3/mcamblor/crash.html (accessed November 2010).

Carter, A. (1975) 'Notes on the Gothic Mode', *Iowa Review* 6 (3/4): 132–4.

Cornea, C. (2003) 'David Cronenberg's *Crash* and Performing Cyborgs', *The Velvet Light Trap* 52: 4–14.

Craven, R. J. (2000) 'Ironic Empathy in Cronenberg's *Crash*: The Psychodynamics of Postmodern Displacement from a Tenuous Reality', *Quarterly Review of Film and Video* 17 (3): 187–209.

Creed, B. (1998) 'The *Crash* Debate: Anal Wounds, Metallic Kisses', *Screen* 39: 175–9.

Cronenberg, D. (1996) *Crash*. London: Faber.

Ebert, R. (1997) 'Crash (1997)', *Chicago Sun-Times* (21 March), http://rogerebert.suntimes.com/apps/pbcs.dll/article?AID=/19970321/REVIEWS/703210301/1023 (accessed November 2010).

Forman, M. (2001) 'Boys Will Be Boys: David Cronenberg's *Crash* Course in Heavy Mettle', in M. Pomerance (ed.) *Ladies and Gentlemen, Boys and Girls: Gender and Film at the End of the Twentieth Century*, pp. 109–27. Albany: State University of New York Press.

Gerstel, J. (1996) 'And You Can See the Skid Marks Left by the Perplexed after Their First Glimpse', *Toronto Star* (17 May): C1.

Grünberg, S. (1996a) 'Entretien avec David Cronenberg', *Cahiers du cinéma* 504: 26–30.

Grünberg, S. (1996b) 'Rencontre avec James G. Ballard', *Cahiers du cinéma* 504: 31–2.

Grundmann, R. (1996) 'Plight of the Crash Fest Mummies: David Cronenberg's *Crash*', *Cineaste* 22 (4): 24–7.

Harpold, T. (1997) 'Dry Leatherette: Cronenberg's *Crash*', *Postmodern Culture* 7 (3), http://muse.jhu.edu/journals/postmodern_culture/v007/7.3r_harpold.html (accessed November 2010).

Hultkrans, A. (1997) 'Body Work: Andrew Hultkrans Talks with J. G. Ballard and David Cronenberg', *Artforum* 35 (7): 76–81, 118.

Lewis, J. (1991) 'An Interview with J. G. Ballard', *Mississippi Review* 20: 27–40.

Kermode, M. and Petley, J. (1997) 'Road Rage', *Sight and Sound* 7: 16–18.

Mathijs, E. (2008) *The Cinema of David Cronenberg: From Baron of Blood to Cultural Hero*. London: Wallflower.

Morris, P. (1994) *David Cronenberg: A Delicate Balance*. Toronto: ECW Press.

Moure, M. (1995) 'J. G. Ballard: *Rushing to Paradise*: Not a Literary Man', *Spike Magazine*, http://www.spikemagazine.com/0901ballard.php (accessed November 2010).

Rodley, C. (1996) 'Crash: David Cronenberg Talks about His New Film Crash Based on J. G. Ballard's Disturbing Techno-Sex Novel', *Sight and Sound* 6: 7–11.

Rosenbaum, J. (1997) 'Sex Drive', *Chicago Reader* (20 March), http://www.chicagoreader.com/chicago/sex-drive/Content?oid=892953 (accessed November 2010).

Ruddick, N. (1992) 'Ballard/Crash/Baudrillard', *Science-Fiction Studies* 19 (3): 354–60.

Sinclair, I. (1999) *Crash: David Cronenberg's Post-Mortem on J. G. Ballard's 'Trajectory of Fate'*. London: BFI.

Springer, C. (2001) 'The Seduction of the Surface: From *Alice* to *Crash*', *Feminist Media Studies* 1 (2): 197–213.

Vale, V. and Juno, A. (eds) (1984) *Re/Search 8/9: J. G. Ballard*. San Francisco, CA: Re/Search.

Chapter 8

FAHRENHEIT 451
Filming Literary Absence

Aristea Chryssohou

The great numbers of films based on novels suggest an abiding human need to transform the linguistic signs into three-dimensional images. However, the relationship between sign and image in the adaptation of novels is complicated, for 'although both novel and film/TV share this storytelling function, there are significant differences in the methods of production, and in the consumption of their various products' (Giddings et al., 2002: 2). Theories of adaptation that assume the superiority of novel to film now seem archaic, especially in their focus on the degree of a film's fidelity to the source novel. The semiotic approaches to cinema of theoreticians such as Roland Barthes, Umberto Eco and Christian Metz demonstrate that film is a distinct discourse, a language with its own syntactical system and expressive devices (shot, and editing) with which to tell stories. This chapter will closely inspect François Truffaut's 1966 adaptation of Ray Bradbury's novel *Fahrenheit 451* (1953) and compare the narrative and structural elements of novel and film. Special emphasis will be given to the issue of orality and how two 'authors' use their medium to describe an artificial oral society.

Ray Bradbury is widely regarded as one of the most accomplished writers of science fiction, horror and mystery. *Fahrenheit 451*, one of his most popular novels, was the expansion of a 25,000-word novella initially entitled 'The Fireman' (1951). The action of the novel unfolds in and around an unspecified city in a fictional future sometime in the twenty-first century. Power has been seized by an absolutist regime whose main agenda involves the elimination of any intellectual activity, resulting in the banning of reading and the persecution of anyone holding books. Safeguarding this new order, firemen have been assigned to uncover illegal libraries and destroy them. Guy Montag is a fireman obedient to superiors until he meets an interesting and rebellious 17-year-old girl named Clarisse, who forces him to re-evaluate the legitimacy of his actions. Montag breaks the law, helped by Faber, an elderly professor, and starts collecting and reading books. The plot reaches a climax when Mildred, Montag's wife, turns him in to the police, forcing him to escape after burning his captain alive. Montag ends up in the forest in a marginal society of educated people who memorize books in order to save them from oblivion while the rest of the world is annihilated in a nuclear holocaust.

The novel has been interpreted mainly as a caustic study of censorship imposed by authoritarian ruling systems, in particular the Nazi's public book-burnings and the suppression of free thought by McCarthyism in the US in the 1950s. For this reason, *Fahrenheit 451* often appears in critical reviews next to George Orwell's *1984* (1949) and Aldous Huxley's *Brave New World* (1932). However, in 2007, Ray Bradbury, commenting on Michael Moore's allusion to his novel in the title of his documentary *Fahrenheit 9/11* (2004), declared that his book was not about censorship but rather how television destroys interest in literature and depicts a distorted reality (Boyle Johnston, 2007). This comment may actually be the invisible thread that seems to connect the 1953 novel with the 1966 film. As George Bluestone noted, Truffaut was drawn to the novel because he loved books and enjoyed speculating about the future and not because he was especially interested in science fiction or dystopias (Bluestone, 1967: 3).

Fahrenheit 451 was released in theatres in November 1966, although the director had already purchased the rights in 1962 and had subsequently sold them to the future producer of the film Lewis Allen. The US$900,000 budget film was considered a rather expensive production for the time, especially compared to the low-budget, black-and-white French films that Truffaut had directed before then (Allen, 1985: 113). Anglo Enterprises and Vineyard Film Ltd production companies handled the production, while most of the film was shot in Pinewood Studios in London. *Fahrenheit 451*, its director's first colour movie, had a 112-minute duration and was filmed by Nicolas Roeg, while its musical score was composed by Bernard Herrmann, best known for his long and successful cooperation with horror master Alfred Hitchcock. It featured actors that had worked with Truffaut before, Oskar Werner as Guy Montag, Julie Christie in the dual role of Clarisse and Linda Montag, while Captain Beatty was portrayed, successfully by general admission, by Cyril Cusack.

Truffaut was one of the leading figures in the French *New Wave* (*Nouvelle Vague*), initially as a critic and later on as a director, and was the main inspirer of the auteur theory. Persisting in technical excellence, outdoor shooting and cinematic modernization, all *Nouvelle Vague* directors (Jean-Luc Godard, Jacques Rivette, and later Roger Vadim and Bertrand Tavernier being some representative names) strongly believed that every film was the incarnation of their personal creative vision. Faithful to the auteur theory, Truffaut had a say in even the minutest detail and apart from directing, he co-authored the script with Louis Richard, despite their limited mastery of the English language. This gave rise to some of the harshest criticism Truffaut ever received, since viewers as well as critics underlined the script's stiff and dry language (Crowther, 1966; Foster, 2006). Truffaut was apparently a lot more pleased with the French dubbing he later oversaw for the film's release in France, since his mother tongue allowed him a more fluent expression of nuances and emotions. In an interview he gave to C. T. Samuels, he admits: 'if I had done the film in French, I would have had complete control of the language; in English, I never quite knew if a line was right'; and continues: 'in *Fahrenheit 451* I was blocked by my imperfect control over the dialogue, and therefore, I was frustrated' (Samuels, 1972). In any case, it is easily understood why the film critic Matthew M. Foster, who views film mainly as a collaborative art form, rejects this one-man show approach; when he characterizes *Fahrenheit 451* as 'a monument of arrogant filmmaking', he sees it as a paradigm for the inadequacies of the auteur theory itself (Foster, 2006). *Nouvelle Vague* supporters often condemn this movie as an unfortunate attempt at a genre that the director had limited knowledge of and describe this meeting between the *New Wave* canon and the science-fiction genre as a 'marriage [that] isn't quite a happy one' (Clinkenbeard, 2011). On the other hand, science-fiction fans are of the opinion that this film barely makes it into the genre since it merely touches on issues of dystopia and futurity. Many Internet users that review the film badly on *IMDb* tend to characterize it as a 'not typical', 'awkward' or 'incidental' science-fiction movie, while others find it 'more hitchcockian [sic] than sci-fi'.[1] In any case, they all lament the non-use of futuristic elements and regret Truffaut's omission of the Mechanical Hound. However, Bradbury himself looked favourably on the film, claiming that 'Truffaut has captured the soul and essence of the book. He has been careful and subtle in his shadings and emotions. He has escaped making a technological James Bond film, and made, instead, the love story of, not a man and a woman, but a man and a library, a man and a book' (Kael, 2000: 81).

If we adopt Geoffrey Wagner's categorization of cinematic adaptations, *Fahrenheit 451* probably falls into the category of transposition, since the literary work has been adapted for the screen *grosso modo* as it was (Kaklamanidou, 2006: 38–9). The narrative line follows the one in the novel, the characters show minimal differentiation and there is no time shift of the plot. The cinematic narrator is extradiegetic, while focalization is sometimes zero, which means that it is totally coordinated with the omniscient narrator of the book, who offers to the reader much more information than any of the characters have access to. When at times focalization becomes internal, it always remains oriented towards Guy Montag's character, in keeping with the frequent use of free indirect speech in the book. However, narrative consistency cannot account for the 'feeling of disappointment or disturbance' (Bluestone, 1967: 3) experienced by science-fiction fans and most of Truffaut's devoted admirers. To do that we must isolate the specific narrative functions that were adapted, altered or omitted in the process. According to Barthes, narrative functions are divided in 'functions proper' and 'indices' (Barthes, 1985: 167). The former denote all those elements that constitute the plot: that is to say, the events that are linearly connected as well as the characters' actions that push the plot to its climax and resolution. These functions are further subdivided into 'cardinal functions', or 'nuclei', and 'catalysers', secondary acts that assist in the delineation of main events complementing the nuclei. By contrast, the indices, including the subcategories of 'indices proper' and 'informants', refer to diffuse pieces of information that enrich character profiles and help create a fuller picture of the heroes' psychology or the narrative ambience (Barthes, 1985: 167–206). How a director chooses to interpret the novel's indices and to what extent those will be altered in the process of shaping the film's *mise-en-scène* may lead a cinematic adaptation in completely different directions.

Truffaut's adaptation of the novel involves the transformation of indices rather than cardinal functions, as there is minimal narrative deviation on the level of plot and fabula, but considerable differentiation on the descriptive level concerning the characters' psychological alienation and the film's dystopian atmosphere. The most important differences in characterization between novel and film consist of the omission of the elderly professor Faber and the change in Clarisse's role. Omitting Faber may be explained by linking it with other negative portrayals of father figures in Truffaut's films, a theme perhaps derived from the experience of rejection and abandonment by his own father and more clearly seen in autobiographical films like *Les quatre cents coups* (1959) and *Baisers volés* (1968). From a psychoanalytic point of view, the novel *Fahrenheit 451* features two powerful father figures that seem to claim Montag, namely the negative figure of Captain Beatty and the positive model represented by Faber, who finally wins Montag over. In the film, Truffaut chooses to make no reference to this opposition, instead making Clarisse the female counterpart of Faber who rescues Montag from 'evil father' Beatty. Whereas in the novel Clarisse is pronounced dead on page 52, in the movie she survives her prosecutors and joins Montag in the Book People camp. She becomes his friend, mentor, fellow-traveller and sister-in-arms but not his mistress. Contrary to the rest of his films, Truffaut refuses to further elaborate the underlying romantic attraction between Montag and Clarisse, not wishing to violate the boundaries of the science-fiction genre which traditionally excludes romantic love stories or treats them as a subplot. Bluestone offers another possible reason, namely that Truffaut belongs to a tradition of French creators who cannot portray sexual fulfilment without at the same time showing love fading over time and being crushed under the weight of society. Truffaut, faithful to this rule that shows love as elusive moments leading to an inevitable destructive end, chose not to have Montag and Clarisse fall in love, since he could not depict their love without finally destroying it (Bluestone, 1967: 6).

On the level of secondary narrative functions, the ones Barthes coined as catalysers, we can perceive certain changes here as well, albeit changes that do not affect the direction of the narrative. Minor incidents, belonging to the scriptwriting ingenuity of Truffaut and Richard, simply assist in drawing a more complete picture of Clarisse. This need arises due to circumstances, given that the time of Clarisse's presence in the film has been extended. The viewer now needs additional information on the life and actions of the young girl that the reader of the book does not, since Clarisse vanishes in the middle of the first chapter in the novel. A series of events, such as the coffee that Clarisse and Montag share, or the visit to the school, from which the former has been fired, are absent from the book. Furthermore, secondary incidents, such as Montag's forced entry in Captain Beatty's office and the secret meeting of the two main characters in the basement where they burn lists of names of illegal library holders, are additions by Truffaut. They do not distract from the plot; on the contrary, their insertion contributes to a smooth transition to the narrative outcome, similar to the original text.

As already noted, the deviation of Truffaut's filmic version from Bradbury's literary text mainly stems from the differentiation on the level of indices proper and informants. Slight changes give rise to quite different aesthetic results, since the so-called narrative ambience is significantly altered in the transition from page to celluloid. *Fahrenheit 451*'s director, trying to convey the dystopian atmosphere

Bradbury describes, opts to emphasize certain aspects that are of interest to him, obscuring or omitting others that do not suit his purpose. Music and *mise-en-scène* take on a leading role, especially if we take into account the absence of a voice-over narrator that would offer clarifying explanations of actions and behaviours. Consequently, while Ray Bradbury remains loyal to sf novel conventions and selects an imaginary twenty-first century future as the theatre of action, whose sole temporal index is the intermission of two nuclear wars from 1990 onwards, Truffaut further complicates temporal location. He attempted to make the future immediate, personal and intimate, to create an atmosphere that is 'strange rather than extravagant', and to 'construct a fable set in the electronic age' (Kael, 2000: 80). The director himself in *Cahiers du cinéma* confessed that he wanted his fable to take place 'in the world as we know it, but with a slight anticipation in time' (Truffaut, cited in Bluestone, 1967: 30).

To achieve the desired effect, Truffaut blurred the boundaries between present and past in a way that reminds one of Godard's *Alphaville* (1965), although the latter insists even more on the dehumanizing aspect of modernist architecture, managing to transform Paris into a nightmare city. Montag's house, Linda's dresses and hair styles, and even the spectacular monorail were all unchanged from the 1960s, with the solitary exception of the enormous flat-screen television sets that disturbingly anticipate our own present. Certainly, this choice denotes neither lack of imagination nor budget restraints. On the contrary, it is the outcome of a totally conscious aesthetic decision to create a neutral and unidentifiable setting that might be found anywhere or nowhere. Truffaut instructed his set and costume designer Tony Walton to create a sterile atmosphere of alienation; the décor was to be 'immediately forgotten', as anything else would signify that 'they had failed' (Bluestone, 1967: 3). At the same time, some props date back to the 1930s, while the house where Clarisse's family resides is nineteenth-century. Truffaut thus leaves untouched all that is related to eras of sincere and essential human communication. Futuristic details, on the other hand, are nowhere to be seen. The frightening Mechanical Hound that appears at key moments in Bradbury's novel, enhancing the dystopian fear of a machine-governed society, is completely absent. So too are jet airplanes, sensory glove holes that open doors, and references to the destructive nuclear war that haunts the whole novel. Truffaut offers a much more immediate, emotional and human portrayal of dystopia. Undoubtedly, his strongest comment lies in the recurrent motifs of alienation and hedonism, such as the close-ups of lonely people on the train touching or caressing themselves. In this society obsessed with speed and visual stimuli, the inability of people to establish contact with fellow human beings turns them into wretched narcissists who only adore their beautiful selves.

In concluding this comparative analysis, special reference has to be made to the transformation of the so-called informants (i.e. the small details that enhance the narrative ambience). The most important change Truffaut makes on that level is linked again to Clarisse. In the novel Clarisse is a 17-year old girl, who faces problems at school due to her eccentricity (stemming from her 'literacy') and the inability to function as a 'socialized' member following the rules of the totalitarian regime. Her young age, her overwhelming enthusiasm and her craving for life and human contact make her the exact opposite of Montag's wife, Mildred, who appears to be totally mesmerized by her tele-family. Apparently of little importance, this shift creates a huge impact on the film because it enables Truffaut to cast Julie Christie in a double role, as Clarisse and as Montag's wife, who is called Linda in the film. Truffaut's artistic experiment puts on the screen two identical women, except for the length of their hair and the difference in their gaze, since throughout the film Linda's alienation shows in her empty and icy look. Montag is thus liberated from the domination of the image and is free to focus on the essence of the two women rather than their stunning looks. Christie's double casting also alludes to Alfred Hitchcock's *Vertigo* (1958), in which Kim Novak played what seem to be two different roles, Madeleine Elster and Judy Barton. Truffaut's decision met with criticism, however; according to Don Allen, it 'simply blurs the distinction between the two characters, contrary to the whole spirit of the novel' (Allen, 1985: 114), and Pauline Kael described it as a movie 'cliché' not in the least effective (Kael, 2000: 79).

The world of *Fahrenheit 451* is totalitarian, violent and hedonistic. Self-absorbed people are entertained by weird interactive TV shows; they depend on medication to induce euphoria and sleep, while they seek to externalize their repressed violent instincts at every given opportunity. Above all, they resent books, have forgotten or never acquired reading skills, and lead their lives immersed in a stagnant nihilistic state rejecting any kind of intellectual activity. It is unclear whether it was the absence of writing that led to the dystopian reality or vice versa. Captain Beatty, as a representative of the regime, explains that books were never banned, and insists that people simply stopped reading due to lack of time, the prevalence of the image and, above all, because books stirred hostilities and rivalries between different social groups.

This idea of writing as a 'source of evil' is not new. In fact it can be traced back to the beginnings of human thought. In Plato's *Phaedrus* (ca. 370 BC), Socrates condemns writing as inhumane, as a construct that destroys memory and weakens the mind. This notion of precedence of the spoken over the written that was further supported by different thinkers such as Rousseau, Saussure or Lévi-Strauss was finally challenged by Derrida. In his work *Of Grammatology*, Derrida opposes 'logocentrism' and argues that writing can be as much of 'presence' as speech is considered to be. For him language develops through interplay between speech and writing, and this leads him to denying that *logos* (the spoken word) can be closer to the 'truth' than writing (Derrida, 1976: 19–25). Strongly reminiscent of the current reservations associated with computer use, writing has for many years been considered an artificial product that simply recorded speech and ultimately detached the author from the text and depersonalized it. But, as accurately pointed out by Walter Ong, in the passing of centuries, writing and later typography were linked to the concept of power, while the written text acquired the almost magical quality of the prophet or the oracle: a book perpetually repeats the author's utterances, without the possibility of his words being directly refuted or discredited. This is the main reason why we tend to regard what we read in a book as true, but it is also the main cause of book-burnings throughout history. 'A text that reports what the whole world knows to be a lie, will forever state its lie, as long as it exists', claims Ong, reaching the conclusion that 'the texts are inherently contumacious' (Ong, 1988: 79).

The modern man, whose conscience is widely believed to be completely shaped by writing, is often found trapped between the need for intellectual strength and the fear of it. This is probably the point that both author and director of *Fahrenheit 451* seek to explore further by assigning the explanation of the book-banning phenomenon to Captain Beatty. However, Beatty, being the most zealous enemy of books, is the only one who knows how to read, also displaying a thorough knowledge of world literature. According to him, books threaten the reader's peace of mind and serenity by deceiving him or her: each book contradicts the other and the writers attack each other through their words, while the reader ends up confused and despondent.

Despite Beatty's little speech on the demonization of writing, Bradbury finally seems to adopt the general rule that regards textual knowledge as a synonym for power. The Captain himself, in order to establish the reality of his words about the history and founding of the firemen profession, refers back to perhaps the only written text that is exempted from the prohibition, the so-called Rule Book: 'Established, 1790, to burn English-influenced books in the Colonies. First Fireman: Benjamin Franklin' (Bradbury, 1953: 34). As Susan Spencer argues, even in an oral society that is fighting for its survival and for the banishment of the last textual trace, the authorities base their power on written speech and invoke it to persuade non-believers (Spencer, 2000: 102).

Truffaut keeps Captain Beatty's character intact and in a scene showing a raid in a hidden library, he has him reproducing excerpts from the original Bradbury text almost verbatim. Truffaut's comment possibly lies in one of the close-ups on the book titles, which reveals Hitler's *Mein Kampf* (1925) among the hidden books about to be burnt. With subtle irony, he reminds the viewer of the relativity of any extreme cause: the book that, in a past absolutist regime, was responsible for the burning of millions of others finds itself in a similar position in the future. (On the other hand, perhaps the very existence of

Figure 1. Fahrenheit 451. Photo courtesy of Universal Pictures/Photofest.

Mein Kampf in the secret library is a comment on what can ultimately be considered canonical literature.)

Bradbury's worship of books as an objectified source of knowledge certainly underlies the writing of *Fahrenheit 451*. But descriptions of book-burnings in the novel are scarce, probably due to the revulsion that this phenomenon caused the author:

> [...] the house jumped up in a gorging fire that burned the evening sky red and yellow and black. He strode in a swarm of fireflies. He wanted above all like the old joke, to shove a marshmallow on a stick in the furnace, while the flapping pigeon-winged books died on the porch and lawn of the house. (Bradbury, 1953: 3)

Bradbury begins his narration with this description and never returns to this unsettling spectacle. By contrast, Truffaut uses the book-burning motif often and very effectively. Don Allen observes that Truffaut's affection for the book as an object, for its look, its feel, even its smell, borders on fetishism. The sight of the book being incinerated appears to shock the director to the point that he chooses to shoot it with the intensity of a human cremation. And it seems quite intentional that in the climax of the film these two images are combined in the scene with the old lady choosing to be burned alive rather than abandon her library (Allen, 1985: 116–17).

For Bradbury, the return to orality brings about a society of linguistic and cultural deprivation. For Truffaut it also means alienation and lack of communication. Nevertheless, his efforts to depict a world 'inhabited by zombies whose linguistic and thus emotional concepts have atrophied during a Dark Age' (Allen, 1985: 116) are not always successful. The film, as well as the book, leaves unanswered the questions concerning the language and reading skills of the characters, while Montag's transition from illiteracy to fluency happens overnight. More satisfactory is Truffaut's depiction of a society ruled by television: the wall screens that Bradbury conceived of are rendered convincingly and the TV shows effectively communicate the state of intellectual dullness.

Television as a visual medium is dominant and exclusively used for propaganda. It shapes consciences, supports government mechanisms and terrifies. The news-report pictures of a young man being bullied in broad daylight by police officers because of his long hair, as well as the staged helicopter pursuit and cold-blooded murder of an innocent citizen who resembles Montag, testify to a negative attitude towards the new medium in Truffaut's film. The absence of any reference to cinema, both in the film and the novel, was noted by several film critics. Bluestone speaks of it as 'a big omission' and contends that 'Truffaut's mistake was making a film about books instead of a film about movies' (Bluestone, 1967: 5). But that is perhaps relative, if we consider Stam's claim that cinema is nothing more than 'a form of writing that borrows (elements) from the remaining forms of writing' (Stam, 2005: 1), and that the absence of literary narration naturally leads to the absence of cinematic narration. Besides, even though Truffaut might have felt threatened as a filmmaker by the emergence of television in the 1960s, it should be noted that nowhere in the movie does television as a medium acquire a narrative function. It does not reproduce events and simply broadcasts fabricated information, functioning as a tool for the mind-control of the masses.

The 'orality vs literacy' topic is persistent in Truffaut's films; it can be traced in *L'enfant sauvage* (1970), as well as in the beginning of *Les quatre cents coups* (1959). In *Fahrenheit 451*, this orality issue becomes more of an obsession expressed through several directorial devices, such as the choice to represent the total omission of writing from the screen with colour-coded medicine bottles, service files containing solely pictures and newspapers resembling comic-strip stories. But the ultimate device conveying the essence of a strictly oral and completely televised society are the film's opening credits, unusual in cinematography history in that they are not written but spoken. The same technique was later repeated in *M*A*S*H* (Robert Altman, 1970), but was used for the first time in *The Magnificent Ambersons* (Orson Welles, 1942), where Orson Welles speaks the closing credits in a voice-over. The *Fahrenheit 451* credits are in fact recited to the audience, combined with subsequent close-ups to rooftops with several TV antennas. Each contributor's name coincides with an extreme close-up on a different antenna, underscored by Herrmann's music. According to Denis Hollier and Alyson Waters, the credits are evidence of Truffaut's successful transition from one medium to another:

> Bradbury's book described a world after the letter. But it was a book. Truffaut's film, however, has broken with the Gutenberg Galaxy. It doesn't simply represent the world of the novel, it inscribes itself in it. Not one word, not one sentence appears on screen to connect the audience to the world of reading. The film is inscribed in a world of images that – with the final passing of the age of the letter – will remain eternally before the letter [avant la lettre]. The authority of the letter has gone up in smoke. It's the end of typography. (Hollier and Waters, 1996: 17)

Contemporary criticism of the *Fahrenheit 451* film adaptation did not manage to break from the snare of fidelity, focusing too much on its deviations from the source novel. Other critics found it difficult to reconcile with Truffaut's other films, while the director himself admitted that he did not feel particularly drawn to the science-fiction genre, since he believed it to be 'far from reality, too arbitrary in its events [and] incapable of rousing any emotions in [him]' (Samuels, 1972). Nevertheless, Truffaut undertook the project and managed to create a strikingly different science-fiction movie which, stripped off of the special effects and imaginary technology, resembled more what Bradbury had earlier called the 'love story between a man and a book' (Kael, 2000: 81). Above all, Truffaut proved that when an artist is inspired by a subject, he should not fear to experiment and explore the boundaries of his artistic vision. I feel that his film bares the stamp of a great director who, inspired by Bradbury's nightmare, did not attempt to render on screen another man's artistic scope. Instead, he treated his original source with respect, dwelled (perhaps too much) on the relationship between man and literature and finally rendered us a sensitive science-fiction film.

Note

1 Quotes are taken from various user reviews on *IMDb*, http://www.imdb.com/title/tt0060390/reviews?filter=hate (accessed September 2011).

References

Allen, D. (1985) *Finally Truffaut*. London: Martin Secker & Warburg Ltd.

Barthes, R. (1985) 'Introduction à l'analyse structurale des récits', in *L'aventure sémiologique*, pp. 167–206. Paris: Seuil.

Bluestone, G. (1967) 'The Fire and the Future', *Film Quarterly* 20 (4): 3–10.

Boyle Johnston, A. E. (2007) 'Ray Bradbury: *Fahrenheit 451* Misinterpreted', *LA Weekly* (30 May), http://www.laweekly.com/2007–05–31/news/ray-bradbury-fahrenheit-451-misinterpreted/ (accessed January 2009).

Bradbury, R. (1953) *Fahrenheit 451*. New York: Ballantine Books.

Bradbury, R. (2007) 'Ray Bradbury on *Fahrenheit 451* Inspiration', *YouTube*, http://www.youtube.com/watch?hl=nl&v=7aKItfLeso4 (accessed December 2008).

Clinkenbeard, J. (2011) 'Oeuvre: Truffaut: Fahrenheit 451', *Spectrum Culture* (7 April), http://spectrumculture.com/2011/04/oeuvre-truffaut-fahrenheit-451.html (consulted May 2011).

Crowther, B. (1966) 'Screen: "Fahrenheit 451" Makes Burning Issue Dull', *The New York Times* (November 15), http://www.nytimes.com/books/99/04/18/specials/truffaut-451.html?_r=2 (consulted September 2008).

De Koster, K. (ed.) (2000) *Readings on Fahrenheit 451*. San Diego: Greenhaven Press.

Derrida, J. (1976) *Of Grammatology*, trans. G. C. Spivak. Baltimore: The Johns Hopkins University Press.

Foster, M. M. (2006) 'Review: *Fahrenheit 451* (1966)', http://www.fosteronfilm.com/sf/dystopia/f451.htm/ (accessed September 2008).

Giddings, R., Selby, K. and Wensley, C. (2002) 'The Literature/Screen Debate: An Overview', in R. Giddings, K. Selby and C. Wensley (eds) *Screening the Novel: The Theory and Practice of Literary Dramatization*, pp. 1–27. Palgrave.

Hollier, D. and Waters, A. (1996) 'The Death of Paper: A Radio Play', *October* 78: 3–20.

Kael, P. (2000) 'The Book's Censorship Metaphor Does Not Work – But the Movie Is Worse', in K. de Koster (ed.) *Readings on Fahrenheit 451*, pp. 76–83. San Diego: Greenhaven Press.

Kaklamanidou, D. (2006) *Otan to mythistorima synantise ton kinimatografo: theoritikes proseggiseis kai sygkritikes analyseis*. Athens: Aigokeros.

McFarlane, B. (1996) *Novel to Film: An Introduction to the Theory of Adaptation*. Oxford: Clarendon Press.

Ong, W. J. (1988) *Orality and Literacy: The Technologizing of the Word*. London and New York: Routledge.

Samuels, C. T. (1972) 'François Truffaut', in C. T. Samuels, *Encountering Directors*, pp. 33–57. New York: Putnam, http://www.industrycentral.net/director_interviews/FT01.HTM (accessed June 2011).

Spencer, S. (2000) 'Literature – and the Literate – Will Prevail', in K. de Koster (ed.) *Readings on Fahrenheit 451*, pp. 100–6. San Diego: Greenhaven Press.

Stam, R. (2005) 'Introduction', in R. Stam and A. Raengo (eds) *Literature and Film: A Guide to the Theory and Practice of Film Adaptation*, pp. 1–52. Oxford: Blackwell.

CHAPTER 9

QUIET EARTHS
ADAPTATION, REPRESENTATION AND NATIONAL IDENTITY
IN NEW ZEALAND'S APOCALYPSE

Andrea Wright

Craig Harrison's 1981 novel *The Quiet Earth* was the foundation for one of the most recognized films produced by a New Zealand director in the 1980s. Significantly, Geoff Murphy's 1985 adaptation of Harrison's novel aligns the narrative with themes prominent in New Zealand's reinvigorated film industry. While the film has gained considerable attention, both as a popular science-fiction text, and as a focus for studies of New Zealand identity on screen, the rarity of Harrison's book has thus far prevented an analysis of the film-as-adaptation.

Although Harrison's novel and Murphy's film follow the same basic premise – that a catastrophic 'Effect' has altered the world – they differ in several important respects. In order to elucidate these differences, this essay explores the notable contrasts between the texts' representation of gender, race and nation, situating both within their national, cultural and historical context. Additionally, it explores Murphy's divergence from Harrison's story within the milieu of the New Zealand film industry.

Of particular significance nationally and culturally is the distinctive image of the New Zealand man alone that is central to both novel and film. The prominence of the lone male is in all likelihood symptomatic of the dominant perception of New Zealand as 'man-made', a view that is evident in gender-specific accounts of nation-building and national identity. Jock Phillips, for example, argues that:

> In New Zealand the male stereotype, rather than the female, has been unusually influential upon the lives of both women and men – it has become identified with the process of national definition. There can be few nations which have so single-mindedly defined themselves through male heroes. (Phillips, 1987: vii)

Claudia Bell, in her examination of pakeha identity (New Zealanders of non-Maori, predominantly European decent), observes that the emerging character of the nation in the nineteenth century was founded on labour and hard work, with the settlers seeing 'themselves as conquerors, tamers and owners of the environment' (Bell, 1996: 36). Such possession and cultivation was achieved through masculine endeavours – farming in particular – which led, perhaps unavoidably, to the creation of particular myths regarding white masculinity. Fundamentally, as Phillips emphasizes, 'New Zealand has been oppressively "a man's country"' (Phillips, 1987: vii). Cultural representations of pakeha masculinity were further defined in the first half of the twentieth century through popular literature. In particular, John Mulgan's 1939 *Man Alone* was highly influential in inspiring the dominant cultural archetype of the eponymous figure. The novel charts the troubled attempts of an ostracized First World War veteran to settle into civilian life and his consequent retreat into the bush after inadvertently shooting the farmer he is working for. Andrew Spicer argues that such 'archetypes need to be conceived, not as Jungian transcendent unchanging universals, but as complex, mutable signifiers operating within specific national and historical contexts' (Spicer, 2000: 1). Indeed, this cultural conceptualizing of masculinity was informed by the masculine gender bias operative in the process of nation-building, in the conditions and nature of colonial settlement and in the country's geography, rather than in universal or fixed notions of a masculine type.

In Harrison's *The Quiet Earth*, geneticist John Hobson is alone for the first half of the novel. Using first-person narrative, Harrison vividly recounts Hobson's mental and physical experience of being isolated in the titular 'quiet earth'. The novel opens with John waking from an intense nightmare of falling. His watch on the nightstand has stopped at 6.12. When he rises from his bed and looks outside, the town of Thames is eerily silent. After leaving his motel room, he investigates his surroundings cautiously, and the realization that he is possibly the last man alive gives him the courage to explore the unoccupied homes and vacant retail and business premises around him. Harrison's detailed homodiegetic account of this investigation is balanced skilfully between focalized descriptions of external sights, sounds and smells and the internalized struggle John experiences adjusting to his new situation. Moreover, this internalization becomes crucial in providing possible explanations for the cataclysmic Effect at the book's climax.

The mysterious nature of New Zealand's apparent apocalypse remains elusive throughout the narrative, and Harrison's prose often hints that the end of the world is yet more intriguing than the disappearance of humankind. For instance, John thinks to himself: 'An enormous isolation and loneliness, a sensation not of being observed but of being ignored, totally abandoned, was all I could separate from the confusion and fear' (Harrison, 1981/1986: 13). As he searches for 'survivors' he ponders:

> The question of whether I was really seeing what I seemed to be seeing kept recurring. I might be mad. This was met with a dodging agility. Madness is a deviation from what is normal, I thought; it is abnormal for people to disappear; I have not disappeared; I *am* now normality. *I think therefore I am.* (Harrison, 1981/1986: 24)

Such philosophical contemplation is precipitated by John's circumstances, but it also resonates with the questions of identity and belonging that preoccupy the New Zealand man alone.

John travels to Auckland, New Zealand's largest city, where, he reasons, there must be someone else alive. Once there, he finds no answers, no living person, just a desolate city and the smouldering wreckage of an Air New Zealand plane that has crashed in a suburb – personal effects from the aircraft and the homes are strewn over the ground, but there are no bodies. At the facility where he worked, John discovers the remains of his former head of research, Perrin, and the presence of the corpse suggests that he had died before the Effect occurred. After accidentally sealing himself in the laboratory by setting off the shutdown procedure to prevent radiation leaks, John escapes with a locked box retrieved from Perrin's office. Upon leaving Auckland he begins his journey south to Wellington. He travels through other formerly vibrant, now deserted locations, and on a road outside Rotorua he swerves to avoid a white, hairless, drooling dog or goat-like biological abomination. He is plagued by the overwhelming sense that an unseen evil stalks him, and this encounter fuels his increasing paranoia. In a dark hotel room at Rotorua, a popular tourist destination and the place where he honeymooned with his ex-wife, Joanne, he sits with a shotgun in his mouth.

With such source material, it is perhaps unsurprising that Murphy's *The Quiet Earth* offers the ultimate example of the cinematic man alone. Spicer has argued that the career of the film's leading actor, Bruno Lawrence, made him typical of the dominant New Zealand masculine archetype: resourceful, independent, itinerant, wary of settling and family life, with a capability for violence (Spicer, 2000: 1). Significantly, the new wave of New Zealand cinema that began in the 1970s was shaped by pakeha men and the period of filmmaking between approximately 1977 and 1985 can be characterized as a 'boy's own cinema' that was predominantly concerned with white, heterosexual male experience. This cycle of films exemplified by productions including *Sleeping Dogs* (Roger Donaldson, 1977), *Smash Palace* (Roger Donaldson, 1981) and *Goodbye Pork Pie* (Geoff Murphy, 1981) shows the persistence of gender and racial bias in New Zealand cultural production. In Murphy's *The Quiet Earth*, Lawrence becomes the quintessential alienated pakeha 'Kiwi bloke' dependent on his own wits and ingenuity. In renaming Lawrence's character 'Zac' rather than 'John' Hobson, Murphy alludes to the apocalypticism of his narrative. Where 'John' is Hebrew for 'the Grace of the Lord', sug-

Figure 1. Bruno Lawrence in *The Quiet Earth.* Photo courtesy of Skouras Pictures/Photofest.

gesting an ambiguous, possibly ironic reading of the character's situation, Zac alludes to Robert C. O'Brien's 1975 post-apocalyptic novel *Z for Zachariah*, implying that his central character is, indeed, the 'last man'.

Murphy divides the film into two acts. The first enunciates the corresponding half of Harrison's novel. Following a title sequence that shows a rising sun (intertextually resonant with most audiences familiar with apocalyptic cinema), the opening shots of the film parallel Harrison's text: Zac wakes up in a darkened room, disoriented, with the clocks stopped at 6.12. However, Harrison's lengthy exploration of the small town is severely abridged, the order of events altered, and Zac makes his way more rapidly to Auckland and then to the laboratory where he worked. Although he does engage in the logical and practical task of attempting to locate other survivors, unlike John, Zac initially appears to relish his last-man-on-earth status. He moves into a luxurious house, surrounds himself with the trappings of wealth and drinks champagne for breakfast. He also breaks into a shopping centre and indulges in consumerist pleasures, which, as Jonathan Rayner points out, imitates George A. Romero's 1979 *Dawn of the Dead* (Rayner, 1999: 15).

Murphy's cinematic articulation of Zac's crisis as he realizes the implications of his situation is less subtle than Harrison's prose. Zac stands in front of a mirror dressed in a woman's satin slip. It appears that this act is not just experimentation with taboo, but realization of what he has lost. This sequence loosely parallels a section of Harrison's book when John gazes into the mirror at the hotel in Rotorua and sees Joanne. This is a moment where an acute sense of loss consumes the protagonist and acts as a prelude to an extended analepsis detailing his troubled marriage and his part in the death of their autistic son Peter. Conversely, Zac descends into mania. He frantically wires up a PA system to give an address to an audience of cardboard figures of assorted celebrities and world leaders, declaring himself 'ruler of this quiet earth'. The next day he challenges God in a church by threatening a statue of the crucified Christ with his firearm and shouting, 'If you don't come out I'll shoot the kid'. He fires and nothing happens. He continues his rampage using a large mechanical digger to destroy everything in his path, but stops abruptly when he runs over a pram in the street. He hurriedly gets out of the cab to check if there is a child inside: there is not. He sits down, the futility of his actions clear, and puts a shotgun in mouth.

This section of the film, while clearly linked to Harrison's text, showcases the performance of its leading actor and is perhaps a more conventional representation of the last-man-on-earth scenario, recalling, for instance, the filmic adaptation of Richard Matheson's *I Am Legend* (1954), *The Omega Man* (Boris Sagal, 1971). Zac gives in to his destructive impulses by running amok in Auckland, but John denies himself such release. John contemplates setting fire to an insurance building, stating: 'Part of my mind was disturbed by the thoughts of destruction and the forward thrill I derived from this' (Harrison, 1981/1986: 71). But, he reasons, 'Burning a tower would be pure spite, no catharsis, just kicking a hollow coffin' (Harrison, 1981/1986: 72). This distinction between the characters is important in situating the film within the first phase of the revival of the New Zealand film industry. Through his actions, Zac seems to embody the countercultural rebelliousness often associated with the Kiwi bloke found in new wave cinema. Reid Perkins, in his discussion of the influence of counterculture on Murphy's films, argues that the character's destructive impulses 'are not meant to be seen as mere acts of insanity but as cries of rage, acts of revolt against a Society which is paradoxically, despite its absence, still present' (Perkins, 1986: 18). Zac's conflict, Perkins explains, is with the materialistic world represented by shopping malls, large houses and top secret installations. For a new society to emerge, the mistakes of the old one that culminated in its destruction have to be avoided. However, as Perkins (1986: 18) points out, the questions of 'what happens now?' remain largely underdeveloped as the film moves into the second act.

Although the protagonists of both book and film effectively conclude the first part of the narrative with a shotgun in their mouth, neither carries out their abortive suicide attempt. Soon after, they discover that they are not the only survivors. In the film, Murphy establishes a familiar sexual triangle between Zac, the Maori Api (Peter Smith) and Joanne (Alison Routledge), thus foregrounding the text's prominent racial theme through the representation of race and the dramatization of racial tensions. The dynamic between the last three people on earth which drives the second half of the film, and motivates its climax, is absent from the book. In Harrison's novel Joanne exists only in John's memory, thus allowing a greater focus on the relationship between the two men. In this way, the book explores more openly the relationship between pakeha and Maori in New Zealand.

After John decides that he will not kill himself in Rotorua, he resumes his journey to Wellington. On a road deliberately blocked by a sheep truck he encounters the first living person he has seen since the Effect. Apirana Maketu is a lance corporal in the New Zealand army and far better equipped than John to survive alone. Nevertheless, John immediately assumes the role of his superior. When they open a bottle of wine to celebrate finding each other, John muses: 'I drank enough to become pleasantly relaxed, and sat there watching him with the thought drifting into my mind that maybe I had acquired Man Friday' (Harrison, 1981/1986: 114). John's attitude towards the Maori seems to stem from his childhood and the racist influence of his aunt and uncle who brought him up after the death of his parents. John admits that he has had little to do with Maoris and that his encounters with them have been infrequent and insignificant. It seems natural to John, therefore, that he should assume leadership:

> . I stood up. He looked around, then turned towards me and said more or less exactly what I wanted him to say.
> 'What's the plan, then?' (Harrison, 1981/1986: 123)

The tension between John and Api is foregrounded in their exchanges over land. In Palmeston North, they arrive at a memorial statue to a Maori chief who was loyal to his colonizers during the nineteenth-century New Zealand land wars, a conflict that was instigated by colonial settlement and the signing-over of significant portions of land to the Crown under the Treaty of Waitangi in 1840. A revival of claims for Maori land rights began in the late 1960s and by 1975 the Waitangi Tribunal was set up to investigate claims for compensation and reinstatement of lost land rights. When Harrison was writing, therefore, the issue of land ownership was a prominent social and political issue. As they contemplate the statue, John once again emphasizes his assumed pre-eminence over the Maori:

> 'Well, you've got it all now,' I said.
> 'All what?'
> 'The land. You can have it back. All yours.'
> He sat up and gave me a look of withering contempt. For a moment I felt almost alarmed.
> 'Oh,' he said, slowly, with heavy sarcasm, 'thank, *you.*' (Harrison, 1981/1986: 131)

In Murphy's film, the hostility between Zac and Api arises as Zac declares himself in charge; he assumes that his superior scientific knowledge and position as the final representative of pakeha patriarchy makes him the natural leader. Api, through his actions and his appearance as the urban warrior dressed in leather trousers, a vest and army boots, is the brawn, racially other, and therefore a follower. But, in what was perhaps an attempt to avoid confronting issues surrounding the land, the rivalry in the film is largely precipitated through their desire for Joanne, the first survivor encountered by Zac. Although she initially sleeps with Zac, Joanne rapidly turns her attention to Api, and Zac realizes that his future does not lie with them. This prompts his decision to drive the truck of explosives into the power grid himself in an attempt to prevent a second Effect from occurring. Ultimately, as Rayner has suggested, by destroying the grid a new world or worlds will be created rather than safe-guarding the old. Joanne and Api's relationship, according to Rayner, is a bicultural compromise that 'cannot accommodate Zac, or rather he does not want to be part of it' (Rayner, 1999: 16). This triangle between Api, Zac and Joanne invites further comparisons with other end-of-the-world cinema that brings together a comparable dynamic, in particular, Ranald Mac-Dougall's 1959 adaptation of M. P. Shiel's *The Purple Cloud* (1901), *The World, the Flesh and the Devil*.

The representation of race in *The Quiet Earth* and its adaptation is perhaps problematic as both texts appear to circulate a narrow portrayal of the Maori that originated in early accounts of the peoples by their European colonizers and nineteenth-century photography. Sam Edwards argues that photographers 'created a series of images which limited potential understanding of Maori and their culture by generalizing social behaviour and cultural characteristics into six main categories' (Edwards, 1989: 19). Of the categories Edwards sums up, which include 'the noble savage', 'the tough aggressive warrior', 'local colour reconstructions of a putative pre-European culture', 'coons and clowns', 'cute kids' and women in 'sexual, mothering or working roles', the most prevalent and regular has been the Maori as warrior (Edwards, 1989: 19–20). Api, in Harrison's book and Murphy's film, is a strong, able, military-trained man with a quick temper and potentially violent nature. Thus, he exists as a contemporary warrior who is often at odds with the white protagonist of the texts. Edwards (1989: 18) notes that while Maori can be visualized as heroic, 'the warrior as aggressor rather than hero has also become a standard figure', particularly in 1980s cinema. However, despite the surface similarities in representation, Harrison's book is more multifaceted in its engagement with New Zealand's underlying racial tensions.

The strain on the relationship between John and Api develops into a fundamental mistrust, with each deeply suspicious of the other. This escalates to a violent conclusion when the young female survivor Api accidentally hits with his car dies. Wild with grief and anger, Api advances on John, who shoots him in the chest. The days leading up to this fatal exchange are interspersed with more analepses as John reads the documents he finds in the box that belonged to Perrin. Additional details of John's work in reactivating dormant genes, the affects of this research on John and his son Peter, and the potential consequences for humankind, are revealed.

John had been struggling to cope with his private life, his health and work. Peter was dead, Joanne had left him, and growing uncertainty about the ethics and safety of genetic experimentation made the continued funding of his research unlikely. Moreover, John had become suspicious that his colleagues, principally Perrin, were conspiring to remove him from the project, and he was suffering from intense headaches and experiencing frequent bouts of confusion, anxiety and guilt. Significantly, this culminates in a mistake in the laboratory, and John is forced to take leave. With his physical and mental state severely compromised, he makes the decision to sabotage the laboratory machinery to kill, or at the very least injure, Perrin, who he considers arrogant and holds responsible for undermining the research. He also makes plans to take his own life. If the world has ended, therefore, it is John's doing; he is driven to it by the unanticipated affects of his research – Peter's condition, the boy's suicide and his own destructive impulses. Similarly, if John now exists in a parallel, distorted world then it is also due his actions and the penalty of his research. In this scenario, the 'real' world continues as it has always done, but John, because of his act of sabotage and his exposure to gene-altering technology, is stranded in an alternative, shifted world.

But, there is also a further possibility. At the end of the story, John once again makes the decision to take his own life. The book ends as it began, and John appears to be stuck in a perpetual, nightmarish temporal loop. Hence, in one interpretation, New Zealand's apocalypse is John's own. As John attempts to unravel what has happened, he proposes that 'There is a world in which doctors discuss the continued brain activity and rapid eye movements of a patient deep in a barbiturate coma and wonder what kind of world he inhabits' (Harrison, 1981/1986: 230–1). Accordingly, Harrison's novel can be read as an exploration of 'that kind of world', a near-empty psychological landscape wherein the prejudices, fears and regrets of the coma-victim are played out in endless cycles.

It is this explanation that makes the inclusion of Api in John's comatose existence particularly fascinating, as Api, in this scenario, would be entirely the product of John's imagination. To an extent, Api is created by a man indoctrinated with racist values, which is evidenced by his recollection of an encounter he had with a Maori boy as a child. One day, a Maori boy new to the neighbourhood had conversed with John, resulting in the latter inviting the youngster into his home (an invitation that was declined when John's aunt appeared). Later, his aunt and uncle had plainly expressed their dislike of the Polynesian families moving into the area, even suggesting that they brought with them undesirable contagions and lice. Although he is initially surprised by their response to this innocuous episode, it confirms a deep-seated recognition that he, too, despised the Maori. It is therefore fitting that in this purgatory-like state, his only companion is Maori, perhaps even the boy from his childhood. John never learns the boy's name and Api is convinced that he has met John somewhere before. These two factors engender sufficient ambiguity to make such an interpretation credible, adding an additional layer of irony to a reading of John's account as a coma-fantasy. Nevertheless, Api is the aggressive warrior who potentially hides a dark and violent secret from his tour of Vietnam, and so is the epitome of the negative racial stereotype. He is what John expects him to be. Harrison's implied position is somewhat ambivalent, therefore, as he appears, simultaneously, to highlight the numerous injustices suffered by the Maori and to enforce common stereotypes.

In Murphy's film all three characters are survivors because they were at the moment of death when the first Effect occurred. Zac was attempting to take his own life because of the weight of responsibility he felt at being part of the secret research programme; Joanne was electrocuted by a faulty hairdryer; and Api was being drowned in a fight with a former friend who held him responsible for his wife's suicide following an affair. Api, consequently, is more straightforwardly the brutish, overtly sexual 'other' to Zac and more in keeping with representations of Maori dating back to the previous century. Like the novel, the film ends ambiguously, but it lacks the complexity of Harrison's text. The final shot of Zac alone on a beach with an unfamiliar ringed planet dominating the skyline does not provide answers to the fate of the central protagonist, Joanne or Api. Equally, its potential as a conceptual breakthrough narrative is also undermined by its lack of diegetic clarity.

Both texts' responses to representations of masculinity and race form part of their engagement with aspects of national identity. However, the itinerant nature of their protagonists indicates the problematic nature of belonging potentially experienced by a post-settler nation; both John and Zac have to find – or avoid – their identity in a new world. Despite being independent since the 1931 Statute of Westminster, New Zealand did not confront serious questions of national identity until the 1970s. The country's 'coming of age' had been forced somewhat by its changing relationship with Britain. In 1973, Britain joined the European Economic Community, thus severing the favourable trade terms that it had previously enjoyed with members of the Commonwealth. Acknowledging Nick Roddick, Stuart Murray labels this period New Zealand's 'adolescence', a time when rapid 'growth' was vital (Murray, 2008: 169). As part of the process of maturation, cultural production was mobilized as a means to explore and affirm a sense of national identity.

An essential feature of the novel is John's journey. The places that he visits are described, sometimes in considerable detail, and named. The reader is given a sense of the varied topography and geographical features of the North Island. John's travelling, whilst a necessary quest to find survivors, reflects Ian Conrich's observation that, arguably:

> the pakeha have experienced difficulties in establishing a sense of place and identity in New Zealand and that they have become 'tourists' overawed by a vast primordial New Zealand Landscape. There is

also the idea that the perpetual journeying is a movement away rather than a movement towards. (Conrich, 2000: 116)

Equally, in Murphy's film, Zac's travels, which allow for shots of the open, empty roads that are so often a feature of New Zealand cinema of the period, emblematize his quest for identity. He struggles to find a new place to settle, moving from his own house to a grand colonial villa to a luxurious bungalow with a sea view as he endeavours to adjust to a radically transformed cultural situation.

The absenting of the human race from the New Zealand landscape that is explored so effectively through Harrison's prose and Murphy's cinematography draws a further distinction between novel and film. Generally, the nature of New Zealand's landscape has often been crucial in building myths of nation. Bell, for example, provides a common understanding of New Zealand as 'clean, green and beautiful' (Bell, 1996: 28), while Conrich and Sarah Davey argue that the country has been described as 'God's Own Country' or 'Godzone', a reference to the pastoral values that the country presents (Conrich and Davey, 1997: 3).

In Harrison's book, the landscape is constant and unaltered by the Effect. John observes:

> The stunned clarity of the landscape seemed almost insulting; but even this was only like an extension of the indifference it had always radiated. I had felt it often when driving through remote hills in the past, on deserted roads. The clear light which scrubbed the hills into such precise definition, which polished seas and rinsed distance from time as well as space, had not changed. (Harrison, 1981/1986: 25)

The ancient landscape is unaffected by the catastrophe that has removed most of humankind. It has a resistance that contrasts with the transitory nature of human settlement, a resistance that renders it sublime in John's perception. Here, and elsewhere, Harrison problematizes the notion of New Zealand as a haven or 'Godzone'; it is not made for humans, nor is it dependent upon them and their efforts towards cultivation. Indeed, its mythic Edenic qualities are subverted in a short exchange between John and Api as they discuss whether or not they are still alive and on Earth:

> 'You don't believe New Zealand really is heaven, do you?' I asked,
> anxious to break the mood. His teeth showed. We laughed.
> 'I reckon not,' he said, then pretended to sniff the air in the direction
> of the sulphur pools; 'could be the other place, though.' (Harrison,
> 1981/1986: 119)

In contrast, the myth of New Zealand as pastoral paradise informs the film's explanation of the cause of the apparent apocalypse. In the film Zac is involved with Operation Flashlight, a project responsible for developing a global energy grid. The project, Zac later tells Joanne and Api, is American-lead, but the Americans were keeping important information from each of the individual laboratories placed in various locations around the world. America is, therefore, ultimately responsible for the Effect.

The film's foregrounding of the threat posed by American authority can be understood within the context of the contemporaneous strain on American–New Zealand relations surrounding the Antipodean nation's stance on nuclear testing. In 1984, the New Zealand's Fourth Labour government banned nuclear armed or powered ships from using New Zealand ports or entering New Zealand waters. This resulted in America suspending its obligations to New Zealand set out in the 1951 Australian, New Zealand, United States Security Treaty (ANZUS). Roy Smith, in his discussion of New Zealand's anti-nuclear stance, argues that it was increasingly difficult to sustain Aotearoa's mythical image as Eden when it was condoning the development of nuclear capabilities through its defence policy; essentially, 'maintaining thoughts of a pastoral paradise is difficult within the context of mutual assured destruction on a global scale' (Smith, 2000: 13). From July 1985 New Zealand was thrust further into the media spotlight when the Greenpeace flagship Rainbow Warrior was sunk off Auckland. In August 1985, New Zealand enforced the dictates of the Treaty of Rarotonga, which outlawed the stationing of nuclear weapons and dumping of atomic waste in New Zealand and in the territories of the other signatories (thirteen nations of the South Pacific). In this context, as Rayner has argued, 'In retrospect it seems impossible to divorce [*The Quiet Earth*] from contemporary national and political issues' (Rayner, 1999: 17).

Harrison's book and Murphy's film can be understood as a product of their historical, political and national context. Their similarities demonstrate the prominence and cultural significance of the 'man alone' archetype and both address, with differing degrees of emphasis, themes relating to the landscape, settlement and race. However, their contrasts appear to be largely symptomatic of the shifts in international politics that had occurred between 1981 and 1985. In particular, the multiple interpretations available regarding the nature of New Zealand's mysterious apocalypse in the novel and the film underline the influence of their context of production. While Harrison's text seems to remark more generally on the dangers of genetic experimentation, the film comments explicitly on the dangers of man playing God. Fears of New Zealand's vulnerability are played out in a film deliberately critical and deeply suspicious of American nuclear capability.

References

Bell, C. (1996) *Inventing New Zealand: Everyday Myths of Pakeha Identity*. Auckland: Penguin.

Conrich, I. and Davey, S. (1997) *Views from the Edge of the World*. Nottingham: Kakapo Books.

Conrich, I. (2000) 'In God's Own Country: Open Spaces and the New Zealand Road Movie', in I. Conrich and D. Woods (eds) *New Zealand: A Pastoral Paradise*, pp. 31–8. Nottingham: Kakapo Books.

Edwards, S. (1989) 'Cinematic Imperialism and Maori Cultural Identity', *Illusions* 10: 17–21.

Harrison, C. (1981/1986) *The Quiet Earth*. Auckland, London, Sydney and Toronto: Coronet Books, Hodder and Stoughton.

Murray, S. (2008) '"Precarious Adulthood": Communal Anxieties in 1980s Film', in I. Conrich and S. Murray (eds) *Contemporary New Zealand Cinema: From New Wave to Blockbuster*, pp. 169–80. London: I.B. Tauris.

Perkins, R. (1986) 'Fun and Games: The Influence of the Counterculture in the Films of Geoff Murphy', *Illusions* 2: 15–23.

Phillips, J. (1987) *A Man's Country? The Image of the Pakeha Male: A History.* Auckland: Penguin.

Rayner, J. (1999) *Cinema Journeys of the Man Alone: The New Zealand and American Films of Geoff Murphy.* Nottingham: Kakapo Books.

Smith, R. (2000) 'New Zealand and the Nuclear-Free Pacific: The History and the Legacy', in I. Conrich and D. Woods (eds) *New Zealand: A Pastoral Paradise?*, pp. 11–30. Nottingham: Kakapo Books.

Spicer, A. (2000) *An Ambivalent Archetype: Masculinity, Performance and the New Zealand Films of Bruno Lawrence.* Nottingham: Kakapo Books.

Chapter 10

Following the Flood
Deluge, Adaptation and the 'Ideal' Woman

Jennifer Woodward

Considered a lost film until its rediscovery by Forrest J. Ackerman in a Rome film archive in 1981, Felix E. Feist's *Deluge* (1933) is a spectacular adaptation of Sydney Fowler Wright's eponymous 1927 disaster novel (Kingsley, 2009). Produced by the independent Admiral Productions Incorporated and distributed by RKO, the film disappeared virtually without trace following its release. Its impressive special effects sequences, most famously the inundation of New York, were recycled, however, and enhanced Republic Pictures' 15-chapter *Dick Tracy vs. Crime Inc.* (John English and William Witney, 1941) and the 12-chapter *King of the Rocket Men* (Fred C. Brannon, 1949). Its reappearance, albeit in a dubbed Italian version with new English subtitles, its release on VHS in 1998 and its subsequent availability online provide a welcome opportunity to assess critically the adaptation of one of Britain's key pre-Second World War disaster novels.[1] Although there are several cultural and political contrasts observable between the two texts, it is in their representation of women that each narrative comments most clearly on its specific cultural context.

As with other British disaster fiction written in the first half of the twentieth century (M. P. Shiel's *The Purple Cloud* [1901] and J. J. Connington's *Nordenholt's Million* [1923] are notable examples), *Deluge* uses the disaster scenario to explore and address contemporary concerns and dissatisfactions. It is an overtly anti-modern novel, elitist in its treatment of class and misogynistic in its representation of women. Originally self-published, it became a bestseller in both Great Britain and North America. Its negative tone echoed the general anxiety concerning the devastating potential of technological advancement that followed the First World War. Furthermore, it captured the social anxieties around the changing roles of women and reflected middle class insecurity at the prospect of the working class gaining wider access to education. Indeed, industrialization, technologization, emancipation, education, declining levels of physical fitness and the oppressive nature of the law are the novel's *bêtes noires*. Central to its consistently critical tone is anxiety over deteriorating masculine authority. Fear of patriarchal decline informs the novel's negative representation of modern comforts and increasingly independent women, and it underpins the narrative's wish-fulfilment depiction of a return to a more primitive and patriarchal existence at its *dénouement*.

While thematically and tonally very different, the novel and film are narratively and structurally similar, with Feist's production offering a condensed version of the source text. In both, most of the Earth's surface is submerged following a number of earthquakes. Whereas the novel is preoccupied with the intricacies of social restructuring in the post-diluvian world, the film focuses to a greater degree on the tense build-up to, and the cinematic spectacle of, the actual disaster. The catastrophe in Fowler Wright's *Deluge* serves as a literary device that leads to the literal 'washing away' of modernity. As such, it is dealt with quickly and largely at a distance, from the perspective of a Wellsian 'observer from a distant planet' (Fowler Wright, 2003: 1), a position which emphasizes humanity's vulnerable position in relation to the forces of nature. The disaster is the result of 'the slightest tremor', which would appear 'trivial' (Fowler Wright, 2003: 1) to such an observer. In contrast, Feist's film rejects such distance in favour of capitalizing on the disaster's potential for dramatic special effects.

Figure 1. Deluge. Photo courtesy of RKO/Photofest.

By shifting the action from the Cotswolds to New York, the film was able to show the destruction of newly constructed high rise buildings (the Chrysler Building was completed in May 1930; the Empire State Building in May 1931) and through the use of back projection and impressive miniature work it showed mass panic and global catastrophe with a realism striking for its time of production.

Following the devastation, both texts trace the converging trajectories of Martin (Sidney Blackmer) and Helen Webster (Lois Wilson) and Claire Arlington (Peggy Shannon). During the flood Martin is separated from his injured wife, Helen, and their children and he presumes them dead. Having established a camp, he finds the body of Claire, who the reader/audience knows to have been trapped on another island with two men, one who claimed ownership of her and one who tried to rape her. To escape this situation Claire swims away to be discovered exhausted by Martin. However, once at Martin's camp, she is kidnapped by gang leader Bellamy (Philo McCullough). Martin rescues her and they become 'married'. Together, they fight Bellamy's gang, and unite with another group of survivors, led by

Tom Aldworth (Matt Moore). Martin assumes leadership of the remaining population and is reunited with Helen and his children. In the novel, the characters agree that he should remain 'married' to Claire in addition to being a husband to Helen. However, in the film no such bigamous arrangement is made, and Claire swims away leaving Martin with his original family.

While both novel and film exploit the disaster scenario's potential for presenting the positive opportunities of rebuilding following a catastrophe, their respective ideological positions differ significantly. Reminiscent of earlier 'back to nature' novels like Richard Jeffries's *After London* (1885), Fowler Wright's *Deluge* rejects the trappings of modernity. More radically, it advocates the complete overthrow of established systems in favour of middle-class patriarchy taming the land, the women and the lower classes. Conversely, Feist's film, produced under the spectre, if not the enforced dictates, of the Motion Picture Production Code (the censorship guidelines of the 1930s which outlined what could and could not be either said or depicted in Hollywood films), focuses on a return to conventional Christian morality and community spirit.

Whereas the novel presents the flood as entirely positive in its obliteration of the modern, Feist's adaptation presents the inundation's effects as an opportunity for a frontier spirit in which people pull together to reconstruct the modern world and re-establish traditional morality. As a film, *Deluge* draws upon the novel's allusions to the Biblical flood as punishment, and develops the disaster's aftermath into a generic western narrative involving the town versus the criminal outlaws. The depiction of townspeople working together to rebuild their lives following a disaster would have been particularly resonant with Depression-era audiences. On the other hand, an unaltered transposition of Fowler Wright's confidence in the contentment achieved through the experience of adversity may have rung rather hollow. The film is, therefore, a metaphor for contemporary America during the Depression, rather than a wish-fulfilment tale about social restructuring.

Nevertheless, the contrast between the novel and its adaptation is most acute in how each represents and objectifies its female characters. Although both texts present patriarchal images of 'ideal women', Fowler Wright's characters are obedient mothers and independent women desirous of enforced submission. Feist's stereotypes, on the other hand, are more conventionally figured as the loyal wife and the punishable, transgressive female, constructed by, and for, the male gaze.

In Fowler Wright's text, wife Helen and the initially independent Claire differ significantly from one another, yet they each represent patriarchally constructed ideal women. Their characterization is defined by their relationship to Martin and demonstrates that women secretly desire enforced subordination to patriarchal authority. As such, the novel embodies cultural fears present in Britain during the first half of the twentieth century when there were a number of debates regarding the nature and efficacy of masculinity. There was a growing fear that, as the influence of women on and in society increased, men would be gradually feminized (Connell, 2005: 195). Modern women were seen as a challenge to patriarchy (John and Eustance, 1997: 54) and commentators since the late nineteenth century had been noting their concern about apparent changes in masculinity. These concerns were compounded during the Boer War (1899–1902) when there was widespread anxiety about degeneracy and the physical deterioration of the population, whose health and fitness levels had declined as a consequence of urban living (Gooch, 2000: 206). At the same time, calls for increased female emancipation seemed to threaten the masculine position further. As a result there was a strong backlash against the women's movement (Porter, 2006: 284). *Deluge*, written by a man who had grown to maturity against this background of anxiety, presents the notion of independent women as a threat to male authority. Indeed, *Deluge* advocates historic, patriarchal constructions of gender roles as natural.

The novel's two female protagonists are both manifestations of an authoritative patriarchal fantasy that contrast with the increasingly emancipated women of the early twentieth century, who are here represented as rejecting their 'natural' position in society. As part of this fantasy, Helen is portrayed as the traditional Victorian 'angel of the house'. She represents what Gamble categorizes as the patriarchally conceived, stereotypical, ideal woman: 'a nurturant wife [and] mother constructed through the scopic gaze of the male' (Gamble, 2001: 306). Beautiful, refined and confined to the private sphere, she spends the novel's duration caring for her children almost untouched by the antediluvian social upheaval. Helen's passive position within the private space is reinforced throughout the text and is exposed particularly when Martin contemplates her possible reaction to Claire, his new 'wife':

> He was sure that it would make no division between them. He had once said to her when a business necessity was taking him away for a month or two: 'I don't believe you'd mind if I found someone else to console me while I'm away.'
> She had smiled her answer [...] 'Not if you wanted to.'
> 'But,' he had added, 'you'd want to know all about it when I came back.'
> 'Why, of course,' she had answered. That was obvious. She was of the temperament that finds it almost as pleasurable to watch life as to share it. (Fowler Wright, 2003: 210)

Helen's characterization as content with her domestic role, subservient to, and understanding of, her husband's infidelities and happy to share in his reflections on past sexual experiences marks her clearly as an idealized patriarchal construct.

The novel asserts that her greatest satisfaction and sense of self derives from her family, an idea central to patriarchal ideology. Clare Burton notes that the idea of the family as the arena for personal fulfilment contributes to women's subordination under patriarchy (Burton, 1989: 41). Helen is a fantasy figure created to contrast with the contemporary 'modern woman' who questioned traditional gender roles. She is part of, and re-enforces, the anti-feminist backlash that occurred early in the twentieth century and reflected concerns about social degeneration stemming from social and political moves towards gender equality (see Izenberg, 2000: 1–21).

Deluge portrays the emergence of the modern woman as the consequence of comfort, cowardice and selfishness. Their increased emancipation, the text implies, serves to accelerate women's removal from their so-called 'natural' roles as child bearers. In contrast to her contemporaries, Helen is defined by motherly love. Although this is clear from the opening of the novel, Fowler Wright makes the distinction explicit when she finds a boat and saves her children during the flood:

> Pillowed on her breasts, the children that she had saved slept peacefully. Born of a race of women that had learned to esteem their children as less than their pleasures, who would even pay to have them murdered in their own bodies, [...] and whether she were dead or living was a little thing. (Fowler Wright, 2003: 37)

This criticism of modern, childless and abortion-practising women highlights Helen's contrary position to the Edwardian woman. Instead, she is equated with what Shirley Foster notes was the Victorian idea that motherhood was 'the apotheosis of womanly fulfilment' (Foster, 1985: 15). Although *Deluge* was published in 1927, the old-fashioned idealization of motherhood still endured. In fact, as Harriett Gilbert and Christine Roche point out when women gained more sexual freedom in the early twentieth century, their independence was 'hijacked by the establishment', which propagated the idea that the greatest joy a woman could obtain was to have children (Gilbert and Roche, 1987: 163). This view was compounded by the fact that, as Lucy Delap highlights, many men and women of the time 'thoroughly disliked the values of Edwardian femininity' (Delap, 2005: 6). They deemed the new woman to be not only un-feminine but also threatening to men (Delap, 2005: 14). Complicit in her own subordination, Helen is a counterpoint to female emancipation. As someone who does not desire freedom or equality she represents the contemporary patriarchal fantasy of returning women to a non-threatening, subjugated state.

Fowler Wright's fiction suggests that women are secretly unhappy with their emancipation, that they are the victims of a weakened masculinity who desire re-submission to a reinvigorated male potency. The misogynistic assumption that women desire to be dominated, and even mistreated, is reasserted throughout the novel and dramatized through the trajectory of Claire. In contrast to Helen, Claire represents the female as threat. Fowler Wright's idealization of her comes from her desire for enforced subordination. Physically muscular, she is practical, strong-minded, violent and independent. Importantly, her autonomous nature can be attributed to her pre-deluge marriage to a symbolically emasculated man; her husband was an invalid confined to a care home. Clearly, her husband serves as a metaphor for what many felt was a weakened masculinity that had allowed the emergence of female emancipation. Hence, Claire's story is the account of her willing re-submission to a patriarchy characterized by renewed masculine virility. Women's assumed yearning for submission to an aggressively asserted patriarchy is evidenced when one male character imagines his gang 'burdened with a score of [...] screaming, weeping, struggling, or secretly-contented [captured] women' (Fowler Wright, 2003: 259).

The idea that the protesting woman may be secretly contented reflects the patriarchally constructed misconception of a woman's 'no'. This misconception is propagated further by Claire. Throughout the text she is depicted as both powerful and vulnerable. She is symbolically phallicized by her weaponry and her ability to disable male attackers (she even murders Bellamy); yet she is rendered sexually vulnerable – and therefore conventionally 'feminine' – by her repeated nakedness in the presence of men. This dual position reflects Claire's attitude of desired enforced submission to the very men she fights. Simultaneously, her asserted and assaulted independence marks her as a barometer for newly reclaimed male virility. Throughout the novel she is an object men wish to acquire; she is 'any man's that can take her' (Fowler Wright, 2003: 296). As such, her progress through the narrative is marked by a number of attempted rapes. During the first of these she fights off her attacker, Norwood, with a piece of wood. The narrator, overtly critical of Norwood's unwillingness to pursue the attempted rape, reflects that 'Probably the game was still [Norwood's], had he played it better. Women have been taken by force often enough [...] and have learnt to kiss their captors' (Fowler Wright, 2003: 58). The narrator's judgement of Norwood is echoed by a scornful Claire, who notes 'the cowardly brutality of the man who had assaulted, and yet had lacked the manhood to overcome her' (Fowler Wright, 2003: 59). It is significant that Claire's lack of respect for her attacker derives from his inability to 'overcome her', a fact that marks him as a coward. His premature acceptance of defeat reinforces the broader themes of the text – that it is male weakness that has failed to keep women in their place. Comparably, Martin questions his masculinity because he did not 'take' Claire when he first met her:

> It crossed his mind that a bolder man would take that which the gods gave [...]. Was he of a lesser manhood? – or more scrupulous? He decided he was nothing better than cautious, and he was not sure that he did not despise himself for the quality. (Fowler Wright, 2003: 88)

Claire also wonders why he has not raped her, finding the prospect secretly appealing: 'she felt that he was hers if she would, and, perhaps, if she would not, he would still take her. There was paradoxical pleasure in the thought' (Fowler Wright, 2003: 104). Eventually Martin does 'take' Claire, and 'not without violence' (Fowler Wright, 2003: 179). This act marks Claire's surrender to patriarchal authority. During the rape, Martin claims ownership of her 'forever and ever' (Fowler Wright, 2003: 179), a symbolic act that marks his power over his female acquisition, while simultaneously defining him as both protector and lover (Cranny-Francis, 1992: 127). The patriarchal reinscription of Claire, whose sexuality is defined by her desire for rape and ultimately submission, is central to the construction of dominant patriarchal masculinity within the text. This is reinforced further by Claire's later reflections on her relationship with Martin. Although she has acted more decisively than and just as bravely as he, she nevertheless decides that he has superior judgement, noting that:

> It was true that he had hesitated where she would not have done so. [...] She did not doubt that he was wiser, as she knew that he was stronger than she. Perhaps he saw more broadly, more truly, than she was able to do. To see all sides does not conduce to prompt action. She had seen that force was the ultimate court of appeal. (Fowler Wright, 2003: 178)

Claire's conclusion that despite her more decisive actions, Martin is the wiser of the two marks the intellectual submission that attends her physical and sexual capitulation. In retrospect, her immediate recourse to violence throughout the text indicates that she has responded to situations emotionally rather than rationally. Such a stereotypically female response distinguishes her actions from the more logical and rational planning of Martin and reinforces the conventional gender binaries established in the text.

In this context, Fowler Wright's *Deluge* is an overt, misogynistic wish-fulfilment fantasy involving the enforced reassertion of patriarchy. For Brian Stableford, 'the end of the book is really a triumphant recognition and acknowledgement of moral responsibility' (Stableford, 1983: 22). In other words, having innocently assumed Helen dead, Martin has entered into another commitment with Claire which he feels bound to honour; he is meeting – according to Stableford – his moral obligations. However, as Paul Kincaid points out, this 'unlikely ménage' at the novel's *dénouement* allows Martin 'sexual freedom without guilt; in a world where there are fewer women than men' (Kincaid, 2005: 216). It is telling that Martin's justification for two wives is not only based on the morality of honouring commitment but also on the premise that any offspring would be able to identify their father. When he contemplates what would have happened if Helen had assumed him dead and entered into another relationship he concludes the scenario would have been 'monstrous' (Fowler Wright, 2003: 181), justifying his position on the basis that future children would be unsure which man was their father. The importance placed on a child knowing its father reinforces the importance of patriarchy to Martin and the society he will establish. As the head of a household, the father's position would be threatened, his authority undermined, if a child was unsure of his parent or if there were two fathers in one family. It is not unreasonable to conclude, therefore, that Martin's position on bigamy is patriarchal rather than moral. His stance is based on stereotypically gendered binary assumptions regarding masculine sexual voraciousness versus female maternal function. Grounded in contemporary ideas of 'natural' gender inequality, particularly the perception that female unfaithfulness 'is, and always will be, a more serious matter than the infidelity of the husband' (Pearsall, 2003: 169), *Deluge* reflects contemporary patriarchal ideas about gendered notions of the acceptability of multiple partners.

The novel offers no challenge to conventional gender assumptions, despite appearing to present a radical movement away from conventional marriage laws. The fact that Helen never assumes Martin dead and so rejects Tom's repeated offers of marriage means that the moral dilemma her acceptance would pose is conveniently avoided.

Where Fowler Wright's *Deluge* actively promotes traditional gender inequalities through its masculine fantasy, whilst remaining radical in its view of polygamy for the powerful, Feist's film seems to celebrate a postdiluvian sexual freedom for its female characters through its advertising campaign. One poster for the film proclaims: 'Ten Men For One Woman With No Law But Desire'. *Deluge*, like many Pre-Code Hollywood productions, not only fails to fulfil such sensational claims but it also actively works against the possibility and desirability of such female sexual autonomy and choice. The film only tentatively makes the viewer question traditional gender roles and relationships before reverting back to endorsing the status quo prescribed in the 1930 Production Code.

Initially, Claire is an exciting, lively alternative to the rather dull Helen. The dichotomy between the sexually appealing partner and the motherly wife is established early in the film. The audience is introduced to a fully clothed (covered up to the neck) Helen praying with her children. She admits to Martin that she is afraid of the storm and looks to him for reassurance and strength. In contrast, when we first see Claire she is semi-naked and preparing for a swim. Informed by an official that the sea is unsafe, her response that 'orders are orders', combined with a mischievous glance at the camera, establishes her playful attitude towards the efficacy of male authority.

From these opening scenes, Claire's representation as an attractive, athletic and independent woman forms a stark contrast to the helpless, dependent and rather plain Helen. Despite their physical differences, however, the enunciation of the two women is relatively faithful to the book. Claire's practical nature is, for example, indicated subtly through visual cues. She uses her skirt as a cleaning cloth to wipe her hands and, in a telling piece of symbolism, wears Martin's trousers when they first live together. Such costuming draws the audience's attention to the equality that defines their relationship for much of the film, especially when she fights Bellamy's gang beside Martin. Conversely, Helen is depicted as a desexualized, loyal and altruistic wife and mother lacking any practical skills outside of the home. Indeed she is much more akin to the way wives would be portrayed after the enforcement of the Production Code on 1 July 1934 (LaSalle, 2002: 171).

According to Harry M. Benshoff and Sean Griffin, Pre-Code Hollywood allowed for the presentation of strong, forthright and sexualized heroines (Benshoff and Griffin, 2004: 218). Similarly, Mick LaSalle remarks that 'Before the code, women on screen took lovers, had babies out of wedlock, got rid of cheating husbands, enjoyed their sexuality, held down professional positions without apologizing for their self sufficiency' (LaSalle, 2002: 1). However, despite this cinematic promotion of gender equality, there was no new model of marriage to incorporate the more independent woman on screen (Benshoff and Griffin, 2004: 550). As a result, the autonomous woman in Pre-Code cinema tended to exist outside of marriage with its prescribed gender roles. In *Deluge*, Claire's self-sufficient status places her at odds with what was expected of women in conventional marital relations. It is no surprise, therefore, that no formal marriage takes place between Claire and Martin. Although they agree to be 'married', their relationship exists outside of the formal, legal marriage structure. Conversely, constrained by her role as a traditional wife and mother, Helen lacks the independence of Claire. As Molly Haskell has observed, in most films 'The implication is clear: all the excitement of life – the passion, the risk – occurs outside marriage rather than within it' (Haskell, 1999: 22). The contrast between Helen and Claire reinforces this perspective. Helen is reliant, plain and functions only as wife and mother whereas Claire is strong, attractive and behaves as an equal partner in her sexual relationship with Martin. At this point, Feist's *Deluge* appears to advocate gender equality and sexual relations outside of a legal framework.

However, the film's sexualization of Claire compromises any progressive politics the film might appear to possess and anticipates its deeply conservative *dénouement*, which re-establishes the traditional family unit. On screen, Claire connotes, to use Laura Mulvey's term, 'to-be-looked-at-ness' (Mulvey, 1975: 6–18); she is constructed by and for the scopophilic male gaze. In this way, Feist's film transforms the novel's identification of beauty with the desexualized 'angel of the house' through Helen to a visual association of beauty with sexuality through Claire. She is presented semi-naked on numerous occasions. As Thomas Doherty observes, Pre-Code Hollywood would often find innovative ways to present women in a state of undress (Doherty, 1999: 118) and Claire's abilities as a swimmer provide ample opportunities for a much more *risqué* representation than would have been permitted a year later outside of a Busby Berkeley extravaganza.

Sustained by Claire's frequent semi-nudity, the film is a barely concealed, guilt-free adultery fantasy for the male viewer – a sharp contrast with the promise of 'Ten Men For One Woman [...]'. Any shame for their adulterous relationship is mitigated by the fact that they both presume Helen dead. The viewer's knowledge that Helen has survived provides much of the film's tension as the potential love triangle unfolds. Martin later admits to Helen that, had he known she was still alive, there would have been no 'bigamous' relationship with Claire. This explanation further mitigates Martin's guilt and highlights that Claire was always 'the other woman', lacking the legal status and rights Helen had secured through marriage. There is no question of Martin ever leaving Helen for Claire.

In his discussion of male sexual fantasies, Reuben Fine writes that 'most men struggle with the idea of another woman for a long time, and not infrequently all of their lives. Movies and plays respond to this fantasy by focusing on the themes of adultery and infidelity. Usually the play or movie is presented with a certain moral to it' (Fine, 1987: 29). Feist's *Deluge* is structured in precisely this way. It utilizes the disaster scenario to create a fantasy space in which adultery is permitted – even excused – but where conventional morality is also restored at the end. Helen, in keeping with her role as the 'ideal' wife mirrors the Helen of the novel. She forgives her husband's transgressions and does not question the short amount of time taken for him to find and 'marry' another woman.

With Helen returned to Martin, the independent Claire is reframed as the dangerous woman capable of undermining the patriarchal order (see Gamble, 2001: 306) and the relationships that bind together the conventional nuclear family. In Fowler Wright's novel she is integrated into, and contained by, a new polygamous social structure; in Feist's adaptation she must leave the reunited family. Claire's departure into the sea in *Deluge*'s final scene mirrors the earlier sequence in which she swims away from Bellamy. Here, however, the situation is reversed. Where her previous movement into the sea to escape her persecutor symbolized her claiming of freedom and opportunity, her withdrawal at the end of the film, though a reclamation of her autonomy, is no longer represented as desirable. Indeed, her independence becomes her punishment for a sexual relationship with a married man. The exciting expedition across the postdiluvian world she had once envisioned now becomes a lonely self-imposed exile into the unknown.

Consequently *Deluge* provides a moral message about the sanctity of marriage while visualizing an adultery fantasy. The film is doubly patriarchal: visually, the female protagonist is sexualized and subjected to the scopophilic gaze; narratively, she is punished for her independence with the very autonomy that she previously claimed. Not only is the independent woman at odds with the dominant patriarchal order in the film, but patriarchy itself transforms female emancipation into its own punishment.

Just as Fowler Wright's *Deluge* is a product of British cultural anxieties, Feist's film advocates traditional Christian values and morality. During the Depression years, in both Britain and America, there was a strong drive to encourage women out of the workplace and back into the home. Part of this drive included the proposition, in America, that women who were married should not be allowed to work (Peterson and Kellogg, 2008: 11). Hence as a woman, one could not be both economically independent and married. Seen in this context, Claire's autonomy and ability to share Martin's workload places her in opposition to contemporary patriarchal opinions about women's roles within society. Although the film seems to hint that an autonomous woman may be a more fulfilling marriage partner, it never commits to this perspective. The fact that Claire finds herself alone at the film's conclusion undermines her positive representation, as does her disregard for conventional morality. When she tells Helen 'I won't give [Martin] up. Not for you or the children', she is shown to be selfish, a quality which now contrasts her sharply, and negatively, with Helen. Her disregard for the family and family values in favour of selfish feelings echoes the novel's representation of independent women as self-centred and lacking morality. Significantly, it is Martin's final speech as the leader of the survivors, in which he calls for the creation of a more lawful civilization for his children, which compels Claire to leave. It becomes clear at this point that she does not conform to the kind of society he represents. Here, the film's trajectory towards a re-establishment of traditional morality reflects the Production Code which was 'designed to put women back in the kitchen' (LaSalle, 2002: 1) by punishing them cinematically for transgressions that placed them outside the patriarchal order.

Where Sydney Fowler Wright's *Deluge* is an overt, misogynistic wish-fulfilment fantasy involving the enforced reassertion of patriarchy, Feist's adaptation is more insidious in its reassertion of patriarchal norms. Beneath the surface of what appears to be a Pre-Code representation of a strong and sexually independent female protagonist lies a scopophilic fantasy that reiterates conventional patriarchal values.

Note

1 http://www.ovguide.com/movies_tv/the_deluge_1933.htm (accessed October 2010).

References

Benshoff, H. and Griffin, S. (2004) *America on Film*. Oxford: Wiley-Blackwell.

Burton, C. (1989) *Subordination: Feminism and Social Theory*. London: George Allen & Unwin.

Connell, R. W. (2005) *Masculinities*. Cambridge: Polity Press.

Cranny-Francis, A. (1992) *Engendered Fiction: Analysing Gender in the Production and Reception of Texts*. New South Wales: UNSW Press.

Delap, L. (2005) *Feminist and Anti-Feminist Encounters in Edwardian Britain*. Oxford: Blackwell.

Doherty, T. P. (1999) *Pre-Code Hollywood: Sex, Immorality, and Insurrection in American Cinema, 1930–1934.* New York: Columbia University Press.

Fine, R. (1987) *The Forgotten Man.* New York and London: Haworth Press Inc.

Foster, S. (1985) *Victorian Women's Fiction: Marriage, Freedom, and the Individual.* London and New York: Taylor & Francis.

Fowler Wright, S. (2003) *Deluge.* Middletown, Connecticut: Wesleyan University Press.

Gamble, S. (2001) *Routledge Companion to Feminism and Postfeminism.* London and New York: Routledge.

Gilbert, H. and Roche, C. (1987) *A Women's History of Sex.* London and New York: Routledge.

Gooch, J. (2000) *The Boer War.* London and New York: Routledge.

Haskell, M. (1999) 'The Woman's Film', in S. Thornham (ed.) *Feminist Film Theory: A Reader*, pp. 20–30. Edinburgh: Edinburgh University Press.

Izenberg, G. N. (2000) *Modernism and Masculinity.* Chicago, IL: University of Chicago Press.

John, A. V. and Eustance, C. (1997) *The Men's Share? Masculinities, Male Support and Women's Suffrage in Britain, 1890–1920.* London and New York: Routledge.

Kincaid, P. (2005) 'Review of Deluge', *Science Fiction Studies* 95: 216.

Kingsley, E. A. (2009) '*Deluge* (1933)', *And You Call Yourself a Scientist!*, http://www.aycyas.com/deluge.htm (accessed October 2010).

LaSalle, M. (2002) *Complicated Women: Sex and Power in Pre-Code Hollywood.* New York: Griffin.

Mulvey, L. (1975) 'Visual Pleasure and Narrative Cinema', *Screen* 16(3): 6–18.

Pearsall, R. (2003) *The Worm in the Bud: The World of Victorian Sexuality.* Gloucestershire: Sutton Publishing.

Peterson, A. T. and Kellogg, A. T. (2008) *The Greenwood Encyclopaedia of Clothing through American History, 1900 to the Present, Volume 1.* Westport, CT: Greenweed Press.

Porter, B. (2006) *The Absent-Minded Imperialists.* Oxford: Oxford University Press.

Stableford, B. (1983) 'Against the New Gods: The Speculative Fiction of S. Fowler Wright', *Foundation* 29: 10–52.

PART IV

NOVELIZATION

CHAPTER 11

EXISTENZ, THE STORY OF A NOVELIZATION
AN INTERVIEW WITH CHRISTOPHER PRIEST

Thomas Van Parys

It is fitting that the author who novelized *eXistenZ* (1999), Cronenberg's last science-fiction film to date, should, in his own distinguished career as a novelist, have so much in common with the master of postmodern horror in cinema; both have strived to explore new horizons while engaging with old traditions, to reinvent themselves while staying true to their idiosyncratic style, and both have remained outsiders to the systems and genres in which they work. Indeed, as Andrew M. Butler remarks, Christopher Priest 'inhabits the margins, the corners' (Butler, 2005: 7); to 'padlock him in a straitjacket of science fiction, metafiction, postmodern fiction, magic realism, slipstream, post-New Wave, [...] is to miss the point' (Butler, 2005: 10). Not surprisingly, then, Priest has also dabbled in that most marginal category of 'serious' literature, and indeed of 'serious' science fiction, the novelization. To set his novelizations apart from his own work – which includes acclaimed novels such as *The Affirmation* (1981), *The Prestige* (1995), *The Extremes* (1998), *The Separation* (2002) and his recent novel *The Islanders* (2011) – he writes them under pseudonyms, viz. 'Colin Wedgelock' for *Short Circuit* (1986) and 'John Luther Novak'

for *Mona Lisa* (1986). It is under this pen name that the novelization of *eXistenZ* (1999) was published in the UK. However, in the US
the novelization carried his real name on the cover, which makes the
US edition the only novelization ever published under 'Christopher
Priest'.

The novelization of *eXistenZ* can easily be placed in that row of
'prestige' novelizations written by literary sf authors, such as Isaac
Asimov's *Fantastic Voyage* (1966), Arthur C. Clarke's *2001: A Space
Odyssey* (1968) and Orson Scott Card's *The Abyss* (1989), even if sf
fans regard it as less of a 'classic' because it does not augment the film
with explanatory information, additional sequences or corrective science. Of course, the film is not in need of any extra explanations, as
its strength is precisely the obviousness of its witty visual metaphors
and black humour. But Priest's work – notably in *A Dream of Wessex*
(1977), *The Affirmation* and *The Extremes* – is arguably much ahead of
Cronenberg's in blurring the boundaries between reality and imagination, or reality and virtual reality.

The following interview attempts to tell the story behind the novelization of *eXistenZ*, but it is not an insider's story like Michael A.
Stackpole's account of his career as a novelizer in the next chapter.
Christopher Priest is still an outsider, brushing against but never
getting involved in the Hollywood system, as he makes clear in *The
Magic: The Story of a Film* (Priest, 2008), his illuminating book on
Christopher Nolan's adaptation of *The Prestige* (2006). *The Magic* is,
as he describes it on the back cover, 'the book of the film' – a literary
film book which offers insights into the adaptation process as well as
comparative analysis and interpretive reading. Symbolic for this position on the fringe is his account of how the film's production company
blocked the use of the film's poster art for the American tie-in edition
of *The Prestige*, most likely because Nolan did not want the novel being promoted too much and hence spoiling his film's ending (which
nonetheless did not stop Nolan from the publication of the screenplay). Happily, the UK publishers, who did manage to obtain the
rights, published an edition with both film art and the phrase 'Now a
major film' on the cover – which now matches well with the *eXistenZ*

novelization (featuring the phrase 'Now a major motion picture') on the bookshelf.

This chapter is a reworked and updated version of the interview originally published in *Image [&] Narrative*, an online journal of visual narratology and word-and-image studies (Van Parys et al., 2004). The interview was conducted via e-mail in May 2004.

How did you get assigned to novelize *eXistenZ*? Did you communicate with David Cronenberg himself at some stage?

I was commissioned by my usual book publisher, and I worked with them. The publisher acquired the rights, phoned my agent to ask if I would be interested, my agent phoned me, and I said yes. I had no direct contact with Mr Cronenberg at any point, so we discussed neither the film nor the book.

How did you approach the novelization?

I tackled it in exactly the same way as I have written other novelizations in the past. I read the script through to get some sense of what the eventual film might be like, thought about it for a bit, mentally decided which scenes would work best in a novel, and which ones would need to be revised slightly to make them work, then got down to it. Time is always short with a novelization. You become involved with the film when they've almost finished work on it, and they want the book to be ready so that it can be on sale at the same time as the film is released. And of course publishing a book takes time. So there's no time to waste.

In general, what you try to do is produce a book that will run parallel to the film. It should try to have the same effect on the reader as the film will have on its audience. It should tell the same story, have the same characters, have the same general 'feel'. But a book requires many more words than a screenplay, so you have the opportunity to embellish a little: work in some back-story, fill out the background, describe the locations, and so on.

But remember: at the time the novel is being written, the author only has a screenplay to work with. It's probably not even a final version, a shooting script. You have no real idea which actors will be in it, or where the film will be shot. You have no knowledge of the music, the pace, what the special effects will look like, the way the lighting will be used, the overall style. All you can do is guess at them, from what's in the script. Other than this, I was free to do whatever I thought was best for the novel.

Why did you choose to dig up your pseudonym 'John Luther Novak' again? And why did it appear on the UK edition only, while your real name was used for the US edition?

'Novak' was used this time because just before working on *eXistenZ* I had written and delivered a novel of my own, which has the title *The Extremes*. I felt that the similarity of the titles could easily lead to confusion. However, when some of the publishers outside Britain (notably in the US) discovered who 'Novak' really was, they said it would 'add value' if my name was on the cover page. Thinking that 'added value' meant they would pay more for it with my name on, I agreed. However, I realized soon enough that they meant it added value for them, not for me.

Many authors, and even some novelizers, regard novelizing as a mere job, as work-for-hire. What is your view on this?

To say that writing a novelization is merely a 'job' makes it sound as if it's written cynically or carelessly, just for the money. That's certainly not true of novelizations in general, and emphatically not true of this one. You obviously wouldn't do the work unless you were paid, but the money's not that good. Every writer takes pride in his work. But you're working with another writer's material, you have only part of the information you need, and you're under immense time pressures. It's going to be inevitable that what you produce simply cannot be at the same level as your own 'real' novels, where you take all the time you want, you're in total command of the material, and so on.

How would you fit in *eXistenZ* with your own novels?

There's no real connection between *eXistenZ* and my other books, except a fairly loose one. I've always admired Mr Cronenberg's films, have usually felt that he and I are probably on the same sort of wavelength. In this sense, I feel I've grown up in the same intellectual or artistic culture as him, that we have interests and concerns in common. I suspect we share many things we like or admire: writers, other films, etc. When I was offered the novelization, I was pleased to accept it for that reason.

In another interview you mentioned that you feel David Cronenberg's view on virtual reality is somewhat outdated (Vernet, 2001). Could you elaborate on this?

This is a tricky subject. I'm sincere when I say I admire Mr Cronenberg's films. Over the years I have generally believed his work to be on the cutting edge of a certain kind of commercial cinema. He's one of the few really innovative and distinctive directors.

Even so, I felt that his take on virtual reality was a bit eccentric and not all that original, frankly. This would have been the impression gained by almost anyone who has, for instance, played any computer games in recent years. Some of the concepts in games are truly mind-boggling. In *eXistenZ*, the characters delve into an artificial reality where they end up in a Chinese restaurant, which leads to a breakdown in what is 'real' and what is not. I felt the mind was not likely to be boggled too much by the Chinese restaurant. Then the story goes off into shifting loyalties, betrayals, a violent insurrection, and an extremely corny ending in which we discover that the two principal characters are not what they have seemed all along.

My first thought was that Mr Cronenberg could not have read any of the novels by Philip K. Dick. Certainly books from the 1960s like *The Three Stigmata of Palmer Eldritch* contained ideas and situations that were many times more interesting and sophisticated than weirdo frog-parts in a Chinese restaurant. Then my second thought was that Mr Cronenberg could not have read any of *my* recent novels. I've been working with quite advanced concepts of virtual reality for at least

Figure 1. Jude Law and Jennifer Jason Leigh in *eXistenZ*. Photo courtesy of Dimension Films/Photofest.

the last 20 years, and most of those were a bit more ambitious than weirdo frog-parts. In particular, the novel I had just delivered, *The Extremes* (which of course Mr Cronenberg couldn't have known about), took the subject of virtual reality into what I considered to be new and advanced areas.

But … my job wasn't to get into an intellectual arm-wrestling match with him. For one thing, screenplays are endlessly rewritten, often to satisfy people in the film business who haven't the vaguest idea how screenplays are written. I could all too easily imagine that by the time the script reached me, it was the product of many compromises, revisions and substitutions. His film needed a novel and I simply played the thing with a straight bat. I took his material and made the best book I could out of it.

You also disclosed that the first version of your novelization was not approved. Can you reveal why?

What happened was that someone in Mr Cronenberg's office (of course, it might have come from Mr Cronenberg himself) said that the novel wasn't dark or menacing enough, that it was too fast-paced, too light. They wanted it made more sombre.

The irony of this, for me, was that one of the things I most liked about the script was its pace, its storytelling flair, and the witty and intriguing dialogue. When I read the script the first time I smiled all the way through, and laughed aloud a couple of times. Cronenberg is an excellent writer. The Jude Law character, in particular, has a nice line in dry asides. The Willem Dafoe character is written in an over-the-top way, which Dafoe, incidentally, translated perfectly on the screen. For some unexplained reason many of the characters spoke English with Russian accents, and I assumed this was some kind of obscure joke. On my reading of the script, I mentally imagined the film as being something like a science-fiction version of *The Big Lebowski*, kind of bittersweet, amusing, oddball. I wrote the book accordingly.

Then the word came down from on high that it needed to be darker, more menacing. This was conveyed to me by the editor at the publishers, who by this time had read and approved my manuscript. She had also read the script. We had a long, long telephone conversation, looking through the script, comparing it with the novelized version. In the end she agreed that I had followed not only the detail of the script, but also the spirit of it. She went back to Mr Cronenberg's office, but they wouldn't be moved. The book was too light-hearted, and needed to be made heavier.

The outcome of this was that an advance screening was set up for me and the editor at Shepperton Studios. Neither Mr Cronenberg nor any of his staff were there. It was here that I saw the film for the first time. At the end of the screening, the editor and I sat in the tiny auditorium and again discussed what differences there were between the film and the book. We remained united in our belief that far from being dark and menacing, the movie was an amusing, interesting, well-made adventure film with a lot of witty dialogue and entertaining scenes. There was some fairly gruesome stuff (such as the scene in which Jude Law suddenly finds himself impelled to eat the disgusting Chinese meal made out of lizards' legs and toad entrails, and the whole business of jacking into virtual reality by having a slimy pod hotwired into your nervous system), but even that seemed to us to be played not as horror but as black humour. Maybe it was a culture clash: our British sense of irony against North American literalism?

Whatever the explanation, the situation remained that Mr Cronenberg was not satisfied, or someone who worked for him said he wasn't. I agreed with the editor that I would run the manuscript one more time through my word processor, and look for every opportunity to introduce a sense of looming threat. This I did. I put in more negative adverbs: nervously, gloomily, darkly, terrifyingly, and so on. I made the weather worse. I kept the hours of daylight shorter. I described worrying noises. I interjected lines of dialogue and description. 'I don't like this.' 'What the hell was that?' That sort of thing. I did what I could.

It seemed to be enough, because after that, up to the present day, I have never heard another word from either Mr Cronenberg or his staff.

In the film, sexuality is quite present on various – mostly metaphorical – levels. In the novel, it is made much more explicit, for instance with Ted Pikul's motivations evolving mainly around sexual desire. Was there any particular reason for this emphasis?

I felt that having a more overt sexual relationship between Jennifer Jason Leigh and Jude Law gave the story a bit more impact, so I made it more detailed. I was also drawing on experience. The sex scenes in films are often shot several times, in varying degrees of explicitness. One version will be intended for cinemas in big cities, another for 'general' distribution. Another might be made with cable TV in mind. Or foreign markets. The actual scenes are often improvised on the day between the actors and the director. The screenplay will confine itself to 'they go to bed together and make love', and will only mention details if those details have a bearing on the characters or the plot. So from the point of view of the novelizer (who hasn't seen the film, and only has a short paragraph to work with) all options are open. My own policy is to try to write such scenes so they are consistent with the characters, the story, what is going to happen next, and so on. It's literally impossible to second-guess the film, so you write the novel the best way you can.

Are you satisfied with how your novelization turned out?

I'm neither satisfied nor dissatisfied with the finished book. I wish, as always, I had had more time to work on it. And I wish I had had a chance to see an early cut of the film before I eventually did. But I feel it's a reasonably professional job, written for the right instincts, that does what it set out to do. I'm sure there are places where it could be improved.

What is your general view on the phenomenon of novelization?

Novels based on films obviously have an appeal. I think people read them partly because they want to recapture some of the magic of having already seen the film and a novel will help them re-imagine it, and partly because they are looking for an explanation of something they found obscure, or an expansion of scenes, or something like that.

I also think a good novelizer can improve things. There was one film I worked on where, unusually, I was shown a rough cut of the film before I even saw the script. At the end of the rough cut there were three endings, one after the other. The director appeared at the end of the screening and explained that he had shot three endings because he couldn't decide which was the best. Privately, I thought all three of them were poor, and gave the film a weak climax. I decided not to worry about it, wait to see what the script said, then deal with the problem at the time. Perhaps by that time they would have decided. But a week later, when I was sent the script, I discovered that it had no ending at all! The writer had simply given up. When I got to the end of the novel I tried to find out what the director had decided to use, but no one would tell me. So I wrote a completely different ending of my own, consistent with the characters, logical within the plot, and with a surprise at the very end. Naturally, I think it's better than any of the other three endings. It's definitely a lot better than the one the director eventually chose. I went to see the film when it came out, and he had picked the easiest, most obvious ending of the three. It was also the weakest. (Of course, now you will want to know what the film was, but I'm not saying. Although I can say that it was not any film of Mr Cronenberg's.)

References

Butler, A. M. (2005) 'Introduction: The Interaction', in A. M. Butler (ed.) *Christopher Priest: The Interaction*, pp. 7–10. London: The Science Fiction Foundation.

Priest, C. (2008) *The Magic: The Story of a Film*. Hastings: GrimGrin Studio.

Van Parys, T., Jansen, L. and Vanhoutte, E. (2004) '*eXistenZ*, a Different Novelization? An Interview with Christopher Priest', *Image [&] Narrative* 5 (1), http://www.imageandnarrative.be/inarchive/performance/vanparys.htm (accessed September 2011).

Vernet, X. (2001) 'Interview de Christopher Priest', *ActuSF*, http://www.actusf.com/SF/interview/itw_priest.htm (accessed June 2004).

CHAPTER 12

PROPOSED TAXONOMY FOR NOVELIZATIONS AND ADAPTATIONS

Michael A. Stackpole

I am a novelist specializing in science-fiction and fantasy books with over 43 novels published since 1988. My career began as a game designer and computer-game designer, which had me working in the role-playing game industry at the time when the success of the *Dragonlance* novels created an urgency among game companies to support game lines with novels. FASA hired me to write a trilogy of novels in their *BattleTech* universe, the first two of which were published in 1988. Well over half of my novels have been set in media universes including, most recently, the novelization of *Conan the Barbarian* (Marcus Nispel, 2011); but the best-known of my franchise work has been for the *Star Wars* book series, including the best-selling novels *Rogue Squadron* (1996) and *I, Jedi* (1998). Because I have done so much work in the field, both as a novelist and as a developer of properties, I have a working professional's view of novelizations and adaptations. The terms 'novelization' and 'adaptation' – as commonly used to reference non-creator-owned works based on another work – are insufficient to adequately describe these works and their complexity. The terms lump together widely divergent works. This creates the incorrect impression that these works comprise a vast but shallow pool of work, disguising completely the true depth of the category.

'Novelization' has been used to describe *all* works from a non-creator-owned series; the term is used in this capacity by a small group of critics who are fighting to classify science fiction as literature. In my opinion, however, this is born out of an embarrassment about enjoying science fiction: only by creating a literary canon, which they hope will garner academic respect, can they make themselves feel good about their guilty pleasure. To create this canon, however, they are dismissive of any work that does not fit their sense of 'classic' science fiction. For instance, even fantasy novels (outside the work of J. R. R. Tolkien and Ursula K. Le Guin) are often viewed as dimly as novelizations are. And it especially seems to rankle them that Isaac Asimov's best-selling work ever was his novelization of *Fantastic Voyage* (Richard Fleischer, 1966). These critics will also call novelizations 'share-cropper novels', which casts the writers as peasants working for a corporate master for a pittance, as opposed to true artists who are willing to starve in order to create great works of art. The virtues of starvation can be argued elsewhere; the clear language bias of 'share-cropper' illuminates the mindset of those who use it. The most important aspect of their denigration of these adaptations is simple: they do not read them. They do not understand how they are put together. The general impression they work from is that an author is given a script, translates it into prose, and adds adjectives or 'he said'/'she said' dialogue tags. While this might be true of some writers and some projects, that impression misrepresents the typical novelization and masks the depth and breadth of adaptations.

Moreover, attitudes toward the work often spill over into attitudes toward the authors. The simple facts that a work is not creator-owned and was written for money form sufficient grounds for the *a priori* dismissal of said work and the writer who produced it. I actually had an editor look at me at the World Fantasy Convention one year and ask in an astonished voice: 'What are *you* doing here?'. If an author dabbles both in original work and work-for-hire, it is not uncommon to hear a critic opine that they hope the author will soon return to his or her *serious* work. The main criticism of work-for-hire books and tie-in novels seems to stem from two erroneous impressions, namely a lack of creativity on the author's part and the fact that the work was done for money. I shall deal with the former point below. The latter point, the anti-capitalism argument, is just silly. Unless a book is being written without a contract – on spec – *all* novels are written for money. Most work-for-hire contracts offer significantly lower advances and royalties. Most are written on very short deadlines. Authors often get paid for the book *after* it is written, so they are working hard for less money. This does not impart any special virtue to them or their work, but neither should that circumstance detract from it. More to the point, however, there are countless reasons to do work-for-hire aside from money. Work-for-hire lets a writer play with properties that he or she may have grown up reading or watching. The fact that the author gets paid to write these stories is a bonus. The author may take on a project as a favour for a friend who owns the property. Deciding to turn out a particular book can be a career-building choice – as in choosing a franchise that will bring the writer to an audience he or she did not already have. (In fact, this rationale played a part in my accepting the *Conan the Barbarian* film novelization; a lot more readers buy Robert E. Howard's fantasy work than they buy mine, so having my name associated with a *Conan* novel might bring Howard's audience to my work.) It can also be a stepping stone to more work from the franchisor, it can be done as a favour to the franchising publisher, or to capitalize the asset – i.e. knowledge of the franchise's universe – the author already possesses. This last point was key in my decision to write *I, Jedi*. Bantam Books offered authors a flat fee for writing the last dozen *Star Wars* novels in their contract. This contract was not popular with the Science Fiction and Fantasy Writers of America (SFWA), but I accepted it because it was very generous *and* because the previous three years had allowed me to develop an incredible storehouse of *Star Wars* knowledge which I could put to work again. Although I did not know it at the time, my willingness to stick with Bantam and do the job inspired Lucasfilm to insist on Del Rey hiring me to write for the *Star Wars* franchise when they took it over, despite Del Rey's intention of never using any of the Bantam authors for their line.

To impart any single motive for doing such work is as much folly as lumping all work together into one category, that of novelization. Breaking out of that restrictive taxonomy is vital because publishers – especially in the United States – are relying much more heavily on franchise work to attempt to make a profit. This field will grow, and new products will be developed within it – a trend which the digital revolution in publishing is exacerbating. In short, novelization is a single-dimensional measure for a three-dimensional phenomenon. My own taxonomy presented here accurately describes adapted works, and is drawn up from experience within the field. It is not reliant on a need to limit, denigrate and dismiss. It is a tool for getting a handle on a branch of literature which is quite robust and acts as a magnet to draw readers into the field.

Let us get down to terms. All of the works under discussion here fall into the broad category of 'adaptation'. Adaptations are works whose content is translated from one medium to another, which includes novels being written from a script as well as scripts being written from novels or short stories. Novels written from a canon also fall into this category, as would graphic novels, short stories, songs, computer games, cartoons, movies, teleplays, radio plays and accent/colour text for cards in collectable card games. On their turn, all of these works can then form part of the whole of the canon from which yet other works can be produced. A 'canon' can be defined as a collection of licensor-owned material provided to contractors for the purpose of producing adaptations. The designation 'licensor-owned' is critical. Much of the denigration of adaptations comes from the incorrect belief that since the source material is not 'creator-owned', the people working with it have zero creative input and, presumably, zero motivation to turn out good work. This sort of dubious logic would suggest that athletes who do not have an ownership stake in their club will not play hard; the notion is silly and unsupportable. A canon can further be broken down into 'primary' and 'subsidiary' sections. Primary works are those works that the licensor considers to be the most important. For *Star Wars*, it is the movies. For *Star Trek*, it is the TV series and movies; for Conan Properties, Inc., it is the original works of Robert E. Howard. Subsidiary work is anything else. Usually this material contributes to the canon, but if there is a continuity error on this level, it is of lesser concern. Subsidiary work may have its own stratification, with writers having to remain true to one set of items, while being permitted to ignore others.

'Novelizations' constitute a first category of adaptations, which consists of works written from a script. Usually, the source work is graphically-based (movie, teleplay, graphic novel) or highly interactive (computer game). It is also possible that an author could be handed a highly detailed outline; these works usually get defined as 'collaborations' – many under the guise of senior/junior parings where the junior does most of the writing. If the originator of the outline owns the property, they are not always seen as adaptations, despite the work being identical to what goes on with other adaptations. While virtually all practitioners in the field will agree with this definition of novelization, novelizations can take many forms. In some cases the licensor grants little or no leeway to the author. The goal there is to take the script and just turn it into prose with no additional content added. Other licensors are far more lenient, allowing the author to add thoughts or scenes. For instance, novelizations sometimes contain scenes which were cut from the final film. The novelization of the *Conan the Barbarian* film is an odd example of this. I received the script six months before I started work on the novel, and a packet of stills about two months out. I finally got to see a rough cut of the film three *days* before starting the novel and, at that point, the studio had not decided which ending they would use. (In fact, the rough cut ending was *not* part of the theatrical release, nor were a number of scenes that made it into the novelization.) The editing process had also moved scenes around so they no longer matched the script. The complete unfamiliarity with the works of Howard meant that the film had a number of continuity errors that included geographical impossibilities and scenes that contradicted both Howard's work and the wonderful graphic novel done by Dark Horse Comics. This put me in a very curious position. To novelize the script straight up would create a novel that did not fit into the Howard chronology. I had no intention of doing that. Fortunately, the folks at Conan Properties had approval, not the studio, so we hit upon a plan. What I wrote was the novel from which the movie could have been taken. I kept it faithful to Howard, accommodated as best I could some Hollywoodisms and created a book that added depth and sense to the movie. The licensor, of course, has final approval of the work product. Authors do get their customary editing passes at the work, but the publishers have a contract and the licensors are responsible for the integrity of any products attached to their property. The changes the licensor wants go into the work, and it is not unheard of for an author to find text he or she did not pen making its way into the printed novel. I myself have found paragraphs I did not write in some of the *BattleTech* novels, and minor editorial changes made in the *Star Wars* books. I do not think readers notice these things, but they creep in there.

Novelizations can be very odd things. Fred Saberhagen novelized the movie *Bram Stoker's Dracula* (Francis Ford Coppola, 1992) by reconciling the script with Bram Stoker's original novel. The novelization was done, of course, as a way to make money from the film, since the novel was already in public domain, so anyone could print up an edition. Most novelization horror stories centre on an author being given an incorrect version of a script. More than once authors have worked quickly to complete a novelization, only to learn that vast sequences have been cut or rewritten. What should have been a simple job now becomes an even more rushed rewrite, since publishing schedules have no flexibility if the book is to be released in conjunction with the film. As noted above with *Conan*, scenes get moved in editing, so while a sequence can be written to set up a following sequence in the novel, the scenes may appear in reverse order in the film – and the author can be tasked with making things match.

The second category of adaptations contains 'elaborations'. Elaborations are works that expand and further develop a property. These can include novels and other literary work, as well as films, cartoons, games, computer games, graphic novels and most other exploitations of the property. Basically, elaborations are authorized pastiches. As with pastiches, there comes an assumption that the writers have little or no creative input on the project. This is not the case, as will be discussed below. Elaborations break down into two further categories: 'expansion work' and 'interstitial work'. While these two categories are, in practice, very similar, the main difference is important enough to split them apart. Expansion work uses the canonical material as a starting-point with an open end. The conclusion of an expansion work is not determined by anything in the licensor-owned canon. Interstitial works, by contrast, occupy a space in the property which is manifestly defined by core canonical events. The works set the stage for or bridge between events. Because of this, interstitial works can be seen as having more legitimacy than expansion novels and yet, depending upon the whim of the licensor, may have had little direction handed to the author.

Licensor disposition determines a great deal of the work an author needs to do. Specifically, their attitude toward continuity is the greatest determinative factor. Paramount, with their *Star Trek* property, decided early on that they would not regulate continuity. They actively discourage it, wanting everything to stand on its own. While some authors might have internal continuity within their works in that property, everything is acceptable as long as a work does not violate core canon. When I worked on the *Star Trek: 25th Anniversary* computer game (1992), the developers all decided that the game would cover year four of the Enterprise's 'five-year mission'. Toward this end we poured through the television shows, pulled out details on worlds, plots and aliens, then crafted a series of scenarios that built on what the show had already done. When speaking with the approval people at Paramount, however, every attempt to tie back into the continuity got shot down. I finally said: 'I'm getting the impression you'd rather we just made up our own aliens than use yours.' Paramount confirmed this. (Yes, I wondered why we had bought a license at that point.) Lucasfilm, on the other hand, is a stickler for continuity and treats all products as part of the canon – though the films have precedence. The novels I have written for them go in for approval with full footnotes referencing games, novels, comics, computer game manuals and radio plays. All of these works, in turn, become canon and are free to use for other creators. There were times, in fact, when I specifically added something new to a novel so another author could use it in his or her book. There were also times when Lucasfilm came to me to plug a continuity hole. General Jan Dodonna appeared in

Star Wars: A New Hope (George Lucas, 1977), but subsequently died in the daily newspaper comic strip that began in the wake of the film's success. When Dark Horse Comics did the first *Dark Empire* series, however, they brought him back. And yet Dodonna had not appeared in Timothy Zahn's *Thrawn Trilogy*, which predated *Dark Empire* by a year in the chronology. It fell to me to establish his survival in *The Krytos Trap* (1996) and his rescue from Imperial forces in *Isard's Revenge* (1999), allowing him to miss the *Thrawn* novels, but show up in time for *Dark Empire*.

The second factor determining the nature of elaborations is the licensor's degree of creative control. While they all review work in outline and completed stages, some licensors feel the need to micromanage every tiny aspect of a work. Most licensors are content with continuity compliance, but may be more concerned when the work involves iconic characters and crucial events. This becomes problematic when the only feedback an author gets is that 'This isn't right', with no indication of what would be right. The worst manifestation of this is when a work has been approved in outline, changes are then demanded after the work has been written to that outline – changes which specifically contradict agreed-to core events. If an author is lucky, the licensor will be reasonable and can negotiate a reversal of the dictate.

The fact that these works go through an approval process is generally seen as evidence that no creativity is involved in the writing. One could argue that if that were that true, there would be no need for approval. The licensor would have handed out a template, and the author would have added names, places, adjectives and adverbs. A spell-check would be all the work requires. In practice, the works are highly creative. Authors understand that while people may be buying the work because of the property's name, *their* name also makes the cover. If the book fails to thrill the most die-hard fan, the author's reputation suffers mightily. He or she will be pilloried on every fan website on the net. If the novel is bad, the reader will blame the writer – no matter that the property-owner approved the novel. Turning out lousy work in a franchise property is a great way to kill a career. Conversely, if·the author does a good job, he or she stands an excellent chance of enlarging his or her audience. The crossover usually runs around 1 or 2 % of readership, which is not much, until you look at the actual numbers. Two percent of the *Star Wars* audience could bring an additional 5–10,000 readers to an author's original work. That is quite a lot of readers, especially in the current market. Moreover, if the works are translated into other languages, a publisher may consider bringing the author's original work over for translation as well.

In terms of the first four novels I did for *Star Wars*, the *X-wing* novels, the project was described to me in this way: 'We want you to write some military science fiction in the *Star Wars* universe.' Building it around a fighter squadron was implied. Later it was suggested that I use Wedge Antilles as a character, since he had a following. Lastly, I was not allowed to use any of the major movie characters without prior permission – a stipulation that I actually suggested and wanted. Having a project that boils down to '*Star Wars* with Wedge, X-wings, and no Luke' is not incredibly restrictive. I made all of the other cast decisions, determined when the stories would plug into the timeline and how the books would go together all by myself. That is the same workload I go into with any novels set in worlds of my own creation. With *I, Jedi*, the project was even more self-directed. Timothy Zahn wanted to use my character Corran Horn in his novel *Specter of the Past* (1997). It was set over a decade after the *X-wing* novels. In a conversation at a convention, I outlined for Tim what was a story I had always wanted to tell about Corran – his development as a Jedi. Tim took notes, and started his book with the assumption that all of that was true – even though *I, Jedi* was not under contract and we had no expectation that it ever would be. I mentioned, in passing, what Tim and I talked about with my editor, Tom Dupree. When Bantam and Lucasfilm started talking about a new contract, he insisted *I, Jedi* be part of it and the project fell back to me. I have mentioned Timothy Zahn's *Star Wars* work, and his *Thrawn Trilogy* points to the power of adaptations. Back before the novel *Heir to the Empire* (1991) premiered at #1 on the *New York Times* bestseller list on 30 June 1991, *Star Wars* was all but dead. That novel blew out of stores: within six weeks Bantam was on its third printing for over 150,000 units in print; and the hardbacks of all three *Thrawn* novels continued to be reprinted in hardback despite the release of the mass-market paperback editions. Those novels rekindled an interest in *Star Wars* which led, ultimately, to the new films and billions of dollars of commerce. The books allowed fans to connect with the universe in ways the movies did not, and their robust response spawned countless new projects.

Breaking things down into these categories and sub-categories is perhaps not exhaustive, but it accurately describes work within the field. There are going to be cases where the work does not fall easily into one classification or another: is it expansion or interstitial? My *X-wing* novels are expansions, since they bring in a new cast of characters and explore a lot of the universe that had not been touched before. Then again, because the novels fit snugly in between *Return of the Jedi* (Richard Marquand, 1983) and the first novel of Timothy Zahn's *Thrawn Trilogy* – and even set up events in that trilogy despite having been written five years after those books were published, one could argue that they were filler novels. And the scripts for the *X-wing* comics served as prequels for my novels, so they might be fillers to fillers. But, to clarify, I would still class those novels and comics as expansions, not fillers. Nothing written in them pointed to or set up anything in the movies. They just fed into and out of subsidiary material. The fact that, at Lucasfilm's request, I papered over a few continuity errors from other works does confuse the issue a little – and means that a lively discussion about where to classify those works could ensue.

I would like to make one more quick point before moving on to a discussion of odd examples of how adaptations function in the real world. An area of criticism that is broader than dealing with adaptations, but into which adaptations fall, is the question of 'speed'. Critics always use the speed with which a work was written as a bludgeon *if* they know how fast it was done *and* they do not like the work. A book that was written quickly but that the critic likes is seldom graced with a comment like 'But it would have been so much better if the author had taken more time to write it'. Some writers write well. Some write poorly. Some write fast. Some write slowly. As many who write well and do it quickly, will write slowly and do it badly. Speed and quality are not inextricably linked. My novel *I, Jedi* is often cited by readers as their most favourite *Star Wars* novel. It came in at 167,000 words and was written in 31 days of a 41-day period. I was working very well and hard on that book, the story came to me easily, and the book needed very little revision. There are times that fast just works. This is not to deny that many adaptations are written on a tight time schedule. More than once I have heard of an author turning in the manuscript before he or she had even got the contract, and having done revisions before he or she got the on-signing money. But many other factors outside of speed determine the quality of a novel, like the availability of core material or support or interference from the licensor. An author who is asked to write the novelization of a film on a tight schedule may do a great job, but adjustments made in editing and with reshoots may totally mess up his or her work. Or, more commonly, the gap in logic which might be dismissed by virtue of a special-effects shot in the film can become a glaring improbability in the novelization. The author can paper it over with a quick rationalization, but the licensor may not allow it.

Classifying these works within a taxonomy is not always easy. Part of the problem is that academics, editors, writers, publishers, property developers and fans all have differing perspectives both of what constitutes proper examples of such work and the purposes to which such work should be put. What might be seen as a legitimate adaptation by one individual may be as much based on how he or she intends to sell it, as what the content truly is. Property owners tend to want to maximize their profits from a product, so they would love to see their property have iterations in novels, graphic novels, animated comics, movies, toys, audiobooks and things waiting to be invented. The line separating adaptations from purer forms of merchandising can be difficult to discern. An action figure might not be considered an adaptation per se, but if a trading card packaged with him has text which expands the canon, it might pull it back into the adaptation realm. To the movie producer it is *all* merchandising, even down to the plastic soda cups at a fast food restaurant, but to a fan into cosplay (i.e. 'costume play'), the variant uniform on that cup is gospel. And a writer who includes that variant in a novel or subsequent script now has brought it back into something most would classify as an adaptation or possibly even canon.

Truly odd things can happen in the realm of adaptations. Stephen Gould's book *Jumper* (1992) was the basis for the movie of the same name (Doug Liman, 2008). In the deal it was decided that the original novel would be reprinted and sold as the novel of the movie – despite the screenplay having taken liberties with the world of *Jumper*. Gould was then hired to write a prequel novel to the movie, *Jumper: Griffin's Story* (2007), which tells the background of a character created for the movie, and involves the world mechanics from the movie, not the world of the original novel. And Gould has also published *Reflex* (2004), which is a sequel to the original novel. So we would have a case where the property-owner wrote a novel based on the canon created by a licensee. For some, this is an adaptation; for others it would not be.

The production of 'prequel' novels, presumably all of which would fall into the realm of interstitial work, is becoming more common. Prequel novels accompanied *Terminator: Salvation* (McG, 2009), *Transformers* (Michael Bay, 2007) and *G. I. Joe* (Stephen Sommers, 2009). Timothy Zahn, who wrote the *Terminator* prequel, said he was given scripts for the movie as well as notes about characters from the film, but was allowed to create his own adventure within the world. He likened the work to the same sort of thing we had done in writing *Star Wars* novels. Other movies and adaptations have not fared so well. Jeffrey Mariotte tells of a four-issue graphic novel miniseries of *Terminator: Salvation* that he wrote from the script. The first of the four issues was approved and printed, but the studio refused to approve any other issues for fear that pre-release images would hit the Internet and reveal the movie's ending, despite the fact that Jeff had not been given the ending of the script to prevent just such a release. Only the first issue ever saw print. With the *Conan the Barbarian* novelization, I was labouring under a similar restriction: the ending of the movie had not been determined, so I did not know which dramatic high point I was writing to. In the end, I wrote the finale I thought was most likely, and did it in such a way that I would only have had to revise the epilogue. It turned out that I had guessed correctly, so I did not have to change anything.

This desire to increase a property's footprint via adaptations is expanding because of the way the market is fracturing. Content is distributed through channels that make it convenient for consumers and imperative for providers to address, to make certain every consumer has a chance to sample their content. Moreover, technology that allows consumers to purchase the next product in a series, or ancillary material with the click of a mouse, creates a great profit potential. Given how much gets spent to produce some entertainment properties, all market opportunities need to be explored. Prequel novels are one way to test the waters for a series of novels set in the movie universe. Choosing franchise worlds for exploitation is a difficult process because the licensors usually want a great deal of money for the rights. At one point it was suggested that television properties that had enough episodes to go into syndication would have a chance at developing the sort of fan base that would make them viable properties for exploitation. I would suggest that another factor to be examined is exactly how much leeway the licensor is willing to give the writers in expanding and exploring the universe.

In the newest season of the *Star Wars* animated television show, *The Clone Wars* (2008–), the episode 'Nightsisters' (2011), written by George Lucas's daughter, Katie Lucas, is set, in part, on the planet Dathomir. This was a world/culture developed by Dave Wolverton for his novel *The Courtship of Princess Leia* (1994). By including it in 'Nightsisters' Katie Lucas invalidated a previous bit of canon concerning Darth Maul's planet of origin and dragged material from the novels completely into the media end of the property. While I suspect she did this because she enjoyed the novel, there is no doubt that Dathomir's inclusion in the animated series will sell a lot more of the books – and she has clearly got a lot of latitude in what she chooses to approach and how. The television series *Castle* (2009–) presents the latest iteration of mutually supportive products. Richard Castle is a mystery writer who is paired with a New York detective, who he is following to use as inspiration for a new series of novels. The novels have been written and sold, and the show regularly references them.

So basically this is a fictional character writing novels about fictional characters. It is not the first time this has been done, but never before have things been so tightly tied together. And if they ever do an episode with a killer following the plot of one of the novels, things will be very confusing. Still, the clear intent is to use one arm of the franchise to support the other.

Digital publication will sorely test notions of 'legitimacy' when it comes to adaptations. If a property holder like Conan Properties were to hire authors to write short or novella-length stories set in the Hyborian Age, and then subsequently published them through an app of some sort, the stories' legitimacy would be challenged on a variety of grounds. Purists would reject them simply because they are digital only, and critics because they are pastiches. Authors would make the decision based on how much they were paying and whether or not the money was worth the effort. Fans would probably come down on both sides of the issue, with those who write fan fiction in Howard's worlds taking the most dim view, since writers would be getting paid to do what they are willing to do for love of the work alone. What might have once been a clean line of descent/development for adaptations will continue to be muddied as we move forwards. *The Clone Wars* provides one example of content that was previously on a lower level of the canon being elevated – and being made that much more legitimate because the person doing the writing is the heir apparent to the entire *Star Wars* franchise. This mixing back and forth has happened previously, and those isolated incidents will likely increase, depending upon the flexibility of the licensor and the willingness of the licensee to be creative.

When Jennifer Roberson offered to write a novel for the *Highlander* series (1992–8), she did so because she was a fan of the television series. She flew to Los Angeles and met with a producer. She talked through the story arc she wanted to write, which included killing off an Immortal character that had appeared in a few of the episodes. The producer said he wanted to think about that, but two weeks later approved the death of that character. As a result, the expansion novel *Highlander: Scotland the Brave* (1996) changed the canon for the primary property. All it took was asking and a reasoned argument to back up why such a change to the canon should be made. Involvement of a writer with series development can also inject major changes in canon. Since 1988 I have written fourteen *BattleTech* novels. Every three to five years, the property owner would have a summit meeting in which staff and a few freelancers would meet to plot out the next five years of story arc. While I did not own the property, I was deeply involved in developing it. I got to craft the characters I wanted to write about, the plots I wanted to explore, the events and consequences to the universe; and other writers would be tasked with turning out work that would fall under that umbrella. Development was not limited to those meetings. When I was working on *Bred for War* (1995), I came up with an interesting twist about the true identity of a principle character in the *BattleTech* universe. I called the president of the property-owner at home on a Saturday, convinced him of my case, and he called his continuity people. They saw no conflicts with the canon, so this twist became canon. Things can get even more convoluted. Screenwriter Lee Goldberg had worked on scripts for the television series *Monk* (2002–9) and then went on to write several novels in the *Monk* universe. The producers liked one of them, *Mr Monk Goes to the Firehouse* (2006), a great deal, and suggested it would make a great television episode. Lee and Bill Rabkin, his screenwriting partner, were hired to write it – though the producer had a suggestion. He thought it would be great if, in the episode, Monk was blind. As Lee writes on his blog, 'So the first thing we did was set aside the sacred text and start from scratch. All we kept from the book were the basic bones of the mystery plot and a couple of clues' (Goldberg, 2006). Here we have another case where an expansion novel turns around and is itself adapted back into a piece of the primary canon.

Interaction with Hollywood – where property development is seen as a collaborative process – may force an expansion of what defines an adaptation. When freelancers are brought in to the collaborative process and become, by dint of being paid, part of the enterprise of the property owner/creator, their work could be considered part of the canon, not an adaptation thereof – at least from the point of view of the property owner. Critics and others might have a different perspective. The collaborative process may end up making it very difficult to determine the true nature of the *original* material, hence making it difficult to precisely place anything else in relationship with it. Regardless of that particular set of problems, the taxonomy I have suggested is sufficient to organize works related to a property by *function* rather than degree of kinship. A clear and concise system for classification of these works is vital to enable study of the phenomenon, and that study is important, since the frequency and scope of adaptations will be increasing with the expansion of our choices in entertainment media.

Reference

Goldberg, L. (2006) 'Mr Monk Can't See a Thing', *A Writer's Life*, http://leegoldberg.typepad.com/a_writers_life/2006/07/mr_monk_cant_se.html (accessed September 2011).

CHAPTER 13

THE ABYSS: BETWEEN FILM AND NOVELIZATION

Thomas Van Parys

In James Cameron's 'Afterword' to Orson Scott Card's *The Abyss* (1989), the novelization of the film of the same name (James Cameron, 1989), Cameron explains how 'the novel has fed into the film, just as the film has nourished the novel' (Cameron, 1989: 352). In his words, the 'book illuminates the film and vice versa, symbiotic partners in a single, multi-faceted dramatic work' (Cameron, 1989: 351). While during the making of the film and book Cameron and Card will undoubtedly have influenced each other (if we can believe their testimony), in this chapter I would like to take a look at how in an actual close reading the novel relates to the film. Are these 'texts' indeed complementary, part of one whole? Or do they in fact differ in significant ways? In that regard, while this novel is not representative of science-fiction novelizations in general, it is a significant case study because the collaboration is so close; as Card himself notes (in his own more substantial 'Afterword'), 'this novel is as close a collaboration between filmmaker and novelist as any other since the collaboration between Kubrick and Clarke in creating *2001: A Space Odyssey*' (1968) (Card, 1989b: 362).[1] In short, since these works are professed to be entirely complementary, this case study is perfectly placed to give a few modest insights into the possibility of a faithful adaptation – in other words, the ever-looming issue of fidelity – and the relationship between film and literature. Along the way, we shall uncover some differences between a regular novelization (the so-called 'hack job') and this kind of more prestigious novelization.

Thanks to Orson Scott Card's fame in the sf field – Card won the Hugo and Nebula Awards for both *Ender's Game* (1985) and its sequel *Speaker for the Dead* (1986) – *The Abyss* (which is Card's only novelization) is indeed one of the more respected science-fiction novelizations. Its prestige places it amongst other instances of novelization by a renowned sf author such as Theodore Sturgeon's *Voyage to the Bottom of the Sea* (1961), Isaac Asimov's *Fantastic Voyage* (1966), Arthur C. Clarke's *2001: A Space Odyssey* (1968), Piers Anthony's *Total Recall* (1989) and Christopher Priest's *eXistenZ* (1999). These novels stand out because it is unusual for the big names in sf literature to cross over into the tie-in business. Novelizations are usually separated from regular science fiction on all fronts, and they are hardly mentioned in histories of sf literature. Novelizations and spin-off novels are generally not highly regarded in sf criticism, the reasons for which are not hard to find. For one thing, novelization derives its material from sf cinema and TV, which not only comes across as unoriginal, but also causes the bad reputation of the latter to reflect on the former. In traditional sf circles, sf cinema has always been considered inferior to sf literature, its stories and ideas being regarded as mediocre in comparison to its literary counterpart. James E. Gunn even contends that most sf films, 'if translated into written form, would be un-publishable because of lack of logic or originality', regardless of 'the success of the novelized versions of a variety of SF films, including *Star Wars* and its sequels' (Gunn, 2004: 45). For another thing, the success of the myriad of novelizations and spin-off novels of certain franchises has led the general reader to equate science fiction with spin-off fiction (which is overrepresented in bookshops in comparison with regular sf). Damien Broderick points out that the 'seductive rise of mass-media "sci-fi" tore sf away from its elaborated specialist roots, carelessly discarded its long history. Science fiction consumers now start again from scratch, again and again' (Broderick, 2003: 62). What is more, as Christopher Priest remarks, many new writers now accept it as a norm that 'selling *Star Wars* or *Star Trek* tie-ins is a way in to the writing of legitimate SF' (Gevers, 2002). However, the remarkable lack of attention to novelization is unjustified, given that, for good or bad, the genre has played an important role in literary sf in the post-*Star Wars* era. As David Pringle notes, 'some sf, fantasy and horror movie novelizations are among the biggest-selling science-fiction, fantasy and horror works of the century' (Pringle, 1994: 40). Not only has novelization emerged as a genre in its own right and as such has had some influence on literary sf, it also forms a bridge between two prolific media, adding by its very nature something to intermedial comparisons between sf cinema and sf literature. That most sf novelizations may be badly written is largely beside the point; thus (ironically) Theodore Sturgeon's classic defence of science fiction itself – that 90 percent of everything is crud – no doubt applies here too. As Pringle argues, even 'if it is despised by critics, the novelization is a form which cannot be ignored' (Pringle, 1994: 40).

Of course, Card's *The Abyss* is not entirely representative of the standard commercial novelization. For one thing, it was written by a high-profile author in sf literature. This overlap of author and literary genre is fairly uncommon with novelizations, for novelization actually constitutes a genre itself, with its own specialized ('hack') authors (e.g. Leonore Fleischer, Alan Dean Foster), cover design, section in bookshops, and so on. For another, regarding content Card's *The Abyss* expands on the script, and does this by way of a collaboration with the filmmakers (which, from the viewpoint of fandom, undoubtedly lends it its 'canonical' status). It can be argued, of course, that novelization is by definition a form of collaboration between the screenwriter and the novelizer: in this sense, 'novelizations can be viewed as artistic collaborations as valid as any other form of literary or creative collaboration' (Larson, 1995: 38). The difference with *The Abyss* is that Card's collaboration with Cameron was simultaneous and proactive (although Card actually collaborated for the most part with Cameron's assistant, Van Ling). The filmmakers' cooperation encouraged Card to try and take this book beyond the commonplace novelization; according to him, he and Cameron tried to make the book 'not a novelization as the term is usually understood, but a novel that stands on its own and yet complements, illuminates, and fulfills the movie' (Card, 1989b: 361). Indeed, Cameron acknowledges this ambition as well:

> More to the point, I have read certain novelizations of my own films and found them to be cursory, mediocre, often inaccurate, and sometimes downright reprehensible. I determined that there would be no *novelization* of this film. There would be a *novel*. (Cameron, 1989: 350–1)

Incidentally, since Cameron directed few films before *The Abyss*, it is not difficult to identify the novelizations he is sneering at (leaving aside David Morrell's *Rambo: First Blood Part II* [1985], which is based on a screenplay co-written by Cameron); Randall Frakes and William Wisher's *The Terminator* (1985) and Alan Dean Foster's *Aliens* (1986) can be taken as typical models for the commercial Hollywood novelization, as they transcribe the screenplay in a pretty ordinary fashion. However, judging such novels on the mediocrity of their writing is as pointless as condemning outright all popular fiction. Instead, such novels are perfectly placed on the one hand to illustrate the significance of novelization as a cultural practice and on the other hand to show how they both do and do not support their source textually, in effect changing the viewer's cognitive experience of the films they are based on. As the case of *The Abyss* demonstrates, though, as soon as there is any form of prestige attached to a novelization, the terminology that is employed by makers and marketers is changed from 'novelization' to 'novel'.

The cover is frequently telling as well, in this regard. Although it is not unusual that the actual term 'novelization' is not used on the cover, it is more likely to be left off when a well-known or literary author is attached to the novelization; for instance, the first hardcover edition of Piers Anthony's *Total Recall* (1989) merely reads: 'A new novel by Piers Anthony'. Often, the cover will then avoid all association with the negative connotations of 'novelization', and even avoid (or at least minimize) the implication that the film came first. This is somewhat similar to the situation of science-fiction literature itself.

Literary authors such as Margaret Atwood, who wrote *The Hand-maid's Tale* (1985), often deny that they have written science fiction and their works have covers in line with regular literary fiction instead of genre fiction. The covers of novelizations can make the general public believe or at least leave them confused whether or not the book came before the film. The phrase 'Now a Major Motion Picture' is key to this obfuscation, since it can be put on novelizations as well as adapted novels that are republished as film tie-ins. While the US paperback of *The Abyss* still specifies that the novel is 'based on an original screenplay by James Cameron', the UK paperback leaves that acknowledgement off the front cover, also changing 'A Major Motion Picture from Twentieth Century Fox!' to 'Now a Major Film from Twentieth Century Fox' (perhaps trying to imply that Card's novel has previously not had a corresponding film). On the UK back cover it is not clarified either that the novel is an adaptation from the film instead of vice versa. It mentions that '*The Abyss* is a major motion picture directed by James Cameron and starring Ed Harris, Mary Elizabeth Mastrantonio and Michael Biehn. Screenplay by James Cameron', but it also reads in bold: 'From Orson Scott Card, one of science fiction's most heralded authors, comes an extraordinary adventure of wonder and terror.' From the cover, a customer/film-goer in the UK might therefore assume that the story originates with Card instead of with Cameron and, moreover, that the film is actually derived from the novel. In this case, the misdirection is not limited to the cover; nowhere within the book itself is it stated that it is based on the screenplay (except in the afterwords). Incidentally, translations of these novelizations in other languages occasionally take this one step further; for instance, the Dutch publication of Card's *The Abyss*, *De afgrond*, has conflicting information on the front cover: while it specifies at the bottom that it is based on Cameron's screenplay ('Gebaseerd op het filmscenario van James Cameron'), the cover is dominated by the double title, the English title being incorporated in the phrase 'Verfilmd als *Abyss*' (which means 'turned into the movie *Abyss*'). In short, by not positioning certain novelizations explicitly as novelizations, these kinds of publication strategies tend to justify the genre's dubious reputation.

I should like to foreground three key elements of the collaboration between Card and Cameron that are essential to the prestige of this novelization. The first is that this collaboration dismantles one of the traditional criticisms of the Hollywood novelization, namely that it is a lesser work because it is never entirely the writer's creation (being a transcription of a screenwriter's work). This is done not by Card making the novel entirely his own, but by further 'diluting' the already hybrid authorship of the novelization, for Card (1989b: 361–2) proclaims that 'it has long since ceased to be possible to go through this book picking out which idea, which nuance, which phrase came from Jim, which from me, and which from the actors'. In short, the prestige does not come from endowing the work with the Romantic notion of authorship, as is often the case with film adaptation, but from playing up the association between novelizer and director and thereby enhancing the validity of the novel.

The second is that Card's adaptation has involved some sort of transmedialization – a translation from one semiotic system to the other (see Baetens, 2005) – in contrast with the regular Hollywood novelization, which often comes down to being a transcription made from the screenplay only. And as Card (1989b: 356) mentions, novelizers 'who work from the screenplay alone either have to remain vague about physical details, or, in being specific they will inevitably contradict the film at a thousand points'; for that reason, the deadline for the novelization was pushed back so that he could also base the novel on the film and not just the screenplay. Indeed, while throwing out what he had written from the script after viewing videotapes of footage, Card (1989b: 358) 'learned for a fact what I had suspected from the start – that a novelization written from the screenplay is worthless compared to a novelization written from the film itself'.

The third element is that a genuine collaboration was established between director and novelizer. According to Card (1989b: 354), there can only be a good novelization 'if the filmmaker had enough respect for the written word to bring the novelist into his confidence and make him a collaborator'. Everyone has interiorized his or her own rules or standards for what constitutes a good film or a good book. For Card, and probably for everyone else too, a good novelization should be adapted from the film itself and not from its screenplay alone; after all, that is what the term promises, namely that an adaptation process has taken place from the screen to the page. Thus, when a novelization is actually adapted from the screenplay, it might be considered inferior, not only because novelization appears to skirt the problem of semiotic translation, but also because the page cannot be an up-to-date reflection of what is on the screen. Indeed, Card's presupposition does not solely come from his belief that a novelizer has a duty to adapt the film and not its screenplay. His terms for accepting this particular novelizing job – even though he had said to his agent: 'Barbara, [...] you know I don't do novelizations' (Card, 1989b: 353) – were: 'If I didn't believe that I could make the novelization utterly faithful to the movie as *filmed* and yet at the same time make it a novel to be proud of, then I wasn't interested' (Card, 1989b: 355). He adds that it 'was vital both to Jim and to me that the novel be quite specific and yet utterly faithful to the film' (Card, 1989b: 356) – but by 'specific' Card means detailed and precise in descriptions (of the actors, their movement, their interpretation of the dialogue and the overall mood). In other words, 'specific' here refers to descriptive accuracy in comparison to the film, and hence to fidelity, yet 'specific' and 'faithful' are antithetically used in his statement. I would argue that this already points to a deeper problem, namely that even when the written word is utterly specific (whether medium-specific or descriptively accurate), this does not guarantee that the meaning of the novel is faithful to the meaning of the film. Also, collaboration does not automatically entail two complementary texts. Even on a superficial level, there will always be incompatible elements: for instance, in the novelization of *The X-Files: I Want to Believe* (Chris Carter, 2008), even though the novelizer, Max Allan Collins, had 'full access to [writer and producer] Frank Spotnitz, [...] who approved everything I did' (Quijada, 2008: 2), the main antagonist is described as '*Rasputin*' – a 'big bulky figure' with 'long, dark, greasy hair and an angular, unforgiving face from which breath emerged like smoke' (Collins, 2008: 4), but is played in the film by Callum Keith Rennie, who has short blond hair and hence does not fit this description. Most differences between the film and novelization of *The Abyss*, however, are not mu-

Figure 1. Mary Elizabeth Mastrantonio and Ed Harris in *The Abyss.* Photo courtesy of Twentieth Century Fox Film Corporation/Photofest.

tually exclusive; as a rule, one text supplies information that the other does not. With the film it is audio-visual information; with the novel it is abstract information. It is in this way that they are complementary texts. In what follows, I will show that this notion is problematic by discussing what the novel adds to the film on the level of 'content' on the one hand, and on the level of 'form' on the other.

On the level of content, Card's *The Abyss* has, like most novelizations, a high explanatory function. Indeed, Cameron himself 'wanted the book to include facts and explanations that were impossible to put into the movie' (Card, 1989b: 355). In science-fiction novelizations, a principal ingredient is the integration of science and scientific plausibility, for it is the norm in sf literature, as opposed to sf cinema, to adhere to the current laws of science and logic as much as possible. In *The Abyss*, the need for scientific elucidation or rectification is not that great, mostly because, as Card himself notes, 'almost everything shown in this film except for the [aliens] themselves is either presently feasible or will soon be within reach of current technology' (Card, 1989b: 358). Still, there is much more elaboration and detail in the novel. For instance, the novel refers to the real scientific background to fluid breathing, to explain how the rat in the film breathes actual liquid (all images of which, incidentally, the British Board of Film Classification cut out of the UK version). The famous 'water tube' – a breakthrough in the area of special effects and possibly the scene that expresses science fiction's 'sense of wonder' best – is also explained elaborately in the novel in scientific (or rather science-fictional) terms. In order to be correct scientifically, Card also provides a reason why at the end of the film the characters do not need to go through a long period of decompression: '[the aliens] reached into *Deepcore* with ten thousand tendrils, touched and penetrated the bodies of the human beings watching there. [...] Then they made simple but profound changes in every cell' (Card, 1989a: 345). In fact, accuracy about decompression is the benchmark for scientific correctness in this novel, and the example above also recalls the infamous error at the end of *Fantastic Voyage* (Richard Fleischer, 1966) – namely that the deminiaturizing ship is left behind in the brain – which Isaac Asimov's novelization (1966) rectifies.

The most important explanatory additions, though, happen on the level of characterization, especially by representing the characters' thoughts through extensive internal focalization. In particular, Card's first three chapters detail the backgrounds and childhoods of each of the three main characters, which Cameron gave to Ed Harris and Mary Elizabeth Mastrantonio, who 'accepted Scott's interpretation as plausible backstory and incorporated it into their preparation for the film' (Cameron, 1989: 352) – even though actual traces of this in the film are impossible to pick up. Overall, the characters in the novel are also developed with much more depth. Whereas the film tries to subdue (to some extent) the conventions or clichés of the blue-collar good guy (Bud) or the obstinate military soldier as bad guy (Coffey) through the acting and the staging of the acting, the novel provides many detailed inner thoughts and motivations, thereby introducing much more ambivalent and multi-faceted characters. For example, Coffey is much more nuanced, and practically becomes essentially a good guy who turns into a victim of both high-pressure nervous syndrome and his own simplistic, strict ethics. Formally, his increasing madness is mirrored in sudden short shifts from external to internal focalization, coupled with chaotic language:

Coffey refused to take any of the things they said personally. Little weasely rat boy thinks I'm crazy? Fine. But the crazy one is you, boy. [...] You watch a woman with a machine, boy. They'll act the same way they do with you. They'll try to make the machine do what they want, and when it doesn't, they'll yell at it, they'll turn their backs and pout, they'll cry, they'll do all the same shit they do with you. [...] Coffey suddenly broke off his train of thought. (Card, 1989a: 245)

Card achieves the heightened level of nuance in the novel by reasoning excessively with the reader over everything (which he rather overdoes in order to play up the 'novelistic' advantages of the novelization): each utterance and each action is being considered, examined and (over)analysed. The reader is given causes, reasons, explanations even for elements that do not necessarily need one and for elements that go unquestioned in the film (perhaps due to the intrinsically different interpretation process that is visual literacy). To a certain extent this can be tied in with the character Bud and a specific character trait that Card has made very explicit, namely Bud's 'ability to handle people' (Card, 1989a: 20). In the novel, the central function and all the actions of this character are connected to this particular gift of his to manipulate and mediate, whereas in the film he remains the conventional good guy who becomes the protagonist because he is plainly the most commonsensical.

What plays a major role in explaining events (and filling in plot holes) in the novelization is the background of the aliens, and more specifically the access to their point of view. As Cameron notes, Card's 'intricately worked-out city of the builders and the rationale for their behaviour goes far beyond the enigmatic images of the film, in ways that can only be explored in the written word' (Cameron, 1989: 351). This additional material can be linked to Card's other work, as Sara Martín Alegre suggests:

All the scenes of the film are in the book, but if the angelic alien monsters of the film are much richer characters in Card's version this is because they bear a striking resemblance to his own alien monsters in *Ender's Game*, his most popular novel. The aliens of *The Abyss*, who call themselves 'builders of memory' and are capable of sharing collectively their memories because they have no sense of individuality are almost the same ones that are unwittingly wiped out by the hero Ender in Card's novel and who later redeem him. Both Card's *The Abyss* and *Ender's Game* end with the aliens' promise – already fulfilled in the former, to be fulfilled in the latter – to teach humankind how to share our memories and thus put an end to our isolating individualism. (Martín Alegre, 1997: 512)

As the novelization uncovers, all events are linked to and controlled by the actions of the aliens. Even the life and death of the characters are dependent on the aliens' actions: 'They watched Coffey fall into the chasm, but they did nothing to help him. Only after he was dead did they move swiftly in and scan his memory, to preserve him' (Card, 1989a: 293). In this way, in a complete reversal of roles, the aliens become the active agents who propel the narrative forwards, with the humans as passive characters that undergo the events (without realizing it). I should note, though, that the aliens come to the foreground more in the 'Special Edition' of the film, which differs significantly from the theatrical cut: in the latter, Bud appears to be really rescuing the aliens (who seem beautiful yet helpless), while the Special Edition's ending shows how the aliens are rescuing the humans by protecting them from themselves. Still, both versions of the film shows the aliens as homogeneous – there is no sign that their state of mind evolves – whereas in the novel they appear as extremely heterogeneous, not only in their actions, but also in their opinion of humanity, and finally in their self-image, which is changed profoundly precisely by the humans (in a nice twist of cross-fertilization). This evolution of their species manifests a few interesting narrative passages: as the concept of individuality is introduced among them, the inner thoughts of their initially unified mind ('us', 'we') gradually become more dispersed with discussion ('I', 'you'), all within internally focalized fragments:

> This very builder who gave the answer to them had been transformed by knowing these humans, and had acted in a way that was different from what any other builder might have done. [...] we fear the change that she has brought to us. (Card, 1989a: 302)

This is too simple an explanation. Is it? Then let me show you another, even simpler. I also see two worlds ahead of *us*. [...] No! Your madness is confusing you, and you are confusing *us*! You're speaking as if these humans were as important to us as we are to each other, as if they were our equals, when plainly they aren't! (Card, 1989a: 330–1)

From a thematic point of view, this is interesting as it points – very generally speaking – to another shift from sf cinema (where it always seems to be the aliens that affect the humans) to sf literature (where aliens and humans affect each other). The profound Otherness of the aliens not only influences the humans (and the readers, if they allow the science-fictional 'novum' to compare things to their own world), the humans' difference also changes the aliens: 'Humans and builders, we're *different* from each other. But we must still value each other, in spite of the differences. Because of them' (Card, 1989a: 332).

Lastly, the three elements I have discussed here, the urge for science-fictional explanation, the narrator's excessive reasoning and the activation of the aliens, are crucially linked by the aliens' ability to communicate 'by directly manipulating memory and emotion at a chemical and electrical level': 'the builders' messages entered Lindsey's brain exactly the way her own thoughts and feelings did' (Card, 1989a: 219). At a certain point in the film, Bud and Lindsey are making a few assumptions about the aliens – what they are, how they function, and so on. These assumptions are educated guesses, but they are not disputed and Cameron does not come back to them. In short, the viewer may assume that these guesses are correct, because the convention of Hollywood narrative cinema is that what the main characters say is authoritative, so there is no need for the viewer to question them at all. Again, the humans become much more passive in the novel; even Bud's pivotal heroic act, the neutralization of the warhead, is done in the novel with help from the aliens: 'They showed him which wire to cut and made him sure of his choice' (Card, 1989a: 332). Even though the texts can still be interpreted as complementary, since they never truly contradict each other, I would argue that this difference influences enough of the actantial model (i.e. the underlying story structure, with characters playing certain roles and instigating certain events) and the narrative causality to change the meaning of the texts. Film and novelization are each susceptible to medium-specificity, genre traditions and conventions, viewing and reading context, and so on, so that the interpretative models the viewer/reader brings to the table for each text are suitably divergent.

On the level of form, the narration in the novel is different from most novelizations. The typical Hollywood novelization has a third-person omniscient narrator, who focalizes continually and alternatively on different characters – which implies many displacements of focus, as Gérard Genette calls this (Genette, 1988: 76). Card's *The Abyss* starts out with precisely such a narrator, who is usually a rather covert narrator. However, he gradually becomes more and more overt:

> I guess that's true about practically everybody – I mean, either we spend our whole lives acting out all the things our parents said and did, or we spend our whole lives deliberately not acting like our folks. (Card, 1989a: 12)

> I told you about that one time because you have to realize that Hiram wasn't holding a grudge against Darrel. He didn't care that much about Darrel Woodward. (Card, 1989a: 30)

> Maybe you're thinking that I'm telling this story because Hiram heard about this [...] (Card, 1989a: 32)

> Any such story you heard was – I was going to say it was a lie, but how do I know? It might have been a hallucination. It might have been a dream. [...] they were near us, but we never really saw them. (Card, 1989a: 43)

> Maybe even with changed circumstances things would have worked out to the same result, except that it wouldn't be me telling you about it. But if things had worked out wrong, there wouldn't have been anybody much to tell it to. (Card, 1989a: 46–7)

This conversion goes from a regular covert narrator to an omniscient narrator who draws attention to himself, to a narrator who purposely tells a story with a message and addresses it to a reader, to a narrator who suddenly does not seem to be omniscient and infallible after all, to a narrator who even appears to be part of the story itself. After this move from a hetero-diegetic narrator (who is not a character in the story) to a homo-diegetic narrator (who is a character in the story), however, the still third-person narrator becomes rather covert again. Only in the closing pages the narrator appears to be Monk, one of the secondary characters, who until then has been addressed in third person, like all other characters. The shift happens in the following sentence: 'The light from the builders' bodies got brighter and brighter, until they – we – couldn't see at all in that direction' (Card, 1989a: 345). At that point, the narrator becomes an I-narrator. Within the diegesis of the novel, this has become possible because the aliens – the builders – are species defined by their sharing of memories and thoughts. At the end of the novel they connect to the brains of the protagonists and pass on all the memories they have collected from the people who are still alive as well as the people who have been killed, which allows Monk to tell the story from various perspectives – in fact, from all perspectives. Monk narrates:

> And they've given us the memories of the people that they scanned, the living and the dead. I've been filled with them, I've lived out their lives from the inside, I've known all their desires, all their fears – […] I have been Bud as he slipped down the cliff, I have been Lindsey as she drowned, I have felt their love for each other, and they have seen every secret in my heart. (Card, 1989a: 347)

He also spells out the message:

> I have learned from them what it means to be alive and human, I've learned why it is that people do the things we do, I've learned how other lives are from the inside. And now I've tried to pass it on to you. […] in these pages I've done my best to give you those memories that will show you what we did and why we did it, we who were down there when builders and humans met and changed each other for all time. (Card, 1989a: 348)

One might consider this Card's ultimate explanation of them all – the explanation of the omniscient narrator that is narrating the story itself

– for Card carries the elaborate reasoning in the novel further here, from content into form. The traditional third-person narrator is given a science-fictional twist, as it is explained precisely how the narrator can have told the story by incorporating him into the diegesis. Nothing comparable – or indeed complementary – to this is found in Cameron's film, with the filmic narrator – which is, following Peter Verstraten's film narratology, an overarching instance that organizes and regulates the visual narrator and the auditive narrator (see Verstraten, 2009) – trying to remain as invisible as possible, in accordance with traditional Hollywood cinema. In this respect, the narratives in both Card's novel and Cameron's film are essentially structured in their own specific and non-compatible way.

In conclusion, while Orson Scott Card's novelization of *The Abyss* indeed 'adds layers of meaning to the original film', I cannot entirely agree with Martín Alegre's verdict:

> After reading Card's novel it is simply impossible to distinguish the characters of the film from the characters of the novel – they become a new type of fictional construction stranded between two media. [...] Because it is exceptional, Card's and Cameron's *The Abyss* challenges us to enter into our critical vocabularies a new concept to complement original authorship, namely, intermedia symbiotic collaboration. (Martín Alegre, 1997: 513)

With regard to characterization and themes, the novel and film are certainly complementary, but only to the extent that neither of them would supplement the other in the Derridean sense (see Derrida, 1974). As soon as medium-specificity is taken into account, the complementary character becomes problematic. This is not to say that, with this particular case or indeed any process of novelization, content is transferable and form is not, to refer to Brian McFarlane's theory of adaptation (see McFarlane, 1996). No text can be entirely faithful to another; meaning always changes somewhere. But the complementary paradigm, which both Card and Cameron impose on the reader/viewer, is only one of a number of ways of understanding the relationship between the novel and the film. Lastly, it seems that even an overt preoccupation with fidelity cannot overcome various structural differences between media. Card's presupposition that a novelization can only be a good novelization if it is faithful to the film is diametrically opposed to the widespread Romantic notion that a film adaptation can only be a good film adaptation if it is unfaithful to and creative with its source material. While much of this actually depends on the authorial status of director or writer, it seems that, generally, film directors will go to great lengths to move away from the source material, whereas novelizers will go out of their way to stick as closely to the film as possible. If texts like *The Abyss* show anything, though, it is that neither fidelity nor infidelity is a very fruitful principle; rather, it is that a disregard for issues of fidelity leads to a more interesting case – both in practice and in criticism.

Note

1 The ultimate step-up from such a close collaboration is of course novelization by the director himself or herself, e.g. Pier Paolo Pasolini's novelization *Teorema* (1968), where it is often not clear which work came first, the film or the novelization.

References

Baetens, J. (2005) 'Novelization, a Contaminated Genre?', *Critical Inquiry* 32: 43–60.

Broderick, D. (2003) 'New Wave and Backwash: 1960–1980', in E. James and F. Mendlesohn (eds) *The Cambridge Companion to Science Fiction*, pp. 48–63. Cambridge: Cambridge University Press.

Cameron, J. (1989) 'Afterword', in O. S. Card, *The Abyss*, pp. 350–2. London: Legend.

Card, O. S. (1989a) *The Abyss*. London: Legend.

Card, O. S. (1989b) 'Afterword', in *The Abyss*, pp. 353–63. London: Legend.

Collins, M. A. (2008) *The X-Files: I Want to Believe*. London: Titan Books.

Derrida, J. (1974) *Of Grammatology*, trans. G. C. Spivak. Baltimore, MD: Johns Hopkins University Press.

Genette, G. (1988) *Narrative Discourse Revisited*, trans. J. E. Lewin. Ithaca, NY: Cornell University Press.

Gevers, N. (2002) 'The Interrogation: An Interview with Christopher Priest', *Interzone* 183, http://www.infinityplus.co.uk/nonfiction/intcpriest.htm (accessed June 2004).

Gunn, J. E. (2004) 'The Tinsel Screen', in L. Anders (ed.) *Projections: Science Fiction in Literature & Film*, pp. 43–59. Austin, TX: MonkeyBrain Books.

Larson, R. D. (1995) *Films into Books: An Analytical Bibliography of Film Novelizations, Movie, and TV Tie-Ins*. Metuchen, NJ and London: The Scarecrow Press.

McFarlane, B. (1996) *Novel to Film: An Introduction to the Theory of Adaptation*. Oxford: Clarendon Press.

Martín Alegre, S. (1997) 'From the Screen to the Printed Page: Orson Scott Card's Novelization of James Cameron's *The Abyss*', in P. Guardia and J. Stone (eds) *Proceedings of the 20th International AEDEAN Conference*, pp. 509–14. Barcelona: University of Barcelona Press.

Pringle, D. (1994) 'SF, Fantasy & Horror Movie Novelizations', *Interzone* 80: 38–52.

Quijada, A. (2008) 'The Truth behind the Novelization – Part III', *X-Files News*, http://www.xfilesnews.com/?view=article&catid=83:reviews&id=837:xfn-exclusive-the-truth-behind-the-novelization-part-iii&format=pdf (accessed September 2011).

Verstraten, P. (2009) *Film Narratology*, trans. S. van der Lecq. Toronto, Buffalo and London: University of Toronto Press.

CHAPTER 14

VALORIZING THE NOVELIZATION
THE AFTERLIVES OF 'TERRY NATION'S SURVIVORS'

Gwilym Thear

The original cult television series *Survivors* (1975–7) is now one of the most celebrated dramas of British 1970s television. It ran for three series between 1975 and 1977 and depicted the aftermath of an apocalyptic pandemic that has wiped out almost the entire population. Those few left alive have to learn to live again almost from scratch as they realize the necessity of growing food, raising livestock, making clothes and furniture and establishing self-sufficient communities. The series chimed particularly with a number of growing subcultural interests of the period, notably communal living, alternative energy and the self-sufficiency movement that also provided the impetus for the BBC comedy series *The Good Life* (1975–8), which made its debut in the spring schedule of 1975 alongside *Survivors* (Sawyer, 2006; Thear, 2010).

This chapter will consider the status of *Survivors* (1976), Terry Nation's novelization of the programme, which he also created. In doing so, it seeks also to try and tease out the complex intermedial relationship between the original series, the novel and the recent BBC series (2008–10). Nation's novel repeatedly stakes a claim for itself as the 'original' source for all other iterations of *Survivors*, yet this claim seems rooted not in any historical or causal relationship but in the conception of Nation as auteur, promoted in his novel and in both fan communities and academic assessments.

Terry Nation remains most celebrated for his work on the long-running BBC science-fiction drama *Doctor Who* (1963–89) and above all for the story he wrote for it in 1963, 'The Daleks', which introduced his most famous and enduring creations. He is also remembered for his 'space opera' *Blake's 7* (1978–81), which he created and on which he acted as script editor. Compared to *Doctor Who*, where Nation was a scriptwriter contributing occasional stories, and *Blake's 7*, where he retained control over the shaping of the narrative through his role as script editor, *Survivors* occupies something of a middle ground. Nation created the scenario, sketched out several of the main characters and wrote seven of the 13 scripts for the first series, including the first and last 'framing' episodes – a contractual requirement that, as Rich Cross and Andy Priestner (2005: 25) have pointed out, helped guarantee the best share of repeat fees. Although he negotiated a role as a script consultant for several episodes written by others (some of which never reached the screen) he never occupied the role of script editor – a position which was in the unofficial keeping of the series producer, Terence Dudley. Following serious disputes with Dudley over the future direction of the series, Nation abandoned the project altogether and started developing other ideas; he was never again to have any input in *Survivors*. His seven scripts for the first series were substantially edited and rewritten and the rest of the series was written by other writers under a separate script editor. He had no input at all into the second and third series.

Given that Nation had little connection with *Survivors* after the opening episodes, the series might be expected to be peripheral to the Nation canon. Certainly, Jonathan Bignell and Andrew O'Day's full-length study, *Terry Nation* (2004), spends considerably less time discussing *Survivors* than *Blake's 7* and *Doctor Who*. Nonetheless, Nation seems indissolubly linked with the programme wherever it is presented. The DVD box sets of all three series, released in 2003, featured on their fronts the words 'created by Terry Nation' directly under the

scriptwriters, is taking a 'somewhat [unfashionable] [...] approach' by '[identifying] and [celebrating] the distinctive contribution to the medium of significant individuals' (Nelson, 2007: 282). Stating their own position in *Terry Nation*, Bignell and O'Day define this neo-auteurism as the identification of 'a "signature" in the programme ideas, genres, plot structures and political subtexts of [Nation's] different works' whilst retaining an awareness of 'the combination of forces of writer, producer, script editor, director and so forth that [are] involved in bringing these works to the screen' (Bignell and O'Day, 2004: 2). Whether or not this approach really does signal a shift in academic attitudes, it undoubtedly chimes with popular auteurist attitudes towards a certain kind of television screenwriter. Andy Sawyer, in his essay on the programme, observes that 'the collaborative nature of *Survivors* obviously precludes ascribing particular influences to individual creators' (Sawyer, 2006: 138). Yet in the title, he nonetheless refers to the show as 'Terry Nation's *Survivors*'.

Approaches to science-fiction television appear to be far more auteurist than other genres. A trawl through the box-sets on my shelves reveals that, while (British) television comedy and serious 'quality' drama are frequently strongly associated with their scriptwriter(s), little or no reference is made to this authorship in the marketing and packaging of these programmes on DVD. *Porridge* (1974–7) may be celebrated as the work of Dick Clement and Ian La Frenais, and *Edge of Darkness* (1985) may be a famous script by Troy Kennedy Martin, but these names are absent from the DVD packaging of these programmes. By contrast, DVD box-sets of science-fiction television series frequently identify an auteur figure prominently on their cover, whether specified as writer or creator: Nigel Kneale and *Quatermass* (1979), Douglas Adams and *The Hitchhiker's Guide to the Galaxy* (1981) and, of course, Terry Nation and *Survivors*. Associating *Survivors* with Nation legitimizes its cult status, which helps to account for his name being identified with the series both on merchandise and in fan discussions even in connection with entire series with which he was not involved.[3]

That Nation should remain such a totemic figure is ironic for several reasons. The nature of his disagreement with the series producer,

Terence Dudley, was about how the survivors should cope in their post-plague world. Nation favoured a more action-oriented storyline, the characters moving from location to location and encountering rival groups, local warlords and various other threats – a formula characterized by one *Survivors* director as his 'four armed men in a Land Rover device' (Priestner, 2004: 16). This was indeed more or less the template for his scripts. Dudley, on the other hand, favoured the survivors establishing a settlement, building an agrarian community and engaging with ideas of self-sufficiency and alternative energy. Together with scriptwriter Jack Ronder he shaped the second half of the first series and, following Nation's departure, the whole of the second series towards these ends. Given the primacy of Nation in contemporary references to the programme, it might be expected that in some sense these developments have been thought to mark a departure from the 'real' *Survivors*; if Nation is the creator-auteur, surely it is his vision of the series which was the most successful and lasting? The audience figures rose for the second series and contemporary critics hailed it as more interesting and more realistic than the first (Cross and Priestner, 2005: 99). This period of *Survivors*, with its focus on community and self-sufficiency, is also the focus of a considerable number of (though by no means all) online fan responses to the programme. Whereas academic assessments tend to view the show as 'sombre', 'bleak' (Sawyer, 2006: 132) or 'fractured', undermining 'any sense of optimism' (Clark), fan sites display a more positive attitude. Although a substantial body of fan opinion would agree with the disgust felt by a poster on a *Digital Spy* forum that *Survivors* deteriorated after its first series into being 'the apocalypse meeting *The Good Life*',[4] other fans celebrate precisely this aspect of the show's history. The 'Terry Nation's Survivors appreciation society' group on *Facebook* invites us in its opening post to 'pull up a chair and relax with a nice glass of nettle wine'.[5]

Nation's influence as series creator is also more ambiguous than is popularly allowed. Although Bignell and O'Day (2004) argue for the primacy of a series creator in terms of influence, above that of individual writers, this is surely compromised when a series creator abandons a project, as Nation did, and leaves further series to be devised, written and produced by others. Certainly, the original scenario of survival within a post-pandemic world remained at the heart of *Survivors*, which thus stayed within the diegesis Nation had established. Yet at the level of plot, character and development, his influence can be considered negligible. Interestingly, though, this ambiguity about Nation's influence can be traced back to the start of the appearance of *Survivors* on television. As Matt Hills has pointed out, an auteur status 'predates fans' involvement through being offered up as an official extratextual/publicity narrative' (Hills, 2002: 133). This is certainly true in the pre-publicity for *Survivors*, which featured a double-page spread in the issue of *Radio Times* for the week beginning 12 April 1975. (*Radio Times* is the UK's leading television and radio listings magazine, at that time owned by the BBC.) Unusually, this article neither featured any images of the cast of *Survivors* nor screenshots from the programme itself; rather, it featured a full-length portrait of Nation himself. The focus of the article was upon Nation's reasons for creating the scenario and his interest in the lack of practical skills held by the general population in the modern age. This leads to a discussion of practical survival skills and self-sufficiency, and inset alongside the picture of Nation are several images of books about poultry rearing, vegetable growing and the great bible of the self-sufficiency movement, John and Sally Seymour's *Self-Sufficiency* (1970). Before the programme even appeared on television, therefore, the publicity material not only foregrounded Nation as originator/auteur, but also contextualized the series within the discourse of self-sufficiency and settlement (inherent in the practices of poultry rearing or vegetable growing) – precisely the direction Nation was unhappy about the series moving in and the apparent reason for his departure. Indeed, as we have seen, the first series itself (in the episodes Nation did not write) explored precisely this territory. The idea frequently ventured by Nation fans that there is a substantial difference in focus (and inevitable drop in quality) between series one and series two is thus open to challenge; the second series, with its focus on settlement and the establishment of viable communities, is a logical development of the first series and arguably expands on ideas that governed the series from its very inception. Nation's fans today may lament his leaving

Survivors and view only the first series as worthy of regard, yet the second series proved much more popular with critics and audiences at the time. Fans' attempts to isolate series one as Nation's work are similarly undercut by the fact that so much of that 'true' iteration of *Survivors* is actually the work of other writers moving the programme in areas contrary to Nation's wishes.

The *Survivors* novel may well have remained a historical curiosity, obscure and largely forgotten except by Nation scholars and *Survivors* fans. Certainly, although out of print for 30 years, the novel was clearly not in demand when I picked up a first edition a few years ago for less than a pound. But what may have remained a minor adjunct to the programme suddenly took on considerable importance when the BBC announced that 'after months of negotiations with Nation's estate' it had secured the rights to remake *Survivors* (*BBC News*, 22 November 2007). The BBC's 'reimagining' began in November 2008 and was axed following the end of the second series in 2010. Rich Cross is undoubtedly correct when he argues that the success of the revived *Doctor Who* helped create favourable conditions for the revival of another cult sf series from the BBC archives (Cross, 2010: 16). The long negotiations and resolution of the 'lengthy dispute' (*BBC News*, 4 August 2004) with the Nation estate to secure the rights to use the Daleks in *Doctor Who* also no doubt played its part in laying the groundwork. However, in reviving *Survivors* the BBC had not attempted the costly and complex process of securing the rights to remake the original television series, which featured the scripts of nine different writers across the three series – a 'hellishly complicated' situation, according to lead writer Adrian Hodges (*Total Sci-Fi Online*, 2008). The BBC had secured the rights solely to Nation's novel, which did not include material from other scriptwriters' work for copyright reasons. The self-proclaimed inspiration for the original *Survivors* had finally become what it had always claimed to be – the source material for a television series. Emphasizing this new-found status, the novel was reissued in 2008 as another TV tie-in, this time featuring the cast of the revived series on the front cover.

It was a further irony that in finally becoming the source material it had always insisted itself to be, the *Survivors* novel should find itself being effectively passed over. In buying the rights to the novel, the BBC had bought the rights to the pandemic scenario and a handful of the characters, yet the revived show did not develop any of Nation's storylines and extensively re-wrote some of his characters so that they remained in name alone. The new *Survivors* did base its overarching narrative arc upon Abby Grant's search for her son Peter, as Nation's novel had done, but it developed into a more conventional conspiracy thriller concerned with secret biopharmaceutical laboratories and the revelation that the virus was man-made. Terry Nation's status as the true auteur of the *Survivors* world seemed even more fragile, despite having been validated by the BBC's purchase of the rights to his novel. Yet when the DVD box-set of the new BBC series appeared, the blurb on its back described the programme as 'A chilling reinvention of the unforgettable 1970's [sic] series [...] based upon Terry Nation's original novel'.

In the end, the position of Nation's text remains odd and ambiguous. Its republication as the original source novel seems intended to validate the new series and give it a sense of authenticity. Yet even though the 'original' *ur*-text has now been 'adapted' into two different televisual representations 30 years apart, it actually has little in common with either. And yet it remains; and in doing so it perhaps helps to assure us that the series and novel alike will always be known as 'Terry Nation's *Survivors*'.

Notes

1 http://bobmeades.pages.qpg.com/index.html (accessed February 2011).

2 http://bobmeades-ivil.tripod.com/ (accessed February 2011).

3 A laudable exception is Cross and Priestner's excellent *The End of the World?* (2005), which, while fully detailing Nation's role and influence on the first series of *Survivors*, resists the portrayal of Nation as an auteurist presence over the whole.

4 http://forums.digitalspy.co.uk/showthread.php?t=698312 (accessed February 2011).

5 http://www.facebook.com/group.php?gid=5659622650 (accessed February 2011).

References

Anon. (2004) 'Daleks Back to Fight Doctor Who', *BBC News* (4 August), http://news.bbc.co.uk/2/hi/entertainment/3535588.stm (accessed November 2010).

Anon. (2007) 'Cult Show Survivors to Be Remade', *BBC News* (22 November), http://news.bbc.co.uk/2/hi/entertainment/7107597.stm (accessed May 2008).

Anon. (2008) '*Survivors*: Surviving the 21st Century', *Total Sci-Fi Online*, http://totalscifionline.com/interviews/1783-survivors-surviving-the-21st-century (accessed January 2011).

Bignell, J. and O'Day, A. (2004) *Terry Nation*. Manchester and New York: Manchester University Press.

Brooker, W. (2005) '"It Is Love": The Lewis Carroll Society as a Fan Community', *American Behavioural Scientist* 48 (7): 859–80.

Bruhn, S. (2000) *Musical Ekphrasis: Composers Responding to Poetry and Painting*. Hillsdale, NY: Pendragon.

Bryant, E. and Ellison, H. (1975) *Phoenix without Ashes*. Greenwich, CT: Fawcett.

Clark, A., '*Survivors* (1975–77)', *BFI Screenonline*, http://www.screenonline.org.uk/tv/id/518741/ (accessed June 2009).

Cross. R. (2010) *Worlds Apart: The Unofficial and Unauthorised Guide to the BBC's Remake of Survivors*. Cambridge: Classic TV Press.

Cross, R. and Priestner, A. (2005) *The End of the World? The Unofficial and Unauthorised Guide to Survivors*. Tolworth: Telos.

Hills, M. (2002) *Fan Cultures*. London and New York: Routledge.

Nation, T. (1976) *Survivors*. London: Futura Publications.

Nelson, R. (2007) 'Review: The Television Series: Terry Nation; Jimmy Perry and David Croft; Alan Clarke; Andrew Davies; Lynda La Plante', *Screen* 48 (2): 281–6.

Potter, J. (1996) *Representing Reality: Discourse, Rhetoric and Social Construction*. London: Sage.

Priestner, A. (2004) 'Viewing Notes', *Survivors: The Complete Second Series*, DVD. London: BBC Worldwide.

Sawyer, A. (2006) 'Everyday Life in the Post-Catastrophe Future: Terry Nation's *Survivors*', in J. R. Cook and P. Wright (eds) *British Science Fiction Television: A Hitchhiker's Guide*, pp. 131–53. London: I. B. Tauris.

Seymour, J. and Seymour, S. (1970) *Self-Sufficiency*. London: Faber & Faber.

Thear, G. (2010) 'The Self-Sufficiency Movement and the Apocalyptic Image in 1970s British Culture', in L. Forster and S. Harper (eds) *British Cul-*

ture and Society in the 1970s: The Lost Decade, pp. 131–9. Newcastle upon Tyne: Cambridge Scholars Publishing.

Wagner, G. (1975) *The Novel and the Cinema*. Rutherford, NJ: Farleigh Dickinson University Press.

PART V

INTERMEDIALITY

CHAPTER 15

THE EYES HAVE IT

Cynthia J. Miller

The theme of the third eye – that unblinking, middle-of-the-forehead icon of alien beings – is a fluid link between science-fiction literature and visual media that has spanned and united generations of writers, artists and filmmakers. Originally adapted from German author Karl Gruert's 1907 story 'Enemies in Space', for the edited volume *Invaders of Earth* (Grunert, 1955), and resurfacing periodically in stories such as Maurice LeBlanc's thriller *The Three Eyes* (1921), the third-eye theme has been adapted for use in numerous science-fiction vehicles from the 1960s to the present, highlighting themes of surveillance, mutation, and the undetectability of aliens among us, both extraterrestrial and earthbound. These images can be found in a range of literary and visual texts, including Ray Nelson's short story 'Eight O'Clock in the Morning', penned in 1963 (Nelson, 1994), which was later adapted as John Carpenter's film *They Live* (1988); the Mexican film *Santo el Enmascarado de Plata vs 'La invasión de los marcianos'* (Alfredo B. Crevenna, 1967); and 'Will the Real Martian Please Stand Up?', written by Rod Serling in 1961 for Season 2 of *The Twilight Zone* (1959–64). The combined influence of these third-eye manifestations can also be seen in other visual media, such as early *Mars Attacks* trading cards, predecessors to the 1988 comic-book series and Tim Burton's 1996 film.

Eyes of Myth and Legend

It is not unexpected that manifestations of a 'third eye' would be pressed into service for a range of expressive purposes. Often cited as 'windows to the soul' (or in French, 'mirrors of the soul' – 'les yeux sont le miroir de l'âme'), eyes have for centuries captured the fantastic imaginings of writers, storytellers and poets. The ancient tradition of the 'evil eye' highlights the eye as a symbol of death and desire – a silent, insidious destroyer of health and happiness – sometimes marked by physical difference, such as variations in colour or each eye containing two pupils, but at other times normal in appearance. Even the Bible notes that 'the lamp of the body is the eye [...] therefore, when thine eye is evil, thy body also is full of darkness' (Luke 11:34). Perseus, the first of the mythic Greek heroes, encountered the Grey Sisters – three dark-spirited hags with but a single eye between them – on his way to kill the Gorgon, Medusa. Greek and Roman mythology both resound with tales of the one-eyed creature known as the Cyclops – a member of a primordial race of giants, each possessing a single eye in the middle of its forehead. In Homer's *Odyssey*, the epic poem of fantastic adventure written at the end of the eighth century BC, Odysseus is captured by, and blinds, the Cyclops Polyphemus, son of Poseidon. Greek poets and playwrights, such as Euripides, Hesiod and Theocritus continued the tradition of the Cyclops, as did the Roman poet Virgil, whose *Aeneid* (first century BC) narrates the fate of Polyphemus after his blinding. In an equally monstrous mythological tale, we find the primordial Argus Panoptes, the all-seeing giant of one hundred eyes, servant of Hera and guardian of Io. Zeus himself was imagined with a fantastic configuration of eyes, and pictured in the temple of Zeus Larissaios with a third eye in the center of his forehead (Burkert, 1983: 168). Numerous such variations on monocular and multiocular sight exist in ancient Greek and Roman mythology, sometimes signifying hideousness, sometimes watchfulness or wariness. However, the overarching function of such deviations from the usual symmetry of human eyes, as David Williams notes in *Deformed Discourse* (Williams, 1999: 151), is to symbolize otherness – physical departure from the natural order signifying departure from the *moral* order – whether as magical guardian or malevolent predator, or in some cases, a combination of both.

This manipulation of eyes, in number, colour, placement, etc., has carried over from ancient mythology to contemporary science fiction and fantasy in a wide range of films. *It Came from Outer Space* (Jack Arnold, 1953) tells the tale of a small town menaced by an alien depicted as a floating eyeball. Two years later, however, *The Beast with a Million Eyes* (David Kramarsky, 1955) earned audiences' ire when the title and promotions lured theatregoers with the promise of grotesque otherness but failed to deliver. Gort, the giant robot in both versions of *The Day the Earth Stood Still* (Robert Wise, 1951; Scott Derrickson, 2008), maintains surveillance through a single glowing eye, while in *Hellboy II: The Golden Army* (Guillermo del Toro, 2008), the Angel of Death is depicted with multiple eyes in his wings and none on his face. In anime, the demon 'Te no Me' (featured in *GeGeGe no Kitaro* [2008]) has eyes in the palms of his hands, as does Kannon (Guan Yin), the Indian bodhisattva, in all one thousand of hers. Similarly, nearly all of the native Pandoran species in *Avatar* (James Cameron, 2010) have four eyes, while even the benign toy aliens in the animated children's movies *Toy Story 2* (John Lasseter, Ash Brannon and Lee Unkrich, 1999) and *Toy Story 3* (Lee Unkrich, 2010) have three.

As these latter examples attest, not all adaptations of the third eye have been malevolent. An early literary adaptation of the third-eye theme can be found in Ray Cummings's Tubby stories, appearing in *All-Story* and *Argosy All-Story* in the 1920s. These stories about Tubby McGuire were short spoofs of science fiction, with formulaic plots in which Tubby, a short, fat, vulgar know-it-all is usually disputing with his cronies about matters that none of them understands. Tubby then has a dream experience that turns their discussions into farce. In the last of these, 'Into the Fourth Dimension' (1926–7), Tubby is in the hospital, suffering from an eye injury. As he and his friends await the surgeon, they begin a discussion on the relationship of vision to dimensions – does one need two eyes to see three dimensions? The conversation is interrupted by Tubby being wheeled out and etherized for surgery. When he awakens, a tall, thin man is in the room – and he has a third eye in the middle of his forehead. He installs a third eye in Tubby's forehead, enabling him to see four dimensions. Looking into the fourth dimension, Tubby sees wealth beyond reason – a seemingly unending horde of 20-dollar gold pieces. The fourth dimension, however, can only be seen, not touched, and Tubby awakens back in his hospital room. So here, rather than functioning as a fearful embodiment of power and danger, the third eye shines a beacon on the human flaw of greed. In this example, the third eye serves as the reinforcer of social and cultural values and a vehicle for commentary on the futility of greed.

Looking Out, Looking In

Other ancient cultures also crafted lore and ritual linked to eyes, both physical and metaphysical, signifying not otherness or social learning, but great power and cosmic learning. An old Igbo (Nigerian) proverb posits that 'People have three eyes. One is the eye with which the spirit is seen, the two remaining ones are used to see people and the material world' (Umeh, 1999: 72). Likewise, in the second half of the first millennium, the Tantric tradition, which originated on the Indian subcontinent as a constellation of rituals and beliefs focused on appropriating and channelling the divine energy that animates the universe (White, 2000), offered an elaboration of the seven chakras, or energy centres, in the body. These chakras, believed to be located in the 'subtle bodies' – the unseen, spiritual dimensions – of the individual, are considered to be the focal points for the reception and transmission of divine (and biophysical) energy. Generally located at major branchings of the nervous system from the base of the spine upwards, the chakras govern increasingly complex energies as they ascend; the higher the energy centre, in relation to the physical body, the closer to God. The sixth chakra, *Ajna*, is the 'third-eye' chakra, located, roughly, in the middle of the brow and linked to both physical and intuitive 'seeing'. *Ajna* is charged with balancing the higher and lower selves and accessing visual consciousness and inner clarity and 'awakening'. As such, it is implicated in psychic faculties and the ability to understand archetypal levels – the 'big' *cosmic* picture of universal cycles of existence. By extension, the third eye carries a connotation of advanced knowledge, power and psychic abilities. These qualities are found in many contemporary third-eye depictions, endowing third-eyed aliens with superior intellects, technological advancement, and the abilities to read and control the thoughts of their human targets.

In later Hindu cosmology, the third eye continued to be a site of power, but in certain mythologies it was a site of more agency and more active, aggressive power. As indologist Wendy Doniger O'Flaherty notes in her book, *Siva: The Erotic Ascetic* (1981), the god Siva – the Destroyer or Transformer figure of the *Trimurti* or Hindu Trinity – is often depicted with a third eye. Siva's third eye, when open, is a creative yet also destructive centre, capable of emitting a powerful ray which, in its beneficent manifestation, created the lake known as the 'Forest of Reeds', yet in its violent manifestation, reduced the god's opponents to ashes. Thus the third eye also has a tradition as a site of danger. Add to this its quality of grotesque 'otherness' – a bizarre aberration in an otherwise human facial appearance – and the third eye becomes a complex locus of power, danger, fear and omniscience.

No small wonder, then, that the third-eye theme was popular in American science fiction in the 1950s and 1960s, when it was feared that a more terrestrial alien – the Communist – had infiltrated American society. That fear was transposed onto the aliens ('like us, but not us') of literary, televisual and cinematic fantasy and often manifested in the grotesque symbolic horror of the third eye. These narratives grappled with the symbolic and existential significance of the third eye – both apparent and hidden – and the otherness, difference and disfigurement it conveyed.

In Search of Alien Eyes

The relationship between popular film and television images and socio-political anxieties is one that has undergone increasing examination by historians, media scholars, and sociologists. Visual adaptations of literature and radio drama create contexts within which mainstream America carries on 'conversations with itself' in eras of rapid social change. The 1950s were one such era – an era marked by the interplay of fear and wonder – and often it was television that created a space of drama and fantasy in which those conversations might occur. The new medium of TV, a work of science fiction in itself, delivered iconic narratives of Americans' most fantastic hopes and unspoken fears intimately and directly into their living rooms.

Cold War era examples of the third eye in science fiction are plentiful. One of the best known is the 1961 episode of *The Twilight Zone*, 'Will the Real Martian Please Stand Up?'. One wintry night, two state troopers investigating a crash are led to believe it is a UFO. They follow footprints that lead them to a diner. The only patrons there are a handful of passengers on a bus to Boston, held up by the snowstorm and a weakened bridge ahead, but a head count yields one more person than passengers on the bus. As the narrative unfolds, suspicion builds as the passengers try to determine who among them is the alien – some fearful, others accusatory, others indignant. One exclaims with excitement, 'This is just like a science fiction! A regular Ray Bradbury!', and asks another patron if he has an eye in the back of his head. Husbands and wives question each other's identities. One patron points out that now they are all going to start looking for invisible clues and one of the troopers observes that 'We're all kids in a closet here. Nobody understands what's going on.' Lights fade on and off, the juke box plays of its own accord, sugar containers explode. Eventually the busload leaves, with all the diner patrons aboard. A while later, one, a businessman, returns to tell the diner's cook that a bridge up the road has collapsed, killing everyone on the bus and the two troopers driving behind them. The cook wonders how the businessman survived, and remained dry. The businessman unveils his third arm – using the hand to light his cigarette – and announces

Figure 1. Barney Phillips in 'Will the Real Martian Please Stand Up?', from *The Twilight Zone.* Photo courtesy of Photofest.

that he is from Mars, an advance scout in a plan to colonize Earth. In an act of extraterrestrial one-upmanship, the cook laughs and reveals his own Venusian identity, along with the news that the Martians have been intercepted and it will be *his* planet that colonizes Earth. Removing his paper hat, he reveals his third eye in triumph. The plot serves up thinly-veiled allegory of American Cold War paranoia, as the passengers turn on each other in suspicion and mirror the various reactions to McCarthyism. In the end, though, it is all for naught, as the plot reveals that the real colonizers of Earth are already here and hiding in plain sight, an unremarkable part of normalized American life.

Another television episode that drew together America's deep ambivalence about developing technology and McCarthy-era fears that subversives had infiltrated the country is 'The Martian Eyes', which first aired in 1950 during the third season of the anthology series *Lights Out* (1946–52). Burgess Meredith stars as Professor Lyman, a crackpot barfly who claims the ability to see the real identities of the

Martians who walk among us (for further discussion of early science-fiction television and technological ambivalence, see Booker, 2004). The episode was adapted from Henry Kuttner's science-fiction short story 'Don't Look Now', which was first published in 1948 and particularly significant in that it prefigured the wave of Cold War alien *doppelgänger* stories, such as *Invasion of the Body Snatchers* (Don Siegel, 1956), *Quatermass 2* (US title: *Enemy from Space*) (Val Guest, 1957) and the short-lived series *The Invaders* (1967–8). Each of these narratives turns on the premise that an alien invasion has occurred and that the invaders remain undetected on Earth, taking control of the human population.

Set in a local bar, where he is seen all too often, Lyman harangues his fellow patrons with warnings of Martians who have conquered the earth, but appear 'normal' to the human eye unless they choose to go invisible. With brief invocations of both Orson Welles and H. G. Wells, he tries to convince his fellow patron, a photographer named Sorrel (David Lewis), that 'They're all around us. We just can't see them', and goes on to explain that all of our irrational and illogical acts and desires are the product of Martian whims and purposes. Criminal confessions, radios, and the torturous discomfort of bathtubs all make no rational sense, and for Lyman are proof-positive that Martians have conquered the earth and control the human psyche. Their influence has been so naturalized that it has become part of everyday life. Lyman says:

> Take wars. Wars don't make sense from any human viewpoint. Nobody really wants wars. But we go right on having them. From the Martian viewpoint, they're useful. They give us a spurt in technology and they reduce the excess population – and nobody ever really wins a war – except the Martians.

Lyman's paranoia is in turn cautious, then animated, as he explains to Sorrel about his ability to see the Martians when no one else can. In Kuttner's story, Lyman's abilities are linked to a laboratory accident:

> Well, I got my brain scrambled, in a way. [...] High-frequency waves, it was. They went through and through me. Should have been inaudi-

ble, but I could hear them, or rather – well, actually I could see them. [...] And after that, I could see and hear the Martians. (Kuttner, 1987: 12)

After the accident, Lyman in Kuttner's story could not only see the Martians, but also resist their commands. In the TV show Lyman experienced the revelation a bit differently. His Martian vision is the result of a special infra-red eyeglass prescription. With these glasses Lyman can see the Martians' one unique physical trait, kept hidden from average humans – a third eye located in the middle of their foreheads. Screenwriter George Lefferts tightened Kuttner's explanatory devices to privilege a strong visual thread throughout the narrative.

As the narrative continues in both the short story and the series episode, Sorrel is won over by Lyman's increasingly paranoid insistence on the existence of alien invaders and reveals his secret – that he, too, has seen the Martians' third eye. In fact, he has the proof long-sought by Lyman – a photograph, taken accidentally with infra-red film. The literary narrative closes with Lyman and Sorrel agreeing to meet again at the bar the next day – forming a bond as co-conspirators in the Martians' exposure and downfall. In the televised episode, however, the terror is just beginning. Lyman and Sorrel agree to meet at the photographer's studio but Lyman is delayed. He places a panicked call to Sorrel, telling him that he has been followed, heightening the photographer's sense of impending doom. Before Lyman arrives, a stranger from the bar, previously identified by Lyman as a Martian that had been keeping them under surveillance, enters and demands the original and the negative of Sorrel's Martian photograph, apparently confirming Lyman's assessment of his extraterrestrial status. Amidst the confrontation, Lyman sneaks in and knifes the stranger from behind. Sorrel takes an infra-red photograph of him for proof of his Martian identity with which to build the pair's case for the authorities. Meanwhile, Lyman goes to the basement to dig a grave in which to hide the intruder's body. Much to Sorrel's horror, however, when the print is developed there is no third eye. The stranger was human. Panic-stricken, he calls down to Lyman to tell him of their ghastly mistake. Lyman, however, ever-so-calmly beckons him to

Figure 2. Burgess Meredith in 'The Martian Eyes', from *Lights Out*. Photo courtesy of Film & History Archive.

bring the body down, informing him that *both* of the graves are finished. Sorrel looks down the basement staircase in confused terror to see all *three* of Lyman's eyes looking back at him from the dark. And in that look we find the most successful aspect of adaptations from page to televised image – the intimacy and directness of the television screen. Lyman was right there, live on TV, summoning viewers out of the safety of their living rooms to the freshly-dug graves in the dirt-floored basement below. The fear was immediate; the three-eyed gaze, penetrating; the betrayal, horrific. And the impact on American television viewers was broad-reaching and simultaneous.

Co-opting the Gaze

The notion of the third eye, in its metaphysical form, gained in popularity in western cultures during the explosion of youth culture in the 1960s, as young people gravitated to Eastern traditions of spirituality and yoga. Peace, liberation, altered states of consciousness, 'new age' ideologies and counterculture values combined to create a dual emphasis on self-actualization, in the form of enlightenment, and universality, with its accent on the unity of not only nations, races and genders, but also humans with the natural world, space, time and the universal energy that animated all things. The Age of Aquarius brought a generation of new travellers down various paths towards Enlightenment, and their journeys led to popular culture's rediscovery of world religions: Tantra, Buddhism, Zoroastrianism, and Krishna Consciousness, along with Native American belief systems, astrology, trance states and the development of psychic abilities and awareness (see Kent, 2001; Sutcliffe, 2003). Inevitably, the quest to activate one's 'third eye', in the spiritual and psychic sense, became key to many counterculture journeys to self-actualization. The symbolism of the third eye returned to its Tantric roots, and countless self-help, spiritual and philosophical texts emerged with analysis, advice and instruction on the path to enlightenment.

Co-opted by mainstream American culture over the ensuing decades, the concept of the 'third eye' continued to advance in personal meaning while diminishing in significance in science fiction. One example of this shift in the status of the third eye is apparent in an example from the 1980s: the short-lived television series *The Third Eye* (1981–4), an anthology series in which the common thread was psychic powers thought to emanate from the third eye. Comprised of stories drawing on both science fiction and the supernatural, *The Third Eye* combined the otherness of special powers with positive messages about those powers' origins and meanings for both the individual and humanity. The voiceover introduction to each week's episode intoned:

> Somewhere in the crowd... sometimes you find someone very special. Someone who sees light in the dark. Someone who hears the unheard. Someone who understands the mystery. Sometimes, there's someone who sees with a third eye!

Intended for a young audience, the series was one of the first programmes on Nickelodeon, a network aimed predominantly at children under twelve. Episodes of *The Third Eye*, however, were somewhat more sophisticated in both content and imagery, and opened with a warning that 'The following is a science-fiction program, and may contain some very startling scenes. This show is intended for older children.' Each of the series' episodes, based on the work of British and Australian writers such as Bob Baker (*Doctor Who* [1971–9]; *Wallace & Gromit: The Curse of the Were-Rabbit* [Steve Box and Nick Park, 2005]), Vivian Alcock (*The Haunting of Cassie Palmer* [1982]) and Dorothy Edwards (*The Witches and the Grinnygog* [1983]), focused on children or young adolescents with psychic abilities – psychometric abilities, telepathy, the ability to communicate with other worlds and other life forms, telekinesis – the use and mastery of which is key to coming to terms with their identities and, more significantly, the moral order of the universe.

As with the physical third eye of early science fiction, the characters' third-eye-generated powers draw the fantastic into the realm of the ordinary, but the fantastic is overshadowed by personal development and social meaning. In all cases but one, the children's powers dissipate or disappear once injustices have been set right or relationships resolved. The common thread throughout the series is that these otherwise unrelated young protagonists are bound together by their abilities to activate powers associated with the third eye, and that such self-actualization is socially and morally valuable.

Here the third eye has a deeply personal significance – it makes an individual 'special' – harkening back to the notion's roots in the Tantric tradition, where the third eye opens as a result of personal development and the proper channelling of energy. Having an active, metaphorical 'third eye' is laudable, something to strive for, and in the series psychic abilities and penetrating insight are linked to positive social status, highly dissimilar from earlier science-fiction usages, when the third eye was something to be feared.

More recent popular culture often subjects aliens, once feared symbols of predatory otherness, to camp and parody, as in the 1967 film, *Santo el Enmascarado de Plata vs 'La invasión de los marcianos'* (released in the US as *Santo vs the Martian Invasion*) and Tim Burton's *Mars Attacks!* In the former, Santo (Rodolfo Guzman Huerta), the legendary Mexican *Luchador*, takes on a force of Martians who, spurred by Earth's failure to use scientific advancements for improvement rather than destruction, intend to take over the planet for the good of the universe:

When you wage war with conventional weapons you are the only victims of your ambition and selfishness. But with the discovery of nuclear energy and your mad experiments with the atomic bomb, you are on the verge of destroying the entire planetary system.

The critical social commentary vanishes, however, in the face of muscular, hypersexualized Martians – bare-chested men in tight silver pants and capes, wearing helmets which contain an 'astral eye' embedded in the centre. The visual comedy of these wrestling Martians, combined with intertextual references to Santo's previous encounters with zombies (1961), vampire women (1962), and witches (1964), robs both the film's Atomic Age warning and the Martians' dangerous third eye of narrative impact.

Similarly *Mars Attacks!*, adapted from the cult trading-card series (1962) and later comic-book series of the same name (1988; 1994), combines political satire with burlesque comedy and science-fiction tropes of alien invasion to create one of cinema's most effective commentaries on Cold War foreign relations. In both films the third eye functions as science-fiction parody, robbing the alien characters, with their excessively obvious otherness, of the terror of their 1950s and 1960s counterparts. The once horrific symbol of alien power is imported into narratives so ridiculous that they cannot be taken seriously, and its wider social power is diminished to the point of comedy.

Conclusion

Contemporary variations on the third eye continue to emerge in film in both subtle and more readily apparent guises. The jagged scar on Harry Potter's forehead marks his mystical sensitivity, becoming pronounced and painful at times of great peril. Noranti, the aging three-eyed Traskan featured on *Farscape* (2002–4), possesses a blend of mystical and scientific knowledge that gives her great insight and ability, yet her good-natured confusion and other mental ravages of ageing make her *accidentally* very dangerous. Both *Monsters, Inc.* (Pete Docter, David Silverman and Lee Unkrich, 2001) and *Toy Story* reduce three-eyed creatures to endearing children's playthings, excising the danger of three-eyed otherness altogether. Conversely, the three-eyed hell-hound Sammael, featured in Del Toro's 2004 film adaptation of Dark Horse Comics's *Hellboy: Seed of Destruction* (1994), is as evil and instinct-driven as any of science fiction's otherworldly monsters, illustrating that the third eye retains its persistent ability to invoke fear as a symbol of malevolence and power.

Taken together, these examples demonstrate the culturally and historically situated and often contradictory nature and range of the third eye in Western culture. Over time and across media it has functioned as both a marker and parody of otherness and danger, as a feature of monstrousness so monstrous that it becomes endearing, and as a symbol of insight and actualization. In the third eye many of our greatest hopes and innermost fears are given form – our mistrust of difference, strivings for certainty, fear of inadequacy, longings for insight, desire for power and need to understand our place in the universe. Refusing to be easily defined – or limited in its functions – the third eye has proved a multivalent symbol. However, its meanings have changed on the path from expressions of Cold War paranoia, to yearnings for self-actualization, to caustic cultural commentary. From an object of fear it has become, on the one hand, a signifier of uniqueness and, on the other, a vehicle for parody and social learning, while retaining its ability to induce fear and revulsion as a violation of the natural order.

Inherent in all of these possibilities, however, are continuing themes that cut across genre, era and narrative intent: themes of self versus other, as characters and audiences alike confront those physically, geographically and cosmically unlike themselves; perception versus objective reality, as ways of seeing are interrogated; and power versus subjugation, as 'vision' is equated with surveillance and control and then challenged. All of these combine, in narratives of the past, present and future, to make the third eye a cultural symbol worth... watching.

References

Booker, M. K. (2004) *Science Fiction Television*. Westport, CT: Praeger.

Burkert, W. (1983) *Homo Necans*. Berkeley: University of California Press.

Cummings, R. (1943) *Into the Fourth Dimension*. London: Swan Publishing.

Gordon, I., Jancovich, M. and McAllister, M. (2007) *Film and Comic Books*. Jackson: University of Mississippi Press.

Grunert, K. (1955) 'Enemies in Space', in G. Cronklin (ed.) *Invaders of Earth*, pp. 182–92, trans. W. Ley. New York: Pocket Books.

Kent, S. A. (2001) *From Slogans to Mantras: Social Protest and Religious Conversion in the Late Vietnam Era*. Syracuse, NY: Syracuse University Press.

Kuttner, H. (1987) 'Don't Look Now', in G. Scithers and D. Schweitzer (eds) *Tales from the Spaceport Bar*, pp. 7–24. New York: Avon Books.

LeBlanc, M. (1921) *The Three Eyes*. New York: The Macaulay Company.

Mignola, M. (1994) *Hellboy: Seed of Destruction*. Milwaukie, OR: Dark Horse Comics.

Nelson, R. (1994) 'Eight O'Clock in the Morning', in F. J. Ackerman and J. Stine (eds) *Reel Future: The Stories that Inspired 16 Classic Science Fiction Movies*, pp. 372–6. New York: Barnes and Noble Books.

O'Flaherty, W. D. (1981) *Siva: The Erotic Ascetic*. New York: Oxford University Press.

Stucliffe, S. (2003) *Children of the New Age: A History of Spiritual Practices*. London: Routledge.

Umeh, J. (1999) *After God is Dibia: Igbo Cosmology, Healing, Divination & Sacred Science in Nigeria, Vol. 2*. London: Karnak House.

White, D. G. (2000) *Tantra in Practice*. Princeton, NJ: Princeton University Press.

Williams, D. (1999) *Deformed Discourse: The Function of the Monster in Mediaeval Thought and Literature*. Montreal: McGill-Queen's University Press.

CHAPTER 16

ADAPTIVE BEHAVIOURS
RAY BRADBURY'S FICTIONS RE-INTERPRETED FOR MEDIA

Phil Nichols

Ray Bradbury is one of the most adapted of all writers in sf and related genres. His major works – including *The Martian Chronicles* (1950), *The Illustrated Man* (1951) and *Fahrenheit 451* (1953) – have all been adapted for feature film or television, and many of his short stories have been adapted for features, short films, radio, television, stage, graphic novels and comic books. Some of these adaptations have been carried out by Bradbury himself.

Bradbury claims that many of his works are already fit for screen (or stage, or radio) and require little or no modification when adapted (Bradbury, 1996a: 131; Warren, 1990: 31). This is a claim which does not survive close scrutiny, even when Bradbury is self-adapting. However, it does call into question the proper relationship between source text and adaptation, especially when we consider that the use of his name in titles such as *The Ray Bradbury Theater* (1985–92) and *Ray Bradbury Comics* suggests that Bradbury is now a 'brand'. The Bradbury brand potentially goes beyond merely announcing that the text is an adaptation and suggests a controlling influence. By considering the nature and extent of this controlling influence in a variety of adaptations of a single short story – 'A Sound of Thunder' (Bradbury, 1953/2008: 113–26) – I will show that, far from being restrictive, such an influence might actually promote creative interpretation of the source.

Bradbury: Hybridity as a Key to Adaptability

Even though Bradbury is one of the most frequently adapted sf writers, it is often said that his work is difficult or impossible to adapt. Three writers who have championed Bradbury's writing, Richard Matheson, Rod Serling and Harlan Ellison, all of them experienced in both screenwriting and the fantasy genre, have stated that Bradbury's work is problematic to adapt. Matheson, who adapted *The Martian Chronicles* for television, thinks the difficulty may be a question of realism: 'Ray's poetic visions are just too difficult to put on the screen [...] they seem realistic when you read them, but when you put them on the screen they lose that poetry' (Matheson, 2002). Serling, who commissioned Bradbury to adapt some short stories for *The Twilight Zone* (1959–64), sees dialogue as a key obstacle: 'Bradbury is a difficult guy to dramatise because that which reads so beautifully on the printed page doesn't fit in the mouth – it fits in the head' (Zicree, 1984: 274). Ellison has written original material for the screen and adapted other writers – but not Bradbury. He characterizes Bradbury (along with Hemingway, Pinter and Stephen King) as 'profoundly allegorical writers. [They] seem to be mimetic writers, but they aren't!' (Ellison, 1989: 181).

Bradbury himself claims he is easily adaptable. He points to his prose style and in particular his use of the visual in his storytelling, and to his own experience of screenwriting. He claims little difference between his writing for print and film and proclaims himself a hybrid writer, who draws on the traditions of print and film and is equally comfortable writing for both (Touponce, 2008: 11). In support of his contention that his work is easily adaptable, Bradbury is fond of quoting the film director Sam Peckinpah. When Peckinpah planned to film Bradbury's novel *Something Wicked This Way Comes*

(1962), Bradbury asked him how he intended to do it. Peckinpah's response was simple and direct: 'Rip the pages out of the book and stuff them in the camera' (Marchi, 1998: 178). This implies a very naive concept of the adaptive process but provides a wonderful metaphor for Bradbury's claim that he is easily adaptable. Alas, the Peckinpah strategy will not work in reality. Apart from anything else, among the pleasures of adaptation identified by Linda Hutcheon is the mixture of repetition and difference (Hutcheon, 2006: 114). If we adapted the Peckinpah way, we would get the 'repetition' but not the 'difference'. Nevertheless, in advocating Peckinpah's approach, Bradbury is throwing down a challenge that few in mainstream cinema have taken up.

The short story 'A Sound of Thunder' has been adapted for radio, television, cinema, computer game and comic book, and has also appeared in various print forms, often with accompanying illustrations. This variety of formats, with their varying degrees of visual accompaniment of the basic narrative, gives us a good opportunity to assess Bradbury's claims about his authorship, his and Peckinpah's view of adaptation, and to consider how the Bradbury brand might influence adaptation.

'A Sound of Thunder':
Short Story as a Challenge to Adaptation

'A Sound of Thunder' first appeared in *Collier's* magazine in 1952, and was collected shortly afterwards in Bradbury's *The Golden Apples of the Sun* (1953/2008). The story is a classic of time-travel, a sub-genre that S. R. L. Clarke has summed up as 'the make-it-didn't-happen story' (Clarke, 1995: 168). The basic premise of 'A Sound of Thunder' is that time-travellers go back in time to hunt dinosaurs, taking care not to stray from a magical path that protects against time paradoxes. Naturally someone does step off the protective path and crushes a butterfly, causing future history to change for the worse, specifically allowing a fascist dictatorship to take over the USA.

'Make-it-didn't-happen' stories create much futile debate and often receive criticism for being implausible or convoluted or both. In fact, 'A Sound of Thunder' was famously rejected by *The Magazine of Fantasy and Science Fiction* in 1952. 'Ha! We don't believe a word of it,' the magazine's editors wrote to Bradbury, '[...] unless you can build up a convincing end and also give a hint at the logic of altered events, this ain't no good for us and our rates' (Albright, 2004: 63–4). Their objections were on the grounds of plausibility, logic, plotting and consequences. But this story has gone on to be the most widely anthologized science-fiction story of all time (Contento, 2008). If the concept is so questionable, what is the appeal of this story? It is tempting to say that it is the image at the centre of the story, the fantasy of confronting a T. Rex. The only problem is that plenty of other stories in the science-fiction genre use that same image, yet have not persisted quite as much as Bradbury's – L. Sprague de Camp's 'A Gun for Dinosaur' (1956) and Brian Aldiss's 'Poor Little Warrior' (1958) to name just two. In fact, it is the imagery of the *very large* and the *very small* that makes this story so appealing: the dinosaur *and* the butterfly. This, and the irony that the pursuit of the large causes the small to be overlooked and that inattentiveness to the small detail, the precious butterfly, causes a catastrophic change in our present.

The narrative is immensely attractive but Bradbury's use of language adds more. He drives the short story forward rapidly:

> They put on their oxygen helmets and tested the intercoms.
> Eckels swayed on the padded seat, his face pale, his jaw stiff. He felt the trembling in his arms and he looked down and found his hands tight on the new rifle. There were four other men in the Machine [...]. (Bradbury, 1953/2008: 115)

This is Bradbury swaying toward what Jakobson calls the metonymic pole (Jakobson, 1987: 95–119): fairly direct language, where the meaning comes primarily from the sequential laying out of visual elements, which makes the text quite similar to the style used in a screenplay. This supports Bradbury's claim that his stories are written like film scripts.

When we get to the moments of powerful, lasting image, however, Bradbury does something different.

> It towered thirty feet above half of the trees, a great evil god, folding its delicate watchmaker's claw close to its oily reptilian chest. Each lower leg was a piston [...] sheathed over in a gleam of pebbled skin like the mail of a terrible warrior. [...] (Bradbury, 2008: 119)

In this passage, Bradbury momentarily stops the action and conjures up a more or less static tableau, and in so doing he flips toward Jakobson's *metaphoric* pole. The meaning comes primarily through non-realistic imagery. Notice that the use of language is suddenly very different from the style typically adopted in a screenplay. Such a scene would not be directly filmable. The challenge for a film-maker adapting this kind of scene would be to find a way of producing an equivalent effect through cinematic means. (Eric Rabkin has suggested that there might be some 'anxiety of influence' at work, to borrow Bloom's expression. That anxiety, in this case, would lead a film-maker to consciously avoid trying to emulate Bradbury in the adaptation, and to try something equally creative but in a different 'direction' [Rabkin, 2009].) Indeed, Thomas Leitch cautions against the fallacy of desiring fidelity in adaptation, arguing that it is ultimately meaningless since the only faithful version of a text is the text itself (Leitch, 2003: 161–2).

However, the existence of brands and franchises – from Stephen King to *Harry Potter* – suggests that there is something of a market and popular taste for straightforward translational adaptations. Playwright and radio dramatist Catherine Czerkawska points out that radio-drama listeners come to an adaptation of a novel with an expectation that certain key scenes will be transcribed, and heaven help the dramatist if they are left out (Czerkawska, 2006). It is certainly the case that studio-system Hollywood tended to 'accommodate the expectations of a knowledgeable audience' when adapting name-brand literature (Edwards, 2006: 45).

It seems to me that this audience expectation is a corollary of Hutcheon's suggestion that an adaptation, by definition, ought to be announced as such (Hutcheon, 2006: 170). When the announcement makes the source text or source author prominent – for example, through the use of the possessive credit, such as *Stephen King's It* – the adaptation becomes strongly branded and cannot help but establish expectations, at least in a proportion of the audience. This would seem to be the case with two successful dramatizations of 'A Sound of Thunder' for radio: a 1984 version produced as part of *Bradbury Thirteen* for NPR radio in the US, and a 1991 version as part of *Ray Bradbury's The Golden Apples of the Sun* for BBC radio in the UK. These productions were able to fulfil the brand expectation through one of the advantages of the medium of radio drama, namely being able to use the author's original language directly in verbal description, benefiting from the old saw that 'the pictures are better on radio'. The screen adaptations of 'A Sound of Thunder', on the other hand, show a significant divergence of approach, arguably also related to the controlling influence of the Bradbury brand.[1]

Screen Adaptations

Bradbury himself once took a stab at adapting 'A Sound of Thunder' for screen (1989), for his TV series *The Ray Bradbury Theater*. As we might expect from his claim to be a hybrid writer, equally at home on the page and on the screen, Bradbury's teleplay demonstrates his expert use of the metonymic pole in key passages, such as this:

ECKLES falls.[2]
In a single move, TRAVIS tromps on ECKLES [sic] ankle, then bends to yank off the short-boot. Holds it up.
CLOSEUP, for all to see: a butterfly trapped in the bottom of the heel.
[...]
ECKLES pulls the butterfly free, holds it out as if to make it live, fly.
[...] (Bradbury, 1989: 22)[3]

Most of the visual directions in the teleplay – as in most teleplays – are in this style; direct language, ideal for the denotative sequential images of a narrative film. When it comes to the potentially more connotative, evocative element of sound, Bradbury somewhat surprisingly swings to the metaphoric pole:

THE TRIGGER IS YANKED.
THE CAMERA, jammed to the rifle hole, explodes. INSTANT
DARKNESS. In the darkness, the butterfly falls down alone into
night.
Thunder, thunder, thunder.
In the thunder we hear all the beasts of time, killed, all the domino
years drop in a thousand avalanches, ending in a cry of the brontosaur
and T-rex, concluding with Thunder in the quick night. (Bradbury,
1989: 23)

Bradbury gives achievable visual events to the film-maker but issues a
serious challenge to the sound designer. It is unusual to see such metaphoric language in a teleplay, as it goes against the idea that a script
is a blueprint for the construction of a film. Unfortunately, as it turns
out, the challenge was never accepted. The TV episode, as broadcast,
shows little evidence of any attempt to use Bradbury's audio ideas,
perhaps because of the series' rather low budgets. Nevertheless, the
episode is a modest but effective adaptation of the story.

I find two things interesting in this adaptation. The first is that
Bradbury's own teleplay is a mere intermediate text, which contains
distinct visual and aural elements that just do not make it into the
finished film, despite Bradbury's name being used to brand the series and despite his status as co-executive producer. The second is
that Bradbury, in his script, has endeavoured to follow the Peckinpah
strategy – but in doing so he has had to abandon some of his own
original literary stylings in the visual descriptions, and has seemingly
found the Peckinpah approach impossible or undesirable when it
comes to descriptions of sound.

The 2005 feature film adaptation of 'A Sound of Thunder', written
by Thomas Dean Donnelly, Joshua Oppenheimer and Gregory Poiri-
er, and directed by Peter Hyams, has no Bradbury 'branding'. Instead
of being announced as 'Ray Bradbury's A Sound of Thunder', the film's
credits simply say that the screenplay is 'based upon the short story
by Ray Bradbury'. It is an announced adaptation, as per Hutcheon's
definition, but it is barely announced in comparison with all of the
adaptations discussed so far. The film consequently seems much freer
to re-shape the story, and re-shape it the film certainly does.

Figure 1. A Sound of Thunder poster art. Photo courtesy of Warner Bros./ Photofest.

A Sound of Thunder retains the central event of the dinosaur hunt, and the idea of accidentally changing history, but it embeds the story in a larger tale of corporate greed and corruption – embodied by Ben Kingsley playing a role as a rich businessman which has no counterpart whatsoever in the original short story. The character of Eckels is present, but demoted to a minor, almost nondescript, character. The discovery of the crushed butterfly serves not as a shocking climax, as in the original text, but as a small plot point along the way to solving a time crisis that somehow is causing waves of de-evolution to sweep the planet. (One wonders what the editors of *The Magazine of Fantasy & Science Fiction* would make of the logic of this version of the story.) Bradbury, incidentally, claims that he had the original director of *A Sound of Thunder* fired for daring to suggest that the butterfly might be dropped from the screenplay (Aggelis, 2004: 194). This was an early indicator, perhaps, of how far the film would drift from the source text as the film's script developed. The film also struggles to accommodate Bradbury's key imagery into its overblown three-act story structure. If one looks at the source text hard enough, one might discern a potential three-act structure already present, but this film has its own overlaid set of characters, all newly invented for the film, and their motivations and conflicts push out nearly every significant element of Bradbury's narrative.

This is not to say that the film is bad simply because it is not true to the source text. Regardless of its origins, the film suffers from high-concept piled upon high-concept, poor characterization and unconvincing special effects. Its troubled production history has left it, in the words of film critic Roger Ebert (2005), looking 'cobbled together from a half-baked screenplay and underdone special effects'. It is tempting to see the relative absence of the Bradbury brand as causing a loss of controlling influence over the adaptation, but it is difficult to sustain an argument from lack of evidence. What is clear, though, is that *A Sound of Thunder* makes no attempt to illuminate the text from which it is derived. If we adopt Dudley Andrew's extension of Bazin's metaphor, in which each adaptation is a flashlight, illuminating different facets of the source text it intersects (Andrew, 1984: 31), then Hyams's film seems to be a flashlight pointing the wrong way.

The radio, television and film adaptations of 'A Sound of Thunder' show us a limited extent of the controlling influence of the Bradbury brand. We can get a greater idea of the range of possibilities – of the way an adaptation can illuminate the source – by considering adaptations in graphic media.

Graphic Adaptations and Illustrations

Bradbury's collection *Dinosaur Tales* (1983/1996b) gathers together all of Bradbury's dinosaur stories, with each tale accompanied by illustrations by a single artist. These might not be considered true adaptations, since the illustrations are designed as accompaniments to the text. However, in some cases it is easy to conceive of the images standing alone, and conveying the narrative without the support of the text.

'A Sound of Thunder' is one such case, and is illustrated here by William Stout.[4] Stout's images interpret the text, add to it, and in some instances lead to a revised reading of the text. His first image of the T. Rex, for instance, emphasizes the monstrous proportions of the creature not only by having it dwarf the surrounding palm trees and circling pterodactyls, but by presenting it across two facing pages, with each page separately framed (Bradbury, 1996b: 66–7). A later image in Stout's sequence, also presented as two framed sections on facing pages, shows the dinosaur hunters being nearly crushed by the felled creature. One faceless human figure breaks from the frame and spreads across the double-page. The man who breaks the frame is Eckels, the transgressor, the character who steps off the path and crushes the butterfly (Bradbury, 1996b: 74–5). Stout's only image showing a clear human face depicts Eckels, centrally framed. His expression shows cowardice, fear and remorse. For this image Stout chooses a single, confining frame. Unlike the gigantic T. Rex, which cannot be confined to a single frame, and unlike the earlier unthinking Eckels who breaks the frame, this later Eckels is resolutely confined by the frame and trapped by the consequences he has triggered (Bradbury, 1996b: 81).

These images are designed to accompany the original story text, and yet they are not simple illustrations of the story's content. They encourage a new reading of the story in which Eckels, at least, shows an awareness of what he has done and possibly recognizes some responsibility for his behaviour. These are aspects of the character which are barely visible in the Bradbury text. There are several senses in which the text is controlling the images – it is Bradbury's book; the images are printed within the story; the images are positioned to tie in with the appropriate section of narrative – but the images also influence our understanding of the text in a way that we do not really observe in the film, television or radio adaptations of the story.

A similar effect is seen in Richard Corben's comic-book adaptation of the story (Corben, 1993). In key sections of his adaptation, Corben divides space and time with some remarkable framing: not limited to a conventional comic grid, the artist is free to divide his page into narrow strips which suggest either simultaneous events or a rapid succession of events. Through this presentation he is able to suggest a relationship or parallel between the T. Rex and Eckels that is not even hinted at in the source text. Eckels's eye is matched with the T. Rex's eye in what in film terms would be called a form edit (Thompson and Bowen, 2009: 93), implying eye contact between them, or a sense of personalized antagonism, or even a sense of identity of one type of monster with another. The events of Corben's narrative are undoubtedly controlled by the source text, as this is a very close adaptation of the story published under a definite Ray Bradbury brand (*Ray Bradbury Comics*), but Corben's selections, use of graphic emphasis and favouring of techniques specific to his medium allow him to illuminate aspects of the characters in a novel way.

Perhaps the most elegant graphic adaptation of the Bradbury story, however, is also one of the oldest: Joseph Mugnaini's line drawing, which was used as the single, original illustration for the story in Bradbury's collection *The Golden Apples of the Sun*, and has been reproduced in most reprints of the book up to the present day. Mugnaini places the dinosaur hunt at the focal point of the image, and his composition uses the pathway as a flourish that frames the tyrannosaur (see Figure 2). But careful, extended examination of the im-

Figure 2. Joseph Mugnaini's line drawing for Ray Bradbury's 'A Sound of Thunder', from the collection *The Golden Apples of the Sun.* Image supplied by and used by permission of Diana Mugnaini Robinson. © The Joseph Mugnaini Estate.

age reveals to us the butterfly, all translucent wings, foregrounded and dominating the scene (Bradbury, 1977: 88). The placement of Mugnaini's drawing at the start of the story in *The Golden Apples of the Sun* arguably gives Bradbury's text a subordinate role. For once, the adaptation/illustration makes its impact before the reader can consume the text, although I would argue that most of the Bradbury illustrations by Mugnaini (who did one for every story in *The Golden Apples of the Sun* collection and also did illustrations for the first edition of *Fahrenheit 451*) repay a second viewing after the story has been read.

These illustrations – Stout, Corben, Mugnaini – are all elegant, enriching interpretations of the text, yet with a quite tightly defined relationship to the source. They show a remarkable freedom of interpretative style, which might go against what we might assume for adaptive work produced under the controlling influence of an author's brand.

Conclusions

Even Bradbury's own adaptations of his own text give the lie to the Peckinpah strategy of ripping the pages from the book and stuffing them into the camera. Bradbury himself appears to follow Peckinpah, but when the need arises he breaks away from the naivety implied by Peckinpah's statement.

In fact, most of Bradbury's own major works turn out to already have something of adaptation about them: *The Martian Chronicles* is a 'fix-up' novel made from older short stories, as is *Dandelion Wine* (1957); *Fahrenheit 451* is a novel adapted from an earlier novella entitled 'The Fireman' (1951); *Something Wicked This Way Comes* is a novel adapted from an earlier, unused, screen treatment. What is more, Bradbury has also adapted all of these works for both stage and screen, and can be seen as something of a compulsive self-adapter. Many of his self-adaptations for stage and screen take extensive liberties with the source material and actually add a fascinating dimension to the study of Bradbury's authorship. 'Peckinpah's method' is a convenient shorthand for one supposed method of adaptation, but it is far from being the practice Bradbury adopts for his own adaptations.

Perhaps Bradbury's advocacy of 'rip the pages out of the book' stems more from his sense of ownership of the Bradbury brand, or from his expectation of his audience's desire to get what they expect of the brand. In the case of 'A Sound of Thunder' we can see that the controlling influence of the Bradbury brand has usually not had a negative effect: dramatizations in radio, television and comics have succeeded in producing vibrant work that at worst merely celebrates the source text but at best leads to a considered re-interpretation. The one exception seems to be the 2005 feature film, where the Bradbury branding is almost non-existent, and where the controlling influence seems to be something other than the source text. In this instance, seriously flawed though the film is, we can perhaps see a much stronger controlling influence coming through the film's director Peter Hyams, as the narrative and physical action reflect his earlier works – such as *Outland* (1981), *Timecop* (1994) or *The Relic* (1997) – at least as much as they reflect Bradbury's short story.

It may seem that this claim of a positive controlling influence in the case of branded adaptations is nothing more than a different way of stating a preference for faithful adaptation. However, the examples I have given of graphic adaptations do show significant points of departure from the source text. The Mugnaini and Stout images sit directly alongside the source text, but do so without anxiety of influence and without the need to be literal, limited or complete. The Corben images create narrative impressions that float freely above a simplified version of the original story. It is precisely this interplay of selected familiar elements from the Bradbury text with original concepts of the illustrators that is shepherded by the controlling influence of the Bradbury brand.

In the instances where Bradbury has himself been responsible for the adapted script, the controlling influence is of a different order, and there is a sense in the adaptation of a re-evaluation of the author's position in relation not so much to the narrative itself, but to the nature of the adaptive process.

Notes

1 Further research is needed to clarify the concept of brand in the case of Bradbury, not least because his active work in media spans several decades during which there have many changes in practices relating to possessive credits (see for example Robb, 1999) which would alter the significance of the 'announcement' of the adaptation. In addition, Brown and Patterson (2010) have shown that the marketing of a literature/film brand encompasses multiple levels of narrativity.

2 This alternative spelling of the character's name is used throughout Bradbury's teleplay.

3 Excerpts from Bradbury's unpublished teleplay of 'A Sound of Thunder' are reprinted by permission of Don Congdon Associates, Inc. Copyright 1989 by Ray Bradbury.

4 William Stout's original artwork can be found at http://www.comicart-fans.com/gallerypiece.asp?piece=725271&gsub=93879 (accessed September 2011).

References

Aggelis, S. (ed.) (2004) *Conversations with Ray Bradbury*. Jackson, MI: University Press of Mississippi.

Albright, D. (ed.) (2004) *It Came from Outer Space*. Colorado Springs, CO: Gauntlet Press.

Andrew, D. (1984) 'Adaptation', in J. Naremore (ed.) *Film Adaptation*, pp. 28–37. New Brunswick, NJ: Rutgers University Press.

Bradbury, R. (1953) *The Golden Apples of the Sun*. Garden City, NY: Doubleday.

Bradbury, R. (1977) *The Golden Apples of the Sun*. St Albans: Panther.

Bradbury, R. (1989) 'A Sound of Thunder'. Unpublished teleplay in the collection of the Center for Ray Bradbury Studies, Indiana University, Indianapolis.

Bradbury, R. (1996a) *Zen in the Art of Writing*. Santa Barbara, CA: Joshua Odell.

Bradbury, R. (1983/1996b) *Dinosaur Tales*. New York: Barnes & Noble.

Bradbury, R. (1953/2008) *The Golden Apples of the Sun*. Burton, MI: Subterranean Press.

Brown, S. and Patterson, A. (2010) 'Selling Stories: *Harry Potter* and the Marketing Plot', *Psychology and Marketing* 27 (6): 541–56.

Clarke, S. R. L. (1995) *How to Live Forever: Science Fiction and Philosophy*. New York, NY: Routledge.

Contento, W. G. (2008) *Index to Science Fiction Anthologies and Collections, Combined Edition*, http://www.philsp.com/homeville/ISFAC/0start. htm (accessed October 2010).

Corben, R. (1993) 'A Sound of Thunder', *Ray Bradbury Comics* 1: 5–16.

Czerkawska, C. (2006) Email to Phil Nichols (22 March).

Ebert, R. (2005) 'Review: *A Sound of Thunder*', *Chicago Sun-Times* (2 September), http://rogerebert.suntimes.com/apps/pbcs.dll/article?AID=/200 50901/REVIEWS/50901002 (accessed January 2011).

Edwards, K. D. (2006) 'Brand-Name Literature: Film Adaptation and Selznick International Pictures' *Rebecca* (1940)', *Cinema Journal* 45 (3): 32–58.

Ellison, H. (1989) *Harlan Ellison's Watching*. Novato, CA: Underwood-Miller.

Hutcheon, L. (2006) *A Theory of Adaptation*. London: Routledge.

Jakobson, R. (1987) *Language in Literature*. Cambridge, MA: Belknap Harvard.

Leitch, T. (2003) 'Twelve Fallacies in Contemporary Adaptation Theory', *Criticism* 45 (2): 149–71.

Marchi, J. (1998) 'An Interview with Master Storyteller Ray Bradbury', in S. Aggelis (ed.) *Conversations with Ray Bradbury*, pp. 175–83. Jackson, MI: University Press of Mississippi.

Matheson, R. (2002) Interview, *Archive of American Television*, http://www. emmytvlegends.org/interviews/shows/martian-chronicles-the (accessed October 2010).

Rabkin, E. S. (2009) Email to Phil Nichols (28 February).

Robb, D. (1999) 'DGA, WGA Battle Over Film Credit', *Back Stage* (6 August), http://www.allbusiness.com/services/amusement-recreation-services/4591841-1.html (accessed September 2011).

Thompson, R. and Bowen, C. J. (2009) *Grammar of the Edit*. Oxford: Focal Press.

Touponce, W. F. (2008) 'Introduction: Situating Bradbury in the "Reign of Adaptations"', *The New Ray Bradbury Review* 1: 9–12.

Warren, B. (1990) 'At Play in the Business of Metaphors', *Starlog* 153: 29–32; 58.

Zicree, M. S. (1984) *The Twilight Zone Companion*. New York: Bantam.

Chapter 17

'Everything Comes from Superman'
Infinite Crises in an Adapting Meta-Text

Martin Zeller-Jacques

When Worlds Collide

In the midst of the chaos of planets smashing together, of worlds being created and destroyed amid all the astonishing visual richness of sixty years of superhero continuity and discontinuity, DC's *Infinite Crisis* (2005–6) provides us with one clear articulation of the superhero genre's complex relationship with its own vast history. As he physically manipulates planets and timelines, seeking to create a single, perfect world from a discontinuous multiverse, Alexander Luthor takes on the role of adapter – choosing, discarding and merging elements from a wide and multifaceted diegesis – in order to create a new, complete text. Luthor is ultimately undone by the one apparently unalterable element of the superhero narrative, the *ur*-text from which all others have sprung: Superman. Staring straight out of the page at the reader, he utters the fundamental truth of all superhero comic books: 'Everything comes from Superman' (Johns and Jiminez, 2006: 163). Alexander Luthor cannot conceive of his perfect world not including a Superman, and yet in a world with a Superman, Luthor always loses. And another would-be adapter falls foul of canonical fidelity. This moment from *Infinite Crisis* is just one, extremely literal, example of a phenomenon that occurs with the production of any new superhero text. Along with its 1980s predecessor, *Crisis on Infinite Earths* (1985–6), *Infinite Crisis* explicitly attempts to rationalize and streamline the superheroic meta-text of the DC Universe, creating one comprehensible world from many divergent worlds. Alexander Luthor, the chief villain of *Infinite Crisis*, occupies the plural position of author/adapter/fan, and is faced with the difficulty of condensing a vast and contradictory body of texts as he seeks to produce a single new, definitive adaptation of all of these 'originals'. More than just a reflexive trope, this is a dramatization of what I will call the 'crisis of adaptation' faced by any new superhero text, in any medium, as it seeks to clarify and characterize its relationship to a great and growing body of texts that, although related, are not necessarily continuous or coherent. Through this crisis, each *Superman* text seeks to position itself as authoritative, as telling *the story* of *the Superman*, and yet to do so it must appeal to some aspect or another of the wider meta-text of *Superman*, drawing its authority from the explicit embrace or rejection of an established part of the *Superman* mythos.

Superhero (Dis)Continuity and Adaptation Theory

Despite the persistence of the term in popular discourse around comic books, most academic treatments of superhero narratives acknowledge that they are not best understood through the idea of continuity. Eco (1979: 114) characterized superhero narratives as existing in an 'oneiric climate [...] where what has happened before and what has happened after appear extremely hazy'. In such narratives time and space are malleable and individual stories occupy no fixed point in chronology: hence Superman's youth, despite 60 years of adventuring. Perhaps because of the persistent concerns of superhero fans, even writers who recognize and draw on Eco's insight persist in writing about continuity. As Eco's work suggests, superhero texts have rarely displayed anything that might justly be called 'continuity'. Instead, they often contradict one another, retell the same events differently, forget past events, or invent new ones, forming a web of interrelated stories – a meta-text – which reaches beyond the story contained in any individual superhero narrative.

This meta-textual view of superhero texts is suggested in the work of Robert Reynolds, whose seminal account of the superhero genre imagined the diegetic worlds of each of the two great comic-book publishers, Marvel and DC, as an 'ideal [...] metatext: a summation of all existing texts plus all the gaps which those texts have left unspecified' (Reynolds, 1992: 43). However, Reynolds was careful to point out that such a meta-text would forever remain unavailable to any individual reader, because of both the vast number of actual texts that contribute to it and the constant production of new texts. Reynolds's analysis remains confined by the discourse around continuity, and in concerning himself with the distinctions made by fans about which texts are and are not part of 'official' continuity, he says little about the potential influences and relationships between texts within the larger meta-textual field. These relationships are crucial to the way superhero texts function and the ways audiences interact with them. Although we might all agree that people all over the world recognize Superman, what exactly do they recognize? Do they know Superman from films, radio, television, comic books? They may know him for little more than the symbol on his chest, but they may likewise know the origin of the Bottle City of Kandor. They might see Superman as George Reeves, Christopher Reeve, Dean Cain, Tom Welling, or any of the other actors who have played him. These differing levels of engagement are not only important to audiences, but are written into new *Superman* texts, which invariably assume different degrees of audience familiarity and thus define themselves in relation to pre-existing aspects of the *Superman* meta-text.

Geoff Klock, drawing on Harold Bloom's paradigm of the anxiety of influence, has argued that superhero texts are written and read from within a web of intertextual relationships. The writing and reading of such texts thus becomes an act of 'misprision', with each writer and reader creating a new text, as he reads it in light of the old. For

Bloom, the influence of an earlier poet upon a newer poet 'always proceeds by a misreading of the prior poet, an act of creative correction that is actually and necessarily a misinterpretation' (Bloom, 1997: 30). Bloom sees this process of misinterpretation, which he dubs misprision, as an inevitable part of the creative process, as each new work must deem old work incorrect or insufficient in order to make room for itself. Applying Bloom's ideas beyond the narrow field of canonical poetry, Klock argues that 'superhero comic books are an especially good place to witness the structure of misprision, because as a serial narrative that has been running for more than sixty years, reinterpretation becomes part of its survival code' (Klock, 2002: 13); and he adds that 'In Eco's oneiric climate, strong work comes to define truth, as narrative continuity is fuzzy at best' (Klock, 2002: 31). Klock's observations are important, but he confines them to the narrow field of revisionary comic books, suggesting that only the 'strong' misprisions of comic-book visionaries like Alan Moore, Frank Miller or Grant Morrison recreate their own narrative realities. However, I would argue that the process of misprision he describes goes into any new superhero text; even those which blankly follow 'continuity' are taking a strong stance in regard to the many 'discontinuous' texts that make up parts of a superhero's meta-text. And certainly, any transfer of a superhero narrative into a new medium requires a strong misprision as the narrative world is reinterpreted for a new audience, making Klock's ideas particularly relevant to the practice of superhero adaptation.

This complex web of relationships draws us closer to the intersections between academic work on superheroes and contemporary adaptation theory. Terrence Wandtke draws attention to the multidirectional nature of influences and adaptations in superhero texts. Writing of *Superman*, he points out that:

> While many claim there is an essential urtext from which all things Superman flow, the truth remains that Superman mythology is very organic [...] [And] most often we see the 'biblical' truth of Superman's story eventually incorporating the most admired flights of imagination [from non-canonical texts]. (Wandtke, 2007: 13)

Wandtke further explains that this kind of multi-directional adaptation has long been common to superhero texts, with even some of the most well-known elements of *Superman* stories, such as Clark Kent's editor, Perry White, or the catch-phrase, 'Look, up in the sky, it's a bird, it's a plane, etc', deriving not from the 'original' comic books, but from radio and television adaptations (Wandtke, 2007: 5–7; 13). Drawing on the work of Mikhail Bakhtin, Richard Berger likewise points out that:

> adaptation in transmedia can alter the authority and status of pre-existing versions of a text. [...] In transmedia an adaptation can become canonical, and eventually the central text. In transmedia, these central texts can serve to connect to and disconnect from a range of other versions [...] [in a] dialogical sphere of influence. (Berger, 2008: 87)

While Wandtke and Berger usefully point towards the complexity of the ideas of canon and continuity, they still seem interested in identifying fixed points of source and adaptation, even while they acknowledge the fluidity of these designations. Berger's contention that *Superman: The Movie* (Richard Donner, 1978) 'marked the genesis of the "transmedia" event – whereby a narrative is deployed across several media, simultaneously' (Berger, 2008: 87) seems to ignore the fact that, long before it was adapted as a film, *Superman* was not a narrative, but many narratives transmitted through many media – simultaneously canonical and non-canonical, mutually contradictory and mutually reinforcing.

Many of these problems are essentially issues of fidelity and will thus sound familiar to students of adaptation theory. Sarah Cardwell has attributed to all adaptations the same quality that I have suggested is particularly visible in superhero narratives, arguing that 'It would be more accurate to view adaptation as the gradual development of a "meta-text". This view recognises that a later adaptation may draw upon any earlier adaptations, as well as upon the primary source text' (Cardwell, 2002: 25). If this view helps to remove us from reductive notions of 'source text' and 'adapted text', it leaves open the question of how adaptations draw upon the existing meta-text.

Thomas Leitch offers some useful observations on this in an essay on adaptations of the mythos of Sherlock Holmes, one of the few literary characters with a widespread multimedia ancillary life comparable to that of an established superhero. Leitch points out that franchises, like that around Holmes, 'are organized around larger-than-life figures whose mythopoetic appeal is iconic' (Leitch, 2007: 207). For Leitch (2007: 208), Holmes's texts are 'hybrid adaptations that depart from their putative originals at any number of points, often choosing instead to remain faithful to unauthorized later versions'. While this clearly echoes Wandtke's observations about superhero adaptations, Leitch goes on to suggest that there are further influences upon contemporary adaptations of the Holmes mythos. In a discussion of Granada's long-running television adaptation of the Holmes stories and novels, Leitch (2007: 228–9) suggests that, 'In rewriting Doyle, the adaptations are choosing fidelity to the appealing macrotext of the Victorian milieu and to a selection of powerful microtexts'. This kind of adaptation performs a powerful misprision of the Holmes mythos, emphasizing particular elements while ignoring or downplaying others. At the same time, it appeals to elements tangential or even foreign to that mythos in order to add a sense of authenticity – the 'appealing macrotext' of Victorian England for Holmes, or of the special-effects blockbuster for a contemporary superhero movie.

Klock sees the multi-layered, revisionist superhero narratives of the last 30 years as responses to and resolutions of the vast and chaotic 'continuities' created by decades of superhero publications (Klock, 2002: 22–3). But I would argue that self-consciousness has been a feature of superhero texts for far longer, and that it is visible in the way that any superheroic narrative, whether conservative or revisionist, defines itself in relation to its own meta-textual tradition. In the most ordinary of superhero texts, this self-consciousness manifests as the repetition of essential tropes of the story's characters. Superman's costume, Spider-Man's credo that 'with great power comes great responsibility', and Wonder Woman's exclamations invoking Greek Gods, are all elements which re-inscribe what non-revisionist texts regard as the essential elements of these characters. While revisionist texts may keep or discard these elements, radically reinterpret them or introduce new ones in ways that are more obviously self-conscious, both conservative and revisionist superhero texts, in whatever medium they appear, define themselves in relation to these elements of a putatively 'original' ur or meta-text. In doing so, these texts enact a crisis of adaptation as they attempt to position themselves as authentic through the explicit re-inscription or rejection of what they regard as the meta-text's essential tropes.

In order to investigate this 'crisis' of adaptation, I will consider *Superman for All Seasons* (1998), *Smallville* (2001–11) and *Superman Returns* (Bryan Singer, 2006), three texts from different media, but all explicitly adapting the character and mythos of *Superman*. Each of these texts offers an adaptation of *Superman*; each exists and is accessible to audiences at the same time; each incorporates many of the same characters, spheres of action and plot elements; yet none in fact represent the same events, or even precisely the same diegetic world. Instead each one is the unique product of its own crisis of adaptation.

Superman for All Seasons

Written by Jeph Loeb, with artwork by Tim Sale, *Superman for All Seasons* is a four-part graphic novel which (re)tells the story of Superman's early years in Smallville and Metropolis. In doing so, it presents a nostalgic view of Superman's story, drawing The Man of Steel among simple small-town folk, and offering the reader four variously sceptical narrators, each of whom articulates his or her own version of the question: 'Why should a man with unlimited power use it to help ordinary people?'.

The first three of the narrators, Jonathan Kent, Lois Lane and Lex Luthor, are unable to satisfactorily answer the question in their own minds, blinded in turn by fatherly love, journalistic scepticism and jealous rivalry. The fourth narrator, Lana Lang, is the one who feels she best understands Superman as an articulation of Clark Kent's simple, human wish to do his best to prevent bad things from happening. This vision of Superman as a good man trying his best – as something at once very ordinary and entirely unique – permeates the story, and is the essential version of Superman to which the text attempts to appeal through its crisis of adaptation. In order to do so, it explicitly contrasts its small-town Superman to the more violent tradition of later superhero narratives, appealing for its authenticity not to the genre's history, but to the macro-text of patriotic Americana, in the school of Norman Rockwell and Frank Capra.

Superman for All Seasons's crisis of adaptation is at its most visible in the third section of the story, and in fact becomes embodied by the character Toxin, a would-be superhero deranged by her immersion in the *Superman* meta-text. In a scene which nods towards Stanley Kubrick's *A Clockwork Orange* (1971), Lex Luthor finds a young woman once rescued by Superman, and now a fervent fan, and subjects her to a prolonged course of brainwashing (Loeb, 1999: 123–5). Her eyes pinned open, a sick caricature of wide-eyed, youthful innocence, she is surrounded by vast screens depicting images of the Man of Steel in action, and her ears are bombarded with slogans glorifying Superman. Although historically these slogans are drawn from comic books, radio broadcasts, and the George Reeves *Adventures of Superman* television series (1952–8), here they are linked with images referencing both the origins of the character, the diegesis of *Superman for All Seasons*, and a simple generic image of Superman deflecting bullets from his muscle-bound chest. This avalanche of words and images expresses something of the diversity and disorganization of the tradition of *Superman*, and certainly does little to suggest 'continuity' in the sense beloved by fans. In fact, the final effect of this treatment is to turn its subject into a delusional would-be superhero – calling herself Toxin, she helps Superman to neutralize a city-wide infection she herself helped to spread, but dies as a result of her efforts.

Her name and outfit redolent of the dark-age anti-'heroes' of the 1990s and the bad-girl heroines which still populate contemporary superhero narratives, Toxin represents the distorting effects of the accumulated size and strength of the *Superman* tradition (and by extension, the whole superhero genre), which now so often churns out heroes who are little but pale imitations of the genre's origins. She embodies *Superman for All Seasons*'s critique of what it sees as the empty, sensational violence of contemporary superhero narratives, becoming the negative focal point of a tradition against which this story attempts to define itself. Her eventual death, simply from the strain of assisting Superman and attempting to live as an equal in his world, presents the spectacle of innocence consumed by the vastness of the superhero tradition.

Even as it uses the character of Toxin to reject the excesses of the superheroic tradition, *Superman for All Seasons* gestures towards a wider tradition of Americana which it tries to position as more 'authentically' relevant to *Superman*. The visual style of the whole graphic novel draws on Norman Rockwell's illustrations of small-town life and also mimics the composition of famous American artworks, such as Grant Wood's 1930 painting, *American Gothic*, and the story incorporates references to Frank Capra's *It's a Wonderful Life* (1946). Although we may find such sources more or less appropriate to the character and tradition of Superman, they can in no way be considered part of his origin or canon. Rather, they position Superman within an alternate meta-text to that created by his own history, marking him as authentically middle-American, plain and simple folk. This represents a drastic example of the crisis of adaptation in a superhero narrative, one which sees the text consciously distance itself from the majority of its tradition.

Smallville

Television's *Smallville*, although part-created by Jeph Loeb, one of the authors of *Superman for All Seasons*, is at once a less radical and a more ambitious adaptation of the *Superman* mythos. Just the latest in a long line of *Superman* television series, notably including *The Adventures of Lois Clark* (1993–7) and the classic George Reeves *Superman* as well as several animated series, *Smallville* tells the story of a young Clark Kent as he grows to maturity and discovers his powers. Although in its early seasons it attempts to leave the future of the character open, refusing to engage too directly with the wider DC universe, in the last few years it has introduced more and more elements from the wider meta-text, and it has now become by far the most expansive screen adaptation of the *Superman* mythos, incorporating a wide array of original and adapted ideas into its diegesis. As a result, the crisis of adaptation is the near-constant subject of *Smallville*, every continuing arc of which offers as one of its viewing pleasures the question: 'How will Clark Kent grow up to become Superman?'

In its early seasons *Smallville* addresses this question by mixing long-established elements of Superman's world with the concerns of the teen TV genre. Clark Kent's discovery of his own powers and limitations is placed alongside his desperate teenage crush on Lana Lang, and many of the show's most effective innovations concern this relationship. Lana wears a kryptonite necklace, early on, crafted from one of the meteors that killed her parents, and this results in Clark, already awkward and shy around her, being physically incapacitated in her presence. Later on, Clark's heat-vision begins to manifest when he is sexually aroused, causing him to light classrooms on fire as he daydreams about Lana. Clark's gradual mastery of his emotions, a typical trope of the teen genre, is thus placed alongside his mastery of his powers, a typical trope of the superhero genre.

As *Smallville* develops over its run, it gradually expands Clark's world, introducing characters drawn from throughout the DC multiverse but providing them with origins and backstories appropriate to the series' increasingly self-sufficient diegesis. The narrative eventually incorporates classic *Superman* characters, such as Lois Lane and Jimmy Olsen, as well as characters from the expanded DC Universe, like The Green Arrow, Cyborg, Aquaman, the Martian Manhunter, and even Krypto the Superdog. It also draws upon 'dark-age' characters such as Doomsday, who share little with the idyllic, middle-American setting of the rest of *Smallville*. In reconciling this wide variety of characters to its central premise, *Smallville* provides an embarrassment of riches to those looking for evidence of the crisis of adaptation. On occasion these are elegant conceits, such as the revelation that Jay Garrick, Barry Allen and Wally West, the three men who in DC's comic books have been known as The Flash, are the names on the fake ID cards of a young super-speedster Clark meets on the streets of Metropolis (in episode 4x05, 'Run').

On other occasions, the crisis of adaptation forms the basis of a whole confluence of characters and events in an episode or arc of *Smallville*. The season-eight episode, 'Legion' (8x11), concerns three superheroes from the future who return to Clark's time in order to assist him in defeating the powerful super-villain Brainiac. These characters are members of the Legion of Superheroes, a group with its origins in DC's comic books, though with little other ancillary life beyond them. They have a comprehensive knowledge of Clark's career as Superman, something still in his future during the diegesis of *Smallville*, but little understanding of how this career relates to his life as the young Clark Kent. They take a position analogous to that of the audience, who have a relatively clear idea of what Superman is supposed to be, and for whom part of the pleasure of *Smallville* is speculating how Clark will develop into the more familiar figure of the Man of Steel. Within the episode's narrative, however, the Legion find this disjuncture between Clark and Superman troubling, with the character of Lightning Lad in particular playing the role of the dissenting fan, complaining: 'Are you sure we've got the right guy? I don't know. No glasses, no tights, no flights. So far, he's nothing like the man of steel.'

Within the episode's narrative, the Legion comes into conflict with Clark over the best way to stop Brainiac, a cybernetic being that has infected Clark's friend, Chloe Sullivan. The Legion maintains that Chloe must be killed in order to prevent Brainiac from stealing every bit of knowledge and memory from every being on Earth, while Clark insists upon finding another way to save his friend. Although the episode presents this conflict as one of personal philosophy, it is also exemplary of the crisis of adaptation, as it centres around one of *Smallville*'s few truly original characters, Chloe Sullivan. Although central to the diegesis of *Smallville* from its inception, Chloe has no previous life in any related *Superman* text. Early on she is conceived as a junior version of Lois Lane – a plucky reporter with a knack for getting into trouble – but without the same attendant sexual tension between herself and Clark. During *Smallville*'s eight years on the air, however, Chloe has developed into a central character, and one of Clark's most important friends and allies. This leads the heroes of the legion to speculate as to why, when they (like the audience) know of Lana Lang, Lois Lane and Jimmy Olsen, they have never heard of Chloe Sullivan. In attempting to reconcile her to their notions of the essential character of the *Superman* mythos, they imagine first that Clark must have asked Chloe to change her name, raising the possibility that she will re-emerge as a more 'authentic' *Superman* character, or that her death was what inspired Clark to take flight in the first place. Effectively, these characters from the future regard Chloe as expendable, because she is non-canonical.

When Clark, as we know he must, prevents Chloe's death and still manages to stop Brainiac, he asserts *Smallville's* authority against the wider meta-text of *Superman*. With the simple statement that 'Chloe Sullivan doesn't die', Clark cements his friend's position in the *Superman* mythos, ensuring her survival both in the diegesis and in the meta-text. Clark upholds one of the fundamental things that the audience know about Superman: that he does not take a human life, under any circumstances. At the same time as it establishes its own authority as a text, *Smallville* reinscribes part of what it sees as an essential element of the *Superman* meta-text.

Superman Returns

In many ways, *Superman Returns* is the most radical adaptation of *Superman* on display here. It is a film which deliberately discards most of the *Superman* canon, instead posing itself as a sequel to Richard Donner's *Superman: The Movie* and *Superman II* (Richard Lester, 1980). In doing so, it not only ignores almost the whole published run of *Superman* comics, but even the two later films in the earlier *Superman* franchise (*Superman III* [Richard Lester, 1983] and *Superman IV: The Quest for Peace* [Sidney J. Furie, 1987]). Despite this, *Superman Returns* takes a narrative leap to get it started, opening in a world without a Superman, where Luthor has escaped from prison and is plotting another fiendish real-estate swindle, and Lois Lane is married and has a child. The film does make a few slight references to the wider *Superman* mythos, having characters speak the famous 'It's a bird, it's a plane, etc.' line, and visually citing the famous cover of *Action Comics* 1 (1938) on which Superman first appeared. In general, however, the film draws its content from a very limited range of *Superman* texts. Nevertheless, its tone is demonstrably influenced by, and responsive to, other contemporaneous superhero film and television texts, most notably *Smallville* and *Spider-Man* (Sam Raimi, 2002).

The whole film seems marked by the complex compromise between its appeal to Donner's *Superman* films as its putative source and its paradoxical reliance upon other texts in order to be relevant and accessible to an audience which may not be familiar with that source. This tension is at its most visible in the film's one flashback to Clark's childhood. The scene recalls a similar one in Donner's *Superman*, where we see the young Clark Kent living a lonely, isolated life, as he hides his powers from the more sociable and popular kids around him. It takes us back to an earlier point, dramatizing Clark's discovery of his powers and focusing on the wonder and freedom that comes with them. It frames this memory with scenes of the adult Clark, having returned to his parents' home in Smallville after a prolonged period of time wandering the galaxy. The framing scene sets Clark in territory familiar to viewers of *Smallville*, even showing him against the background of the Kent family barn, the setting of many of the television program's emotional and narrative high-points. Meanwhile, the flashback directly recalls not only Donner's *Superman* but Raimi's more recent *Spider-Man*. The scene of Clark running and jumping through the cornfields visually references similar scenes depicting Peter Parker running and jumping across rooftops as he experiments with his newfound powers in *Spider-Man*. The scene in *Superman Returns* is constructed in order to assert, or create, an essential difference between the *Superman* mythos and the *Spider-Man* mythos. Specifically, Singer's Superman is a character with the weight of the world on his shoulders (at one point he quite literally hoists a whole continent and lifts it skyward), one who sacrifices himself to save humanity and then rises from the dead. The biblical scale of these events creates a pointed contrast to the very personal conflicts that predominate in the *Spider-Man* films. This contrast is further borne out in the scene displaying Clark's discovery of his powers. While in *Spider-Man*, the

Figure 1. Stephan Bender in *Superman Returns.* Photo courtesy of Warner Bros./Photofest.

scene ends with Peter slamming into a wall – the free exercise of power being curtailed by its sudden and severe limitations – in *Superman Returns*, although Clark initially stumbles as he leaps onto the roof of the barn, he stops in mid-air just as he is about to hit the ground, and hovers there, his ability to fly representing the fullest extent of his freedom. This difference sits at the heart of the way *Superman Returns* seeks to present its hero, establishing the lack of limitations on his power as key to his identity and to the film's narrative. Rather than relying on the large and, to many audiences, inaccessible *Superman* meta-text to establish this, *Superman Returns* resolves its crisis of adaptation through an appeal to the powerful micro-text of Donner's *Superman* films in combination with the widely known macro-texts of more contemporary film and television superhero narratives.

Conclusion

In each of these texts we can see evidence of the crisis of adaptation at work. As they attempt to reconcile their own, adapted version of *Superman* with the wider *Superman* meta-text and with the various macro-texts of genre, popular art and popular culture, they comment upon their own adaptation and attempt to establish their own authenticity. They may each begin with *Superman*, but they end as texts that attempt to assert themselves in place of all the *Supermen* who have come before. If this process is particularly apparent in superhero adaptations, which are often associated with widespread, multi-media franchises, it is surely not only apparent here. The more commonly adapted works are, and the more widely those works circulate within popular culture, the more likely it is that each new iteration of that work will show evidence of a crisis of adaptation.

References

Berger, R. (2008) '"Are There Any More at Home Like You?": Rewiring Superman', *Journal of Adaptation in Film and Performance* 1 (2): 87–101.

Bloom, H. (1997) *The Anxiety of Influence: A Theory of Poetry. Second Edition.* New York and Oxford: Oxford University Press.

Cardwell, S. (2002) *Adaptation Revisited.* Manchester: Palgrave.

Eco, U. (1979) *The Role of the Reader.* Bloomington: Indiana University Press.

Johns, G. and Jiminez, P. (2006) *Infinite Crisis.* New York: DC Comics.

Klock, G. (2002) *How to Read Superhero Comics and Why.* Continuum: London.

Leitch, T. (2007) *Film Adaptation and its Discontents: From Gone with the Wind to The Passion of the Christ.* Baltimore, MD: The Johns Hopkins University Press.

Liebowitz, J. (ed.) (1938) *Action Comics 1.*

Loeb, J. (1999) *Superman for All Seasons.* New York: DC Comics.

Reynolds, R. (1992) *Superheroes: A Modern Mythology.* Jackson: University of Mississippi Press.

Wandtke, T. (ed.) (2007) *The Amazing Transforming Superhero.* Jefferson, NC: McFarland.

Wolfman, M. and Perez, G. (2001) *Crisis on Infinite Earths.* New York: DC Comics.

CHAPTER 18

EXTRAORDINARY RENDITIONS
THE MANY LIVES OF FLASH GORDON

Mark Bould

To the extent that *IMDb* users' comments can be taken as representative, Sci Fi Channel's *Flash Gordon* (2007–8) was greeted with universal derision, gaining only a few supporters over the course of its 22 episodes. Many positioned it in relation to Sci Fi's supposed inability to produce original sf programmes, likening it to such 'bad' Sci Fi films and series as *Frankenfish* (Mark A. Z. Dippé, 2004), *Mansquito* (Tibor Takács, 2005), *Painkiller Jane* (2007) and *The Dresden Files* (2007). Some compared it unfavourably to such contemporary space operas as *Stargate SG-1* (1997–2007), *Farscape* (1999–2003) and especially Sci Fi's *Battlestar Galactica* (2003–9). Others dismissed it as a hideous blend of *Sliders* (1995–2000) and *Beverly Hills, 90210* (1990–2000) or *Dawson's Creek* (1998–2003), contrasting its desecration of a much-loved character/story-universe with the 'successful' revisionings of another 1930s character in *Lois and Clark* (1993–7) and *Smallville* (2001–11). User 'Vang' states: 'I thought that CBS's "re-imagination" of *Kolchak the Nightstalker* [2005–6] was the worst remake ever. Sci Fi Channel has proved me wrong once again', and 'Hint-of-Smega' concludes: 'If it had a grave, I'd spit on it'.

Negative responses to fresh iterations of *Flash Gordon* are not uncommon. Although Mike Hodges's 1980 *Flash Gordon* film was nominated for the World Science Fiction Convention's Hugo Award and the Academy of Science Fiction, Fantasy and Horror Films Saturn Award, popular guides to sf are unanimously disdainful. John Brosnan (1991: 211–12) describes it as a 'garish, crass and patronizing [...] sorry mess'. Douglas Menville and Robert Reginald (1985: 102–4) argue that a 'lack of understanding, and contempt for the material and his audience, blight every frame of this overblown, mindless turkey' – 'ashamed' of the source material, the filmmakers did not treat it with sufficient 'respect'. John Clute (1995: 282) grumbles that the 'whole point of Flash Gordon is to believe in him'; Peter Nicholls (1984: 60; 87) contends that 'its cardinal crime [...] was not to take its subject matter seriously', thus failing 'to reproduce the innocent lunacy of its comic-strip origins' and Phil Hardy (1985: 361) deplores Hodges's 'knowingness and literalness [for working] completely against the sense of pulp poetry so essential if we are to believe in Flash'. More recently, John Scalzi (2005: 41) can muster only a single parenthetical listing of its title.

This critical belittlement seems also to be the source of the mistaken belief that the film was a commercial and critical flop. *IMDb* and *Box Office Mojo* estimate a US$35m budget, but *Variety* disapprovingly reported that it 'cost around $20 million' (Brown, 1992: 45), and Hodges suspects producer Dino De Laurentiis of exaggerating the budget (Bould, 2007b: 29). It took a respectable US$27m at the US box-office, receiving favourable reviews from Pauline Kael and Roger Ebert and begrudging admiration from *Variety* for its sets, costumes and cinematography. In the UK, where it was nominated for three BAFTAs and a British Society of Cinematographers award, it was 'in the top 25 grossers in the 1980s' (Bould, 2007b: 29).

Intriguingly, for many *IMDb* users, Hodges's film was the 'original' that the television series failed to live up to by eschewing those very qualities of self-consciously pantomimic camp that provoked such ire in its critics. Where Hodges opened up the obsessional erotics of Alex Raymond's 1930s comic strip even more effectively than *Flesh Gordon* (Michael Benveniste and Howard Ziehm, 1974; see Bould, 2002), Sci

Fi abandoned what had become for many *the* defining characteristic of the character/story-universe in order to develop those aspects of Raymond's strip (and other versions) intended to appeal to a family audience. For these viewers, no amount of unintentionally camp moments could make up for this systematic betrayal of a beloved 'original'.

As this suggests, the notion of an original is profoundly problematic. The Flash Gordon character/story-universe emerged from the economics of competition across several media and commodity forms. In 1928 and 1929, the pulp sf magazine *Amazing Stories* published Philip Francis Nowlan's novellas 'Armageddon – 2419 AD' and 'The Airlords of Han', in which Anthony Rogers accidentally falls into suspended animation, wakes up in a future US dominated by Mongolian warlords, leads an uprising and perpetrates genocide. However, even before 'Armageddon' appeared, Nowlan circulated it to various newspaper comic-strip syndicates. He was commissioned by National Newspaper Syndicate, Inc. to write a daily strip illustrated by Dick Calkins. With its protagonist renamed Buck Rogers, its first instalment appeared in January 1929, before the second novella was published. A Sunday strip (drawn by Russell Keaton and Rick Yager) followed in 1930, and both ran until 1967. While the novellas might have reached 100,000 readers, the strips 'eventually appeared in nearly 400 newspapers and reached over 50 million readers' (Benton, 1992: 11). Their phenomenal popularity immediately prompted further adaptations: a radio series, a movie serial (which was also edited down into a feature film), books and merchandizing, including the first toy ray-guns. Such lucrative business attracted imitators and competitors.

King Features Syndicate commissioned Raymond's Sunday strip, *Flash Gordon*, which debuted in 1934 (and ran until 2003). This is where the problem of identifying an 'original' begins. Since the strip was created to be both like and not like *Buck Rogers*, its identity was determined outside of the strip itself. The premise of a contemporary hero adventuring among futuristic technologies is common to both, and thus *Flash Gordon* is defined by qualities possessed by *Buck Rogers*. Likewise, Raymond's preference for swashbuckling adventure on exotic worlds among scantily-clad men and women over Nowlan and

Calkins's fascination with engineering marvels also locates *Flash Gordon's* particularity outside of the strip, in its differences from its rival. Its immediate success also prompted numerous spin-offs and adaptations in various media, including: two radio serials (1935; 1936); *New Fun Comics's* 1935 copycat 'Don Drake on the Planet Saro'; a single issue of the pulp *Flash Gordon's Strange Adventure Magazine* in 1936; Alex Raymond's 1937 novel *Flash Gordon in the Caverns of Mongo*; at least half a dozen Big Little Books between 1934 and 1945; two daily strips (1940–4; 1951–92); and three movie serials. *Flash Gordon* (Frederick Stephani, 1936), starring former Olympic medal-winning swimmer Larry 'Buster' Crabbe, had an unprecedented US$350,000 budget (three times the norm for a serial) and, unusually, played evenings in first-run theatres (see Kinnard, 1998: 30–40). Universal's second biggest grosser of the year, it was edited down into two feature films, *Spaceship to the Unknown* (1936) and *Perils from the Planet Mongo* (1936), and was followed by *Flash Gordon's Trip to Mars* (Ford Beebe and Robert F. Hill, 1938). Cashing in on the success of Orson Welles's Halloween radio play *The War of the Worlds* (1938) later that year, it was hastily re-edited into the feature film *Mars Attacks the World* (1938), and was sufficiently successful for yet another feature-length release of the first serial as *Rocket Ship* (1939). Before producing *Flash Gordon Conquers the Universe* (Ford Beebe and Ray Taylor, 1940), Universal made the *Buck Rogers* movie serial, also starring Crabbe, by which point the precursor looked like the imitator. Later adaptations include two television series (1951; 2007–8); the Turkish film *Baytekin fezada carpisanlar* (*Flash Gordon's Battle in Space*) (Sinasi Özonuk, 1967); comic books by King Comics (1966–7), Charlton Comics (1969–70) and Gold Key/Whitman Comics (1978–80); half a dozen novels in 1974, attributed to Raymond but written by Ron Goulart and Carter Bingham; a further half-dozen novels by David Hagberg in 1980–1; two cartoon series (1979–80; 1996) and a role for Flash as one of the *Defenders of the Earth* (1986); the softcore movies *Flesh Gordon* and *Flesh Gordon Meets the Cosmic Cheerleaders* (Howard Ziehm, 1989); Dan Jurgens and Bruce Patterson's nine-part DC comics series (1988); Al Williamson's two-part Marvel comics series (1995); Warren Ellis and

Gianluca Pagliarani's five-part *Ignition City* comics series (2009); and a still-in-development new feature film.

This brief overview of *Flash Gordon*'s cross-media circulation (for a fuller account, see Bould, 2007a) is important for an understanding of the critical judgments passed on Hodges's film. It is evident that Raymond's *Flash Gordon* was created as an imitation-with-differences, a commercially motivated 'misprision' of *Buck Rogers*, 'a misreading [...], an act of creative correction that is actually and necessarily a misinterpretation' (Bloom, 1973: 30). If this relationship to *Buck Rogers* renders it problematic to treat the Sunday strip – let alone the movie serial – as the 'original' by locating its essential aspects outside of the strip itself, so too does the rapid proliferation of other *Flash Gordon* texts and artefacts. This is why it is unclear what precisely the critics of Hodges's film consider to be the 'original' it sullies. They seem to conflate the strip and the movie serials (and overlook other versions), ignoring the medium specificities and processes of adaptation that render them, despite similarities, radically different from each other. They then attribute to this uncertain amalgam a particular set of values (primarily, innocent adventurous fun) from which any variations appear as aberrations. They refuse to acknowledge or allow significance to those elements within their textual conflation that contradict, trouble or escape their imaginative reconstruction of a pure 'original'. And, perhaps most significantly, they fail to recognize that their understanding of the 'original' is itself an act of misprision, and this is exacerbated by an underlying, but fallacious, assumption that the various *Flash Gordon* texts were intended solely for children (and that audiences in the past were more naive). This ignores the specific contexts of production, distribution and consumption – newspapers and cinemas aiming for audiences composed of entire families – and the ways in which different variants sought to cater to a range of ages and tastes. The critics of Sci Fi's *Flash Gordon* reveal similar tendencies, assumptions and prejudices, albeit with a different 'original' in mind.

This admittedly sketchy reception history is instructive on multiple levels, but I will use it to explore some debates in adaptation studies. In 1948, André Bazin wrote that 'one must first know to what end the adaptation is designed: for the cinema or for its audience. One must realize that most adapters care far more about the latter than about the former' (Bazin, 2000: 21). This opens up several interrelated concerns for students of adaptation.

Adaptations and their sources are commodities bound up in the realms of production and consumption. In order critically to comprehend them, it is necessary to come to terms with the nature of intellectual, creative labour required by both producers and consumers of textual commodities. That is, we need to develop the means by which to 'examine the historically specific conjunctures in which interests and meanings are brought into being and actively negotiated' (Grainge, 2008: 8). This requires attention not only to 'the diversity of attitudes and practices that exist among consumers, audiences and subordinate social groups' privileged in cultural disciplines since the 1980s, but also, 'with equal sensitivity to context and complexity', to 'the interests and meanings worked out within the field of cultural production' (Grainge, 2008: 8). Thinking about adaptation therefore requires us simultaneously to consider not only the processes by which we make culture out of commodities but also those by which capital is made out of culture. Both processes are reflected in the responses to two versions of *Flash Gordon* outlined above, with each generation being offended by the new version's crassly commercial attempt to transform culture – an earlier version of *Flash Gordon* that has been subsumed into their cultural habitus – into a commodity, as if earlier versions were not equally attempts commercially to exploit a commodity. For adaptation studies, one of the advantages of considering such a proliferation of commercial texts is that they are undeniable outputs of a mode of production in which Romantic-bourgeois notions of the author and the original are as dead as post-structuralism could wish. Such examples also highlight the cultural transformations that have accompanied the reconceptualization of ownership away from authorship/copyright to reproducibility/trademark as technologies of mechanical and electronic reproduction have proliferated (see Lury, 2004).

Bazin's essay concludes:

it is possible to imagine that we are moving toward a reign of the adaptation in which the notion of the unity of the work of art, if not the very notion of the author himself, will be destroyed. If the film that was made of Steinbeck's *Of Mice and Men* [...] had been successful [...], the (literary?) critic of the year 2050 would find not a novel out of which a play and film had been 'made,' but rather a single work reflected through three art forms, an artistic pyramid with three sides, all equal in the eye of the critic. The 'work' would then be only an ideal point at the top of this figure, which itself is an ideal construct. The chronological precedence of one part over another would not be an aesthetic criterion any more than the chronological precedence of one twin over the other is a genealogical one. Malraux made his film of *Man's Hope* before he wrote the novel of the same title, but he was carrying the work inside himself all along. (Bazin, 2000: 26)

In terms of decentring priority, origin, influence and the status of the medium, Bazin's examples are problematic because of the ways in which they continue to privilege the notion of authorship. However, he does suggest the possibility of wrestling with the cycles and flows of adaptation processes – in terms of production and consumption, of achronological encounters between audiences and texts and of 'the discursive properties of intellectual properties: their sole legal authorship, their ubiquitous proliferation, and their multiple social authorings' (Coombe, 1998: 38). Indeed, the reception of both versions of *Flash Gordon* sketched above reveals something of the 'social worlds [...] in which social actors with specific interests, agendas, histories, and social positionings voice their aspirations and irritations, identifications and affiliations, reverences and resentments through the media of commercial culture' (Coombe, 1998: 38). It is through such interactions that capital, in the form of commodity-texts, becomes the kind of culture that can be turned back into capital.

The earliest Anglophone discussions to wrestle with the problematic notion of fidelity to a source recognize different approaches to adaptation. Geoffrey Wagner describes 'three types of transition of fiction into film' that 'can help us clarify the meaning in each, and appreciate the norms of both' (Wagner, 1975: 222; 230–1): transposition, 'in which a novel is directly given on the screen, with the minimum of apparent interference' (Wagner, 1975: 222); commentary, 'where an original is taken and either purposely or inadvertently altered in some respect' (Wagner, 1975: 223); and analogy, 'a fairly considerable departure for the sake of making *another* work of art' (Wagner, 1975: 227). Michael Klein and Gillian Parker divide adaptations between those which 'attempt to give the impression of being faithful, that is, literal translations of the text into the language of film' (Klein and Parker, 1981: 9), those that retain 'the core of the structure of the narrative while significantly reinterpreting or, in some cases, deconstructing the source text' (Klein and Parker, 1981: 10) and those that regard 'the source merely as raw material, as simply an occasion for an original work' (Klein and Parker, 1981: 10). But the structure of each of these schemes privileges source over adaptation, unwittingly reproducing and re-inscribing 'the axiomatic superiority of literary art to film, an assumption derived from a number of superimposed prejudices' (Stam, 2000: 58) deeply rooted in our culture about the superiority of older and linguistic arts over newer and visual ones. For example, Dudley Andrew – who offers his own tripartite scheme of borrowing, intersecting and transforming sources (Andrew, 1984: 98–104) – argues that the very process of adaptation 'insist[s] on the cultural status of the model' and that 'in a strong sense adaptation is the appropriation of meaning from a prior text' (Andrew, 1984: 97). I will highlight two problems with this claim.

First, adaptation as 'the appropriation of meaning' construes the source as a fixed object rather than as site of multiple contested meanings. Brian McFarlane, drawing on Roland Barthes, proposes distinguishing between 'what may be transferred (i.e. from novel to film) from that which may only be adapted' (McFarlane, 1996: 13), thus providing a more complex sense of the varieties of information that it is possible to appropriate. In his terminology, distributional functions (or functions proper) are concerned with doing, with actions and events horizontally or syntactically arranged in linear sequence. There are two varieties. Cardinal functions are narrative hinge-points where the action could head off in a completely different direction; strung together, they form the basic narrative structure and are transferable between media. Catalysers are small actions that root the

Figure 1. Flash Gordon. Photo courtesy of Universal Pictures/Photofest.

cardinal functions in the details of a particular story-world and enrich them through adding particularity. They, too, are transferable. Integrational functions (or indices) are concerned with being, with character psychology, with atmosphere and place. Again, there are two kinds. While informants – specific data, 'such as names, ages, and professions of characters, certain details of the setting' – are 'amenable' to transfer, indices proper, which are closely related to character and atmosphere, are diffuse, difficult to transfer and 'therefore more broadly open to adaptation' (McFarlane, 1996: 14).

Although it still tends to presume that texts are fixed objects that can be analysed without subjective interpretation, this terminology is helpful in anatomizing an adaptation's transformations. For example, although Hodges's film begins by following the narrative of Raymond's 1934 strip closely (albeit in modern dress), it diverges from the original's cardinal functions when Ming orders Flash's execution. However, visual catalysers – the set-design and costume-design – continue to anchor the film in Raymond's distinctive vision of Mongo (indeed, the transparent chamber in which Flash is 'executed' is based on the strip for 16 January 1938).

The pace and tone of the film enable Hodges – and Williamson's comic-book adaptation – to avoid providing his characters with any substantial or complex interiority. In contrast, Arthur Byron Cover's novelization rounds out the narrative to an appropriate length with some curious attempts at characterization consonant with the period in which it was written. The characterization of Flash has always been rather fluid: in the 1950s television series, he was an agent of the Galactic Bureau of Investigation; in Dan Barry's daily strip of the 1950s, he was a space-pilot-for-hire (with an air of officialdom) in a more 'realistic' future solar system; and in the 1996 cartoon series, he was a hoverboarding teenager. In Cover's novelization, he is – for no discernible reason – described as having grown up poor in Alabama (which requires Cover to concoct an explanation for him no longer having an Alabama accent). His mother died in childbirth, his remote father five years later, and he was raised by an Aunt who died when he was in his teens. He grows up to be a loner with vague countercultural values and existentialist pretensions that Zarkov shares. Sexually active, but with no long-standing attachments, Flash yearns for true love. Zarkov and Dale Arden have sexually diverse pasts – his includes transvestism, hers orgies – but for both, such experimentation was largely driven by their respective partners' desires. Such catalysers and indices proper ground the characters in a popular fiction realism of post-countercultural coke-and-disco hedonism (although Cover's treatment of sexuality is rather ambivalent: while Hodges keeps the 'bore worms', with which Princess Aura is to be tortured, an off-screen and unexplained threat, Cover makes them monstrous through linking them to painful and damaging anal sex). Despite their distance from earlier versions of the character/story-universe, these sorts of information follow the pattern of Hodges's film in opening up Raymond's erotic textuality. Cover's presentation of this information, much of which occurs in chapters before the events of the film, does not break the film's chain of cardinal functions. However, it does produce some fascinating moments of dissonance between film and novelization. For example, when Flash and Dale are reunited in the Hawkmen's city, Dale says 'Boy, have I got some crazy stories to tell you!'. Flash responds, 'Save them for our kids', to which she replies, 'Ooh, I accept'. In the novelization, however, before accepting Flash's proposal, Dale thinks '*Our kids? Should I tell him now about my opera-*

tion? Oh well, there's plenty of time. He'll take it well because he's such a liberal' (Cover, 1980: 154).

IMDb users' complaints about Sci Fi's series were particularly focused on indices: the 'caucasianization' of Ming; the replacement of spaceships with interdimensional portals and of Hawkmen wings with cloaks; and especially the casting of Flash and Dale as twenty-somethings who could be mistaken for teenagers. 'Supercygnus' suggests that 'It would have been better off being its own thing and not trying to simply leech off the Flash Gordon name' and 'Obelix 1971' argues that 'If you name your show *Flash Gordon* then give us Flash Gordon and NOT the sequel to *Sliders* where the main character just happens to listen to the name Flash Gordon'. Sci Fi's decision to use little more than the most basic of informants (trademarked names) is perhaps related to the sense that 'we are in the era of a permanent *marketing* campaign, where the selling of an entertainment environment is ongoing, an activity punctuated by commodity texts' (Acland, 2003: 77). As Barbara Selznick argues, throughout Sci Fi's existence, its branding efforts have been preoccupied with the commercial need to attract a mass audience for whom sf is not a primary concern without alienating too much a considerably smaller audience who identify themselves as sf fans or viewers (see Selznick, 2009). Hence, the channel's recent name/logo change to Syfy, intended to appear as a connotation-free station ident for a potential mass audience while continuing to reach an sf audience phonetically. Hence, also, Sci Fi's claim, uncritically repeated by obliging journalists throughout its run, that *Battlestar Galactica* is not sf but a drama that just happens to take place in an sf context. Such attempts to reach different audiences provide a useful framework for understanding Sci Fi's attempt to create a version of *Flash Gordon* by reorganizing distributional and integrational functions so as to draw in a minority audience familiar with earlier versions while concentrating on attracting other audiences for whom the character/story-universe has little cultural resonance.

The second problem with Andrew's claim is that his 'appropriation of meaning' involves an attempt to efface 'the memory derived from reading the novel by another experience – an audio-visual-verbal one – which will seem, as little as possible, to jar with that collective memory' (McFarlane, 1996: 21). This opens up the possibility of conceptualizing the adaptation as a Derridean supplement. Derrida suggests that 'to supplement' has two related meanings: 'to add to' and 'to take the place of', and so while the adaptation might be seen as an additional version of the text, it can also work to take the place of it. The status of the supplement is always 'undecidable' – 'a plenitude enriching another plenitude' (Derrida, 1974: 144) or adding 'only to replace' (Derrida, 1974: 145) – and ultimately, Derrida concludes, it is both of these things, accretion and substitution (Derrida, 1974: 200), in an endless series of supplementary mediations in which the original is created by the copies, and is never graspable, always deferred.

I was 12 years old when I saw Hodges's *Flash Gordon* in the cinema. Growing up before domestic video technologies were commonplace, my memories of and passion for it became inextricably bound up with spectral supplements: occasional screenings on broadcast television of the film (although some content, such as Klytus's death, was bowdlerized) and the 1930s movie serials, which I already knew quite well; Cover's novelization (that expanded the narrative in ways I did not then find so amusing) and reissues of the 1970s novels (which had photos from the film on their covers); Williamson's comic adaptation (which always seemed too hasty, too compressed) and Queen's soundtrack album, the B-side of which more-or-less replicates the climax of the film (although I generally disliked Queen, even more so when they broke the South African boycott in 1984). Because of this particular experience of a plenitude of not-always-satisfactory texts constantly substituting for each other (without necessarily constituting an enrichment), my relationship to variant versions seems to be very different to those of their critics cited earlier. Despite having preferences among the many versions of *Flash Gordon*, my relationship with them has more in common with the sense of the text underpinning Stam's work on adaptation, which construes the text as an 'open […] structuration […] reworked by a boundless context. [It] feeds on and is fed into an infinitely permutating intertext, which is seen through ever-shifting grids of interpretation […] All texts are tissues of anonymous formulae, variations of those formulae, conscious and unconscious quotations, and conflations and inversions of other texts' (Stam, 2000: 57; 64). This applies as much to a source as it does to an adaptation; a source is every bit as fragmented, fluctuating and *derived* as its adaptation; an adaptation is necessarily every bit as informationally complex as its source; and both source and adaptation have multiple sources. Adaptation therefore is a complex series of negotiations, selections, suppressions, emphases, divergences and variations. Consequently, as examination of such a commercial property as Flash Gordon™ suggests, adaptation studies should abandon any residual notion of fidelity and embrace instead the notion of extraordinary rendition – not in the sense of a source being illegally abducted and tortured (which is how many still seem to feel about adaptations) but in the sense of each variant being a cover version, ordinary in its repetition of elements but *extra*ordinary in its transformations of them.

References

Acland, C.R. (2003) *Screen Traffic: Movies, Multiplexes, and Global Culture.* Durham, NC: Duke University Press.

Andrew, D. (1984) *Concepts in Film Theory.* Oxford: Oxford University Press.

Barthes, R. (1977) 'Introduction to the Structural Analysis of Narratives', in *Image-Music-Text*, pp. 79–124. Glasgow: Collins.

Bazin, A. (2000) 'Adaptation, or the Cinema as Digest', in J. Naremore (ed.) *Film Adaptation*, pp. 19–27. London: Athlone.

Benton, M. (1992) *Science Fiction Comics: The Illustrated History.* Dallas, TX: Taylor.

Bloom, H. (1973) *The Anxiety of Influence: A Theory of Poetry.* London: Oxford University Press.

Bould, M. (2002) 'Not in Kansas Any More: Some Notes on Camp and Queer Sf Movies', *Foundation* 86: 40–50.

Bould, M. (2007a) 'Oh My God, This Film's Really Turning Me On!: Adapting *Flash Gordon*', *Film International* 5 (2): 18–26.

Bould, M. (2007b) 'Soufflés and Sexual Tightropes: An Interview with Mike Hodges', *Film International* 5 (2): 27–29.

Brosnan, J. (1991) *The Primal Screen: A History of the Science Fiction Film.* London: Orbit.

Brown, J. (ed.) (1992) *Variety Science-Fiction Movies: Illustrated Reviews of the Classic Films.* London: Hamlyn.

Clute, J. (1995) *Science Fiction: The Illustrated Encyclopedia*. London: Dorling Kindersley.

Coombe, R. (1998) *The Cultural Life of Intellectual Properties: Authorship, Appropriation, and the Law*. Durham, NC: Duke University Press.

Cover, A. B. (1980) *Flash Gordon*. London: NEL.

Derrida, J. (1974) *Of Grammatology*. Trans. G. C. Spivak. Baltimore, MD: Johns Hopkins University Press.

Ebert, R. (1980) 'Flash Gordon', *Chicago Sun-Times* (8 December), http://rogerebert.suntimes.com/apps/pbcs.dll/article?AID=/19801208/REVIEWS/12080301/1023 (accessed October 2010).

Grainge, P. (2008) *Brand Hollywood: Selling Entertainment in a Global Media Age*. London: Routledge.

Hardy, P. (ed.) (1995) *The Aurum Film Encyclopedia: Science Fiction*. London: Aurum.

Kael, P. (1986) *Taking It All In*. London: Marion Boyars.

Kinnard, R. (1998) *Science Fiction Serials: A Critical Filmography of 31 Hard SF Cliffhangers: With an Appendix of the 37 Serials with Slight SF Content*. Jefferson, NC: McFarland.

Klein, M. and Parker, G. (eds.) (1981) *The English Novel and the Movies*. New York: Frederick Ungar.

Lury, C. (2004) *Brands: The Logos of the Global Economy*. London: Routledge.

McFarlane, B. (1996) *Novel to Film: An Introduction to the Theory of Adaptation*. Oxford: Oxford University Press.

Menville, D. and Reginald, R. (1985) *Future Visions: The New Golden Age of Science Fiction Film*. San Bernadino, CA: Borgo.

Naremore, J. (2000) 'Introduction: Film and the Reign of Adaptation', in J. Naremore (ed.) *Film Adaptation*, pp. 1–16. London: Athlone.

Nicholls, P. (1984) *Fantastic Cinema: An Illustrated Survey*. London: Ebury.

Scalzi, J. (2005) *The Rough Guide to Sci-Fi Movies*. London: Rough Guides/Penguin.

Selznick, B. (2009) 'Branding the Future: Syfy in the Post-Network Era', *Science Fiction Film and Television* 2 (2): 177–204.

Stam, R. (2000) 'Beyond Fidelity: The Dialogics of Adaptation', in J. Naremore (ed.) *Film Adaptation*, pp. 54–76. London: Athlone.

Wagner, G. (1975) *The Novel and the Cinema*. Rutherford, NJ: Fairleigh Dickinson University Press.

Index